Practical social work

Published in conjunction with
the British Association of Social Workers
Series Editor: Jo Campling

Social work is at an important stage in its development. The profession is facing fresh challenges to work flexibly in fast-changing social and organisational environments. New requirements for training are also demanding a more critical and reflective, as well as more highly skilled, approach to practice.

The British Association of Social Workers has always been conscious of its role in setting guidelines for practice and in seeking to raise professional standards. The concept of the *Practical Social Work* series was conceived to fulfil a genuine professional need for a carefully planned, coherent series of texts that would stimulate and inform debate, thereby contributing to the development of practitioners' skills and professionalism.

Newly relaunched, the series continues to address the needs of all those who are looking to deepen and refresh their understanding and skills. It is designed for students and busy professionals alike. Each book marries practice issues and challenges with the latest theory and research in a compact and applied format. The authors represent a wide variety of experience both as educators and practitioners. Taken together, the books set a standard in their clarity, relevance and rigour.

A list of new and best-selling titles in this series follows overleaf. A comprehensive list of titles available in the series, and further details about individual books, can be found online at :
www.palgrave.com/socialworkpolicy/basw

Series standing order ISBN 0–333–80313–2

You can receive future titles in this series as they are published by placing a standing order. Please contact your bookseller or, in the case of difficulty, contact us at the address below with your name and address, the title of the series and the ISBN quoted above.

Customer Services Department, Macmillan Distribution Ltd, Houndmills, Basingstoke, Hampshire RG21 6XS, England

Practical social work series

Joyce Lishman

Communication in social work

Second edition

palgrave
macmillan

First edition 1994
Reprinted fifteen times
Second edition 2009

Published by
PALGRAVE MACMILLAN
Houndmills, Basingstoke, Hampshire RG21 6XS and
175 Fifth Avenue, New York, N.Y. 10010
Companies and representatives throughout the world

PALGRAVE MACMILLAN is the global academic imprint of the Palgrave Macmillan division of St. Martin's Press, LLC and of Palgrave Macmillan Ltd. Macmillan® is a registered trademark in the United States, United Kingdom and other countries. Palgrave is a registered trademark in the European Union and other countries.

ISBN-13: 978–1–4039–1620–4
ISBN-10: 1–4039–1620–9

This book is printed on paper suitable for recycling and made from fully managed and sustained forest sources. Logging, pulping and manufacturing processes are expected to conform to the environmental regulations of the country of origin.

A catalogue record for this book is available from the British Library.

A catalog record for this book is available from the Library of Congress.

10   9   8   7   6   5   4   3   2   1
18 17 16 15 14 13 12 11 10 09

Printed and bound in China

Contents

Preface

In preparing this new edition, I am pleased to see that, for me, it has stood the test of time and reflects the essence of why effective communication is essential to social work and, indeed, to social care. In revisiting *Communication in Social Work* I will explore briefly the contextual changes in the provision of social work and social care which have occurred since 1994. First I consider continuity. We need to ensure that 'we escape the insidious error that wisdom shall die or was born' within our or any generation (Ashdown and Clement Brown, 1953, p. 228).

What have remained the fundamental aspects of social work? In 2002 I wrote:

- 'a concern about individual people and the enhancement of their lives and relationships;
- a commitment to social justice and the eradication of poverty and discrimination;
- a commitment to social work as a moral and ethical activity;
- a holistic approach to practice, where relationships and process as well as outcomes are addressed;
- a commitment to partnership and involvement with users in the development of services to meet their needs;
- a commitment to evaluating practice as a means of developing it
- a recognition that the worker's use of self is integral in social work activity' (Lishman, 2002, p. 95)

However, social work operates in an ideological and political context, a fact which I underestimated as a student 'bored' with social policy and as a social worker working with individuals and families. Now I realize that it is essential that social workers understand the social, economic and political context within which they practise and how it affects the delivery of social service. Under the Conservative Government (1979–97) the prevailing ideology promoted market forces, consumerism and managerialism in the public sector. It was critical of post-war welfarism and the perceived ensuing dependency culture (Butler and Drakeford, 2001).

According to Butler and Drakeford, the aims of the Conservative government were:

> to extend the rationalities and technologies of the market place to the provision of public services, to reduce the burden of social responsibility accepted by the state and to transfer the delivery of residential services for which it retained an obligation, away from public bodies and towards voluntary or independent providers. (Butler and Drakeford, 2001, p. 8)

Since 1997 social work under Labour Governments has continued to operate in a context of economic and financial concern about containing public sector spending, given its growth in proportional terms relative to the private sector. The detailed attention to economic and financial concern still emphasizes efficiency savings and ensuring value for money based on the three Es – efficiency, economy and effectiveness – with a particular focus on economy and efficiency.

Social work has always operated in a context of rapid legal and organizational change with significant policy changes in relation to social work. Within this complex context, social work practice itself is uncertain and ambiguous, involving an ethical base, legal accountability, and responsibility for complex assessment and decision making about relative risks, safety, harm and protection and intervention in the lives of people who are in distress, conflict or trouble. Ethical issues in social work involve:

> tensions between individual rights and public welfare, between individual responsibilities and structural inequality and oppression; they lead to moral dilemmas and a balancing of rights, duties and responsibilities for which there may be no right answer. An ethical response may conflict with financial accountability and resource availability: it may inform or conflict with legal accountability (Lishman, 2002, p. 96)

One fundamental social policy and legislative change introduced by the Conservative Government was the National Health Service and Community Care Act 1990. Other social policy and legislative challenges enacted by the Conservative Government included the Children Act 1989, the Criminal Justice Act 1991 and legislation for the local government reorganization in 1996. More than ten years after the election of a Labour Government in 1997, the policy context within which communication in social work and social care occurs needs to be more explicitly addressed.

While the 1997 Labour Government made the distinction between 'the selfish individualism of the Tory years and the compassionate communitarianism of Labour' (Butler and Drakeford, 2001), it maintained much of the Conservative Government's critique of public service in its modernizing agenda. Its programme proposed to reform public services and improve partnership working to provide seamless services and develop new approaches that cut across old boundaries (Scottish Executive, 2001).

In particular this agenda was based on a commitment to:

- social inclusion;
- integrated service delivery between health, education, social services, housing and the police as well as relevant services in the voluntary and independent sector;
- an increasing emphasis therefore on interdisciplinary practice;
- increased public accountability and scrutiny;
- strategies to improve local democracy, create community responsibility and initiative, and remove dependency;
- increasing emphasis on the role of users and carers in developing policy and service delivery with an emphasis on diversity, access, user and carer rights and advocacy;
- increasing emphasis on personalization of social services (Leadbetter, 2004);
- increasing specialization e.g. between community care, child protection and criminal justice or probation, with a continuing blurring of boundaries between social work and social care;
- an emphasis on the use of IT: the E-government strategy emphasizes the use of information and communication technology to widen customer choice and flexibility in service delivery;
- an increased emphasis on evidence-based practice (Lishman, 2000, 2007; Smith, 2004) where the agenda may be skewed to 'what works' and outcomes rather than reflective evaluation of both processes and outcomes.

While these agendas have dominated the social policy context in the United Kingdom since 1997, the impact of devolution in 1999, with Northern Ireland, Wales and Scotland each having an independent Parliament or National Assembly with specific devolved powers, has influenced the development of social work and social care policy and practice in each of the four countries slightly differently.

For example, in Scotland, tensions between the power-sharing agenda of devolution and the centralist New Labour United Kingdom agenda have continued to exist. The outcome of the 2007 elections for the Scottish Parliament, which led to a minority Scottish National Party Government, means that the future policy development in devolved Scotland is slightly unclear at the time of writing. In the late 1990s, the Scottish Executive's clear vision of social justice and the defeat of child poverty within a generation (www.scotland.gov.uk) reflected the wider New Labour agenda as well as Scotland's rejection of Thatcherite policies and a commitment to a more democratic and egalitarian agenda. In Scotland the policy desire for integration, in particular between health, education and social work, led to a perceived fragmentation of the social work policy agenda in the Scottish Executive (Trinder and Reynolds, 1998) where social work functions were divided and integrated into broader departments, for example:

● Community Care in the Department of Health
● Children and Young People and Social Work Education in the Department of Education
● Adult Offenders and Victims in the Justice Department

While there were anxieties that such restructuring might lead to a perceived fragmentation of the social work policy agenda in the Scottish Executive (Trinder and Reynolds, 1998) this division of responsibility, mirrored throughout the UK, attempted to deal with the need to integrate health and social work services in relation to community care and to integrate education and children's services for children and families. Criminal justice in Scotland has remained part of social work services. In England probation is not part of local authority social work provision: its education and training is separate. In England, while education and training for social work in children's services and community care remains integrated, service delivery is not. However the complexity and challenge of ensuring an integrated approach to adults and children in need of social services – whether in terms of disability, mental health, criminal justice, old age, child care prevention and protection – is a major policy context for this book.

The change in Scotland from the Scottish Executive to the Scottish Government led to changes in the structure of Scottish government departments but not to a separation of children's and adults' services: criminal justice remains part of social work.

However the Scottish Government's decision to base its policy on five strategic objectives – to make Scotland wealthier and fairer, smarter, healthier, safer *and* stronger and greener – and in the main to remove ring-fenced funding has implications for social service authorities *and* voluntary organizations. These changes may come at the expense of service delivery to vulnerable people by local authorities, and for social work education with the loss of a ring-fenced training budget.

Recent policy developments in social work in Scotland, England and Wales are also reflected in 'Changing Lives: Report of the 21st Century Social Work Review' (www.scotland.gov.uk/Resource/

Doc/91931/0021949.pdf), 'The State of Social Care in England 2004–5' (www.csci.org.uk/about_us/publications/the_state_of_social_care_in_en.aspx) and 'Social Work in Wales: A Profession to Value' (www.all-walesunit.gov.uk). Major themes of which social work students need to be aware include:

- A focus on service users', carers' and citizens' needs and aspirations and, in particular, the need for more personalized services (Leadbetter, 2004).
- The need for greater integration of service provision.
- The need for an inbuilt culture of performance improvement.
- The need for improved leadership in social services at all levels including practitioner level.
- The need for improved practice governance so that social work services are personalized and empowering, but are also accountable to employers and wide stakeholders.

In Scotland, as in the other countries of the UK, there is recognition of the need to have confident, competent and articulate social work practitioners who are properly accountable organizationally for their work.

The modernizing agenda of the Labour Governments since 1997 also led to developments in social work education across the four countries, each of which now has an honours degree in social work education as the minimum qualification for entry to the social work profession. In all countries these new degrees drew on both the Benchmarking statement in social work and National Occupational Standards. In Scotland these two sets of requirements have been helpfully integrated into SiSWE (Standards in Social Work Education) (2003). The new degrees involve a much greater emphasis on the knowledge base and its integration in practice, on research mindedness and on evidence-based practice (Lishman, 2007).

Communication in social work and social care in the 21st century needs to be set in this social and political context. This is the environment in which we practise and, as social and social care workers, we should be constantly aware of these issues. Before moving on, reflect on these questions which create the context for considering everything that follows:

- What political, economic and social policy influences are the contexts of the organization you work in? How do these affect its value and ethics base, its service delivery and how it supports and enhances the role of social work and social care in social service delivery?
- How do these political, economic and social policy influences affect and even determine your social work practice?

To Roly, Tamsin and Benjamin
for their love, support and encouragement
over even more years

To Elaine Webster for her support in ensuring
that this manuscript was translated
from author's pen to Windows document

1 | Introduction

Effective communication is an essential component of social work and social care which includes, for example, providing basic care, giving advice, making assessments, providing care packages, counselling, writing reports, acting as advocates for service users, and working in interdisciplinary settings with health, education, housing and criminal justice. It is necessary for social workers to have effective communication skills if they are to promote self help and empowerment. While the language of community care planning, with its emphasis on care management, brokerage, the purchaser/provider split and devolved budgets, sounds technocratic and impersonal, care managers and providers need to use a range of communication and interpersonal skills if community care is really to mean real choice and personalized services for service users. Social workers in childcare, whether protection or prevention, field or residential, and staff providing professional care and control in criminal justice also need to use a range of communication and interpersonal skills.

While major problems facing users of social work services remain those of poverty and discrimination or oppression on the basis of race, class, gender, age, disability and any amelioration or solution requires political and structural change, social workers and social care workers are faced with the immediate impact of structural problems on individuals and families and the need to work with them to improve on or ameliorate their particular situations. They are also faced with more individual problems, for example, in relation to attachment and loss (Aldgate, 2007; Rochford, 2007). This engagement in direct interaction requires the use of the range of communication skills examined in this book.

One reason for wanting to write this book, therefore, was that communication skills are at the core of social work and social care, and, indeed also interprofessional work in health, education and criminal justice. A second reason was that understanding and knowledge about effective communication is derived from a variety of sources, for example social psychology, evaluation research, social work theory, and research into users' and carers' perceptions of social work. This range of knowledge requires integration and application to social work. A third reason is that, while training in social work acknowledges the importance of communication skills, our knowledge about their use in real practice is very limited. Partly this is because in many settings, particularly fieldwork and secondary settings, social work has been an 'invisible' profession, practised in private and unobserved (Pithouse, 1987). Partly it is because few research studies examined, even descriptively, workers' behaviour and interaction with clients (Baldock and Prior, 1981; Lishman, 1985), let alone attempted to evaluate the effectiveness of different communication techniques and styles.

My aims in this volume are:

- to draw together knowledge from different sources about the communication skills we need for effective social practice in social work and social care and to present these in a clear, readily available way;
- to apply this knowledge to social work and social care in a range of contexts and settings;
- to help the reader then draw on this knowledge to apply to his or her own practice;
- to help the reader reflect on and be aware of his or her own communication and its impact.

Let us consider the following two social workers. The first is interviewing a female service user who referred herself to her GP because she was anxious that she was punishing her seven-year-old son excessively. In the interview the social worker's voice is gentle and soft. She appears attentive and listens carefully. She checks that she has understood what the woman is saying. She smiles frequently, her face is expressive and she appears warm, interested and sympathetic. Her responses are supportive to the woman and she reinforces positive behaviour on her part, e.g. 'Don't play it down. Aren't you pleased to have managed that?' She clarifies what the woman says, and shows verbally that she is understanding her.

In contrast a worker is interviewing a young man who is on a probation order, and who has just re-offended by serious housebreaking. In the interview the social worker's voice sounds rather cold and harsh. She fidgets and moves about impatiently as if she has heard it all before. She does not smile and her face is impassive and serious: her only facial expression is to frown. She questions in quite an abrupt way, 'Well, what was it about, then?' and rejects the answer, 'I know it was about housebreaking but ...' She does not appear supportive and does not check out her understanding of the young man. Her responses are often critical and she confronts the probationer with her scepticism about his future behaviour and ability to stay out of prison.

These are two very different service users with different problems and agendas observed in two different interviews and two different communication styles on the part of the worker. Interestingly, the social worker is the same person!

The interviews are described because they raise central questions about communication in social work. What skills are used? Do these skills change in response to the person requiring a service? Does a social worker use the same skills regardless of the user of service or the problem? Can we say that individual social workers have individual communication styles? The answers to these questions are descriptive. We need also to ask what communication skills are effective and, more specifically, what communication skills are effective in what settings, with which specific users of services and for what purposes? These questions are evaluative. As workers in social work and social care we need to reflect on both of these questions. What is my preferred individual communication style and how am I perceived? How effective is my communication?

The answers, in so far as there are answers, are drawn from a range of sources. Social psychology can help us to understand the meaning and interpretation of our non-verbal and symbolic behaviour, the relevance of class, race and gender to verbal communication, and influences on interpersonal perception, such as stereotyping. Behavioural theory reminds us of the importance of reinforcement and modelling.

Research into clients' perceptions in the 1970s and 1980s and into the views of service users thereafter, gives us clear feedback about social workers' communication skills or lack of them (Trevithick *et al.*, 2004). Evaluative research in social work, psychotherapy and counselling highlights the importance of the worker showing empathy, warmth and genuineness – the 'core conditions' for effective helping – and of the use of contract-based intervention and focussed intervention methods such as task-centred work.

Practice theory in social work has confidently prescribed how we ought to behave and communicate. Unfortunately the evidence to support such prescription is more limited. Although a great deal has been written about the beliefs, knowledge and qualities expected of social workers, there remains a debate about the nature of social work practice and a lack of empirical knowledge about the skills we use which distinguish social work from other professions.

This book draws upon practice theory, even where it has not been rigorously researched, provided it is supported by collective practice experience and evidence from relevant sources such as social psychology or evaluation research.

It also draws on colleagues', students' and my own practice experience: practice experience and wisdom must contribute to the development of knowledge and theory in social work, but equally social workers need to draw on relevant research and evidence (Lishman, 2007).

Policy development, as outlined in the Preface, is the social policy context in which communication in social work and social care is practised. Particular relevant policy agendas are:

- the involvement of service users and carers in the development and evaluation of policy and practice;
- the importance of providing personalized service (Leadbetter, 2004);
- the necessity of developing and using evidence-based and research-minded practice;
- the importance of integrated services and interdisciplinary work;
- the relevance and application of new information and communication technologies (ICT).

In relation to the involvement of service users and carers we also need to pay attention to the views of users of services who feel they are *involuntary*, e.g. in criminal justice and in childcare and protection and in mental health.

Terminology in relation to people who use social work and social care services is complicated. As Cree and Davis (2006) comment, 'The term "service user" has been used for a number of years in preference to the term "client" as a convenient and neutral shorthand expression to denote those who are receiving social work services' (p. 3). The term 'patient' in relation to the National Health Service and health care is universal. However, in social work and social care people who receive services are not a homogeneous group. For example, carers who receive services may have specific requirements which are very different from those of service users who receive services. Not all users of services wish to receive the service they are given: in child protection and criminal justice they are compelled to receive service as involuntary 'service users'. Professionals engaged in social work and social care may themselves be service users or carers. They may historically have been involuntary service users.

In this edition I use the generic term 'users of services' to include voluntary and involuntary service users and also carers. Where different perceptions in relation to communication emerge I will define more specifically which group of 'users of services' is being referred to.

In relation to the personalization of services agenda (Leadbetter, 2004) for all users of services, voluntary or involuntary, carer or service user we need to draw on the range of their perceptions about what they experienced. Did the communication between the agency, worker and user of services contribute to a personalized experience rather than a more routine one? Did it contribute to useful and effective outcomes? Where might the limits of a personalization agenda lie? Cox (2008), for example, is very clear in relation to family group conferencing: 'Not all families are their own experts' (p. 80). In order to attempt to address these questions we need to use an evidence-based approach (Lishman, 2007) where it is available, but also a critical reflective approach to practice (Fook, 2007). We need to practise by using and applying the best available evidence *and* our critical reflective analysis of this evidence.

Chapter 2 examines research findings on what users of services believe constitute helpful and effective communication. Rees and Wallace (1982) argued that these judgements were the most important criteria in evaluating social work and the personal social services. They believed that social workers' accountability to users of services should take 'precedence over accountability to agency or profession and that, in response to problems which are largely structural, social workers' responsibility is never to lose sight of the needs of the most powerless people' (p. 58). This must involve seeking and actively responding to their perceptions and evaluations.

This tension between accountability to the agency and accountability to users of services has remained, as has the tension between resources available and the requirements of and need to empower users of services.

The chapter integrates relevant findings from the earlier client-based literature with an examination of how, more recently, users and carers have evaluated the effectiveness of the communication they experienced from social workers and more generally in social care.

Chapters 3 and 4 examine different kinds of communication: symbolic, non-verbal, verbal and written. Symbolic communication involves aspects of our behaviour and presentation – such as punctuality, dress, the kind of food we provide in residential care, and the kind of basic care we give – which convey a symbolic as well as literal message to users of services about our respect or basic care for them or about the power relationship between us. Non-verbal communication is precisely that; not spoken communication but communication through behaviour such as facial expression, gaze, orientation and body movement.

Verbal communication is what we say and includes questioning, reflection, focussing, summarizing, challenging and confrontation. Verbal communication involves the use of language, and we need to be aware that the worker and the users of services may not share the same language. Interpretation, with its implications for clear communication, may be necessary. Written communication is essential work, not least in terms of recording and accountability. Communication by information technology has begun to replace written communication as a means of case recording but it is also a means of direct communication with vulnerable users of service (Rafferty, 2000). The use of information technology in communication with users of services is therefore an integral part of this book.

Subsequent chapters apply different kinds of communication to different purposes of social work. Chapter 5 examines relationship building and maintaining, and the skills of conveying genuineness, warmth, acceptance, encouragement, empathy and responsiveness. Chapter 6 examines the skills involved in attending and listening, including the use of silence. Chapter 7 is about sharing information: getting information by using reflection, paraphrasing, clarification, questioning and probing, and giving information and advice in either verbal or written form. Chapter 8 examines the use of contracts and the skills involved: summarizing, focussing and negotiation. Finally, Chapters 9 and 10 examine intervention skills and means of helping users of services to achieve change in attitudes or behaviour. Here we are concerned with the use of influence, both with skills like questioning, probing, advising, summarizing and focussing which were examined previously and with new skills such as interpretation and confrontation.

The skills identified and examined throughout the book are transferable skills. They are applicable across a range of settings, including group care, fieldwork and secondary settings, and to a range of users of services, including children, older people, people with learning difficulties, people with mental health problems and people with disabilities. They need to be applied with full understanding of the implications of structural differences, e.g. class, gender, age and ethnicity, for effective communication.

These transferable skills need to be used with colleagues. The skills involved in engaging, listening, negotiating and challenging are equally relevant to communication in work groups and multidisciplinary teams. I hope that readers will find the examination and discussion of skills applicable not only to working with users of services, but transferable to interdisciplinary communication in their work settings.

Finally, writing about communication is inevitably limited and problematic. Communication is an activity which has to be performed and practised. In order to develop skills, feedback has to be sought and acted upon. The reader must therefore first consider and reflect on the discussion in this book, but also, and more importantly, consider how to apply, use and practise the skills identified in each chapter, and seek feedback from users of services and colleagues or video in order to develop further competence in using them.

---

putting it into practice

Knowledge about communication is drawn from a number of disciplines. Reflect on your own sources of knowledge about communication skills. They may not refer to areas of social care but your own experiences of who you perceived to communicate effectively and why and how.

Consider the two service users described in this introduction and how they were treated by the same social worker. Reflect on how you, like the social worker, communicate verbally and non-verbally with different people, and why and how.

Recommended reading

The SCIE website (www.scie.org.uk) provides useful knowledge reviews, for example 'Teaching and Learning Skills in Social Work Education' (2004), 'Teaching Learning and Assessment Skills with Children and Young People in Social Work Education' (2006), 'Types and Quality of Knowledge in Social Care (2003).

2 | Helpful and effective communication – the views of users of services

In Chapter 1 we saw that an underlying principle of this book is that the views of users of services should influence, underpin and, more importantly, teach us about how we best can engage in effective communication in social work and social care. We also saw that terminology had changed in the last thirty years reflecting changes in the way in which users of services and social service providers work together. In the 1970s and early 1980s an extensive research-based literature examined *clients'* views of social work. The focus in the early 1970s on the importance of clients' views about the services they received was innovative, and a precursor to the importance we now attribute to partnership with users and carers and ensuring we incorporate their perspectives into changes in our practice. Current research-based literature focusses on the views of *users* and *carers* who require and receive social services. It is important here to be clear about terminology. As discussed in Chapter 1, Cree and Davis (2006) address this complicated issue, and I draw on their useful distinctions and terminology.

It is also important to be clear that, while we always need to pay careful attention to the views of users of services, we also have a duty to consider issues of risk, safety, child protection and adult protection. We may then take a view and make an assessment and propose intervention which does not accord with the views of the user of services.

This chapter explores the views of users of services, voluntary or involuntary, about helpful and effective communication in social work and social care. The term 'users of service' includes carers: if their views about helpful and effective communication diverge from those of direct service users the divergence will be discussed. We must also acknowledge social work's innovative history in researching and listening to the views of users of services about their experience of service delivery.

Mayer and Timms (1970) first highlighted the importance and complete neglect of seeking clients' views about the social work services they received. The subsequent growth of studies of the views of clients and users of services reflected a developing recognition that they were consumers of social work and social care and should have a voice in its appraisal and development. Any commitment to the empowerment of social work clients and users of services was meaningless if their views were neither sought nor taken into account.

While clients were not a homogeneous group who spoke with one voice (see also Cree and Davis, 2007, about service users), Rees and Wallace's (1982) review of the literature on clients' evaluations of social work identified common themes. Rees and Wallace distinguished between client satisfaction relating to the worker's style of response or perceived helpfulness, and client evaluation based on the outcome of contact and its effectiveness. This distinction can be made in terms of communication and its effectiveness and remains important in current examination of effectiveness and evaluation of social work and social work services.

These clients' evaluation of social work practice focussed on how they experienced relationship-based social work. Relationship-based social work was not a prominent part of social work methods in the late 20th century but has been a focus of re-emerging attention in the early 21st (Sudberry, 2002; Trevithick, 2005; see McIvor and Raynor (2007) in relation to criminal justice). This chapter initially examines the 'client'-based literature about helpful and effective communication, which was well researched and stressed the need to pay attention to the views of people who used social services (Mayer and Timms, 1970; Rees and Wallace, 1982; Sainsbury et al., 1982). Social work was unusual and innovative, particularly in comparison to health-related professions including medicine and nursing, in researching and publishing about the views of clients or users of services regarding the service they received. However this research literature was not necessarily translated into changes in practice or social services delivery as more recent research into users' and carers' views makes only too clear. More recent literature about the views of users of services in relation to communication (helpful and effective) is examined. Interestingly these suggest that what users of services currently perceive as helpful or unhelpful, in terms of social workers' communication, is not dissimilar to the findings of the earlier 'client'-based literature pre-1994.

We begin with the 'client'-based research: the literature referred to may appear dated but the lessons for current social work and social care are not. What can we learn from social work's past and apply now more effectively than we appear (from the literature about the views of current users of services) to have done so far?

Helpful and effective communication from the clients' perspective

Clients coming for help reported that they were likely to be bewildered, confused and ignorant about social work and social services. Many clients came during a crisis when they were likely to be particularly sensitive to their first point of contact – reception. This remains true. Hall (1974), investigating reception in children's departments, observed receptionists who appeared unsympathetic to clients and asked them to discuss personal problems in front of a waiting room of people. Such a reception was perceived as insensitive, uninterested and devaluing. More generally the literature on client perceptions indicated the need for greater sensitivity, individualization and tact on the part of social work receptionists. The current personalization agenda for social services (Leadbetter, 2004) reinforces this. From the social worker, clients initially appreciated warmth, informality and friendliness. They valued social workers who showed personal concern and interest and did not seem to be 'just doing a job'. As Davies (1994) suggested, client studies showed that 'the true professional is not someone who is cool, detached, career minded and disinterested' but is someone who shows friendliness, understanding and warmth in a way which convinces the client of his/her concern: a more personalized approach to the delivery of social services also requires these qualities from the social worker. (Leadbetter, 2004).

Clients saw this concern to be communicated if the worker expressed interest about their families, activities or hobbies, symbolizing professional *and* personal concern (Sainsbury, 1975). Lack of concern was communicated by the worker appearing bored or inattentive, e.g. staring out of the window when the client was talking, (Reith, 1975), keeping clients waiting (Hoffman, 1975) or breaking appointments at the last minute.

Clients valued social workers who listened attentively. Parents whose daughter had died very suddenly appreciated 'having someone outside the family just to sit and listen' (Lishman *et al.*, 1990). This act of listening was often valued in itself, independent of other help given. Patience and an unhurried approach were also appreciated by clients. Again this was seen to convey a personal concern, individualization (and personalization) and acknowledgement of the importance of the client's concerns: 'I was quite surprised they had time to bother because they've lots of people to deal with and maybe my case, it was big to me, but it was quite trivial to them' (Rees, 1974, p. 259).

Some clients, arriving at a social work agency, had ambivalent or negative feelings about asking for help (and this is still true). Clients who felt ashamed or apprehensive valued social workers who were able to put them at their ease. How did social workers help clients to feel more at ease? Rees and Wallace (1982) stressed the importance of the social worker empowering the client, especially by anticipating potential requests and putting them into words. Social workers who stressed clients' entitlement to money were seen as helpful, whereas stressing the cost of the help or shortage of resources increased clients' feelings of dependence (Blaxter, 1976) – something that is currently extremely relevant to care management and single shared assessments.

Where clients felt anxious about seeking help with interpersonal problems, they appreciated an individualized and friendly reception, patient, attentive listening and understanding. They emphasized the importance of a non-judgemental approach. Although they realised that social workers had to ask questions they appreciated a non-intrusive style. Rees and Wallace (1982, p. 32) suggest that 'too many questions, too early in contact can at times only confirm a client's suspicion that he or she is being judged or cross examined'. These early impressions about the perceived meaning of social workers' communication re-emerge, for example, in the debate about the refocussing initiative in relation to vulnerable children and its impact on social work practice. Is it about the investigation of child protection issues or an initial assessment of child concerns (Platt, 2006)?

The anxiety expressed by clients in the 1960s and 1970s about the authority and power of the agency has continued. As one service user commented:

> ...my health visitor and all that were going behind my back and things. And I said 'I'm not doing anything behind your backs. I want you to be honest and truthful with me.   (Platt, 2006, p. 277).

While authority is inherent in the role of social work, some fears could be unrealistic. A client at a child and family psychiatry clinic exemplifies this:

> I was frightened. I thought they would say I was a bad mother and take him away from me. When they took him away (to see a psychiatrist while she saw a social worker) I wondered where he was going. I did not ask.
> (Lishman, 1978)

I was the social worker and was unaware at the time of this intense anxiety. For me the initial encounter was a regular everyday experience. For my client it was unique and I should have been more aware of her anxiety and conveyed my recognition of it.

While warmth, empathy, patient listening and a non-judgemental approach were important to clients, they did not necessarily overcome clients' negative perceptions of social work and social work agencies. A client might trust an individual worker but remain suspicious of the agency. This finding is still relevant and we need to be aware of how our employing agency may be perceived.

Finally, clients found *activity* by the social worker helpful. Rees and Wallace (1982) suggested that '[b]y "doing things" or attempting to do things social workers confirm their concern and willingness to help.' Activity included giving advice and making arrangements on behalf of clients. Such activities had not always been valued historically in the social work literature: for example, giving advice had been seen as contradicting the principle of client self-determination (Biestek, 1965) and making arrangements on behalf of clients as encouraging the client's dependence. Clients did not appear to share these reservations. For example, one client gave the following reasons for finding his social worker helpful: 'he gave advice about social security, would go along to court or write a letter – I don't have to stammer out to someone who has no sympathy' (Lishman, 1985). Recent anecdotal evidence from young offenders is about the importance they attach to the social worker helping them to manage practically, for example in negotiating jobs and social security.

Because social workers' communication and behaviour are perceived as *helpful* it does not mean they are effective in terms of achieving a desired outcome. By 'desired outcome' we mean a positive change in a problematic situation, for example improved self-esteem, getting a job, managing a limited budget, improved family relationships or reducing offending. Maluccio (1979) argued that while warmth and friendliness initially could give clients a sense of hope and raise their expectations, clients felt let down if the expectations were subsequently not met. Maluccio suggested that different qualities and skills were required at different stages: warmth and sympathy initially, competence and knowledge later. This is an important distinction for current social work where we must, as professionals, evaluate outcomes for users of services and our effectiveness, and expect these to be examined and assessed by inspection agencies (see, for example, SWIA, 2006).

What did clients see as contributing to social worker's effectiveness in helping them achieve desired outcomes? Clients stressed knowledge and expertise, use of authority, agreement between client and worker about the purpose of contact, a task-centred approach and provision of advice and material help. All of these elements remain important for users of services but the context has changed: empowerment is crucial for voluntary users of services, but it is more problematic in working with involuntary users of services where the use of authority by the social worker is fundamental. In all these situations, knowledge and expertise and agreement about the purpose of joint work remain crucial.

Three main areas of knowledge and experience were valued by clients (Rees and Wallace, 1982):

1. Clients valued workers who had the maturity, whatever their age, to listen non-judgementally to what might appear to be shocking aspects of their lives, for example, violence, deprivation, loss or deviance. A non-judgemental attitude is not synonymous with condoning destructive, anti-social or sadistic behaviour, but if a social worker expresses shock, disapproval, or a kind of salacious over-inquisitiveness, any basis for effective work by client and worker is lost.

2. Clients valued workers who had enough life experience to understand clients' problems from their own experience. For example, experience of marriage or parenthood was seen as important if the client's situation involved child rearing, marital or family problems. Dissatisfaction about perceived youth appeared to relate more to clients' wish for the capacity to be understood, as well as wisdom and knowledge on the part of their social worker.

3. Clients appreciated specialized knowledge and training, or rather criticized workers for lack of specialized knowledge. In particular, parents of children who were physically disabled complained about workers' lack of knowledge of the disability itself and of relevant benefits and facilities (Butler, 1977; Robinson, 1978). However social workers need to be careful not to 'preconceive' from their knowledge rather than listening to users and carers as experts by experience.

Appropriate use of power and authority was an essential component of effectiveness as perceived by clients, but appropriate use was perceived differently by different clients. Some clients appreciated a relationship based on equality with the social worker in problem-sharing, and did not wish the social worker to exercise power and control over them. Instead they saw the social worker as someone with expertise to be consulted. This preference was particularly expressed by foster parents and parents of children with physical disability or learning disability. Currently we need to be aware that many adults with physical disabilities see social workers in this light, and also as someone who may have access to the resources they require.

In contrast, other clients preferred the social worker to be directive and exercise authority over them. According to Rees and Wallace (1982) such clients tended to be poor, to experience themselves as having little control over their lives and to have had past experience of people in authority which led them to assume the social worker was an expert and the relationship was of unequal power and knowledge.

For such clients, effective power and authority was seen to be exercised in two ways: by advice and guidance, and by control and limit-setting. Some clients perceived the social worker as more effective the more advice was given. They expected that after they have told the social worker their problems some kind of diagnosis and solution would be given and if it were not 'the clients feel somewhat let down and disappointed' (Rees and Wallace, 1982). In a sense this reflects the medical world, where there remains an expectation that we go for a diagnosis and an expert view. Some clients appreciated the social worker exercising authority over them by being firm, for example, by instructing them to carry out certain tasks, demanding certain behaviour or giving strong guidance (Sainsbury, 1975). This remains a relevant concept, for example in criminal justice and the 'What Works?' agenda (McGuire, 1995), but needs to be balanced against the views of other users of services who would wish to be involved in partnership as 'experts by experience'.

Other clients, particularly parents, wished the social worker to exercise control over others, their children. Fisher et al. (1986), commenting on parents' passive acceptance of loss of authority over their children, suggested that 'if difficulties had reached the point where a parent could not exercise proper authority over the child, it was logical in the parents' eyes to exercise responsibility by calling in external help' (p. 61) even if this meant admission to care. As one mother said, 'it's for control that they're in care'. This remains an issue for parents who feel they have lost control in relation to their care of their children.

The implications for social workers about these views of appropriate use of authority are complex. The worker needs to be aware of different approaches to the use of authority and control by users of services: where the expectation is of empowerment, user-led service delivery or power-sharing, worker control is resented. On the other hand, where the expectation is of worker control, e.g. in problematic behaviour by children or adolescents, an attempt at a more mutual approach may be seen as ineffectual. However, even where clients expected some form of authority, they did not wish this to be imposed arbitrarily and valued understanding, honesty and an empathic response from the worker (Rees and Wallace, 1982; Sainsbury 1975).

The differing views on purpose of contact and use of authority in studies of client perceptions suggested a 'clash in perspective' between worker and client. In a seminal study of clients of the Family Welfare Association, Mayer and Timms (1970) found that clients who felt they needed *material* help perceived the social worker as offering *relationship* help instead. Similarly, clients who went for help with *emotional* problems actually wanted something done about *another person* (spouse, child) whereas the social worker tended to focus on the client. As Davies (1994) points out, '[s]o numerous are such examples in the literature that one might be forgiven for thinking that what have been called "pervasive disagreements" are an inherent part of the social work process' (p. 22).

Maluccio (1979) found that lack of agreement between worker and client about the nature of the problem was one of the most important factors associated with a poor outcome in social work interventions. In one small-scale study, agreement about purpose emerged as an important factor affecting outcome (Lishman, 1985). If clients and social workers did not share a contract and sense of purpose, then, however understanding or positive the social worker was, the client felt nothing was achieved. This lack of a shared purpose was conveyed in the following perceptions:

Service User: 'I didn't know what he was after, he wouldn't say. I thought he would try and find some way of it being my fault.'

Worker: 'He came for advice and management of the children but that's not what we tend to do. He is very strict and controlling – the children's problems may be a response to this.'

Clearly the interests and purpose of clients and social workers did not always coincide. The lesson from these client studies, however, was not that social workers and their clients can always agree totally, but that social workers had the responsibility for clarifying expectations and checking how much they were agreed. Even where they differed, honest acknowledgement of the differences was a better base for successful, outcomes-focussed work than discrepant assumptions on both sides which were never checked or challenged.

If agreement about purpose was established, the act of unburdening and the worker's ability to listen, to be empathic and to be non-judgemental could be effective from the client's point of view. Particularly if clients were experiencing interpersonal or mental health problems such an unburdening was a relief. As one client (Lishman, 1985) expressed it: 'I got a lot off my chest – it had been inside for a long time'. How effective was such unburdening in the long term? For it to be effective it must lead to something: material help, advice and guidance or insight.

Families with multiple problems stressed the importance of mate-rial or financial help and still do. People who were physically disabled stressed the importance of practical help such as aids and adaptations. They valued practical help which was regular and reliable such as home helps. These views remain relevant for users and carers accessing (or not) services through care management and direct payments.

People who were in prison or on probation orders appeared to have relatively clear expectations of social work: for people in prison, practi-cal help in relation to housing, material resources and children's behav-iour; for people on probation, practical help with employment, school or finance (Gandy et al., 1975; Sainsbury and Nixon, 1979). People on probation and their families also valued an advocacy or negotiating role. Again these findings remain relevant. Perhaps however, in implementing the What Works agenda (McGuire, 1995) and other elements of statutory social work, we have not as assiduously sought the views of 'involun-tary' users of services as we have of those who require services but are not compelled by the state to use them.

As we have already examined, clients were likely to perceive direct advice and guidance as more effective than a passive approach, and this was particularly true if they had interpersonal problems e.g. a child care problem. Unburdening could sometimes be effective if it led to insight rather than to advice. For example, one client said, 'I realised, I was too possessive with my daughter', and another, 'I found I was channelling anger from my husband onto my son and using my daughter as a buffer' (Lishman, 1985). However these insights were only effective because they led to changed behaviour and relationship patterns.

Lessons about helpful and effective communication from the client-based literature for current social work and social care

In summary, what lessons from the client-based research remain relevant to practice with users of services in social work and social care now? In relation to helpful communication they include the following:

● the recognition of anxiety and fear people may have in approaching social services: consider, for example, parents who misuse drugs and may be very anxious about seeking help because of their fears about the possible removal of their children;
● the importance of the quality of the reception, in terms of waiting areas and receptionists' communication skills (including telephone skills);
● the importance of warmth, informality, friendliness and concern from the social worker or social care worker;

- the importance of listening and, as users and carers currently would wish, in doing so, recognizing them as 'experts by experience';
- the need for sensitivity to users' and carers' concerns about accessing social services and in particular the importance of recognizing their entitlement;
- the importance of activity by the social worker including advice and information giving which can contribute to the empowerment of users of services.

In relation to effective communication the lessons of client-based research include the fact that, while age and experience were of importance to clients, they are not aspects of self an individual social worker can change. Given the recent problems in recruitment and retention in social work and the concomitant expansion of recruitment of younger applicants including school leavers, the question of how social workers address the views of users of services about their age and experience or lack of it, is extremely important. The implications, in more detail, are:

- any young social worker or care worker needs to be aware that her or his youth may initially be perceived as problematic by a user of services;
- being young does not mean being naive or easily shockable. All social workers and care workers should use training to examine their own attitudes to a range of complex, distressing or shocking situations, which may arise from structural oppression or discrimination, or personal tragedy, loss or abuse, or a combination of personal tragedy and structural oppression. No individual social worker or care worker can have direct experience of all problematic life experiences. The need for transferability of understanding and knowledge e.g. of loss, abuse, oppression or discrimination is necessary for all users of services and their problem situations.

More generally we need to recognize that:

- all social workers have to take responsibility for the continuing development of specialized knowledge. This does not imply that a social worker needs to know everything a user of services might ask: rather that she or he 'has a responsibility to have at her/his fingertips detailed, accurate and up-to-date knowledge about the law, welfare rights and local community facilities, and be willing to turn to help to others in the agency' (Davies, 1994). Social workers need to be able to say honestly 'I don't know' but such a statement should imply a responsibility to find out and feed back the information to the user of services.
- social workers need to consider carefully and critically how users of services view their authority, and when it is usefully and

appropriately applied, and when its use may promote dependency and disempowerment.

● the agreement about clarity of shared purpose is fundamental.
● the concept of a potential 'clash in perspective' needs to be recognized in our communication with all users of services.
● we need to monitor and review shared purpose and a potential clash in perspective if we wish to achieve shared and useful outcomes for the user of services.

The findings discussed from research about client perceptions of social work remain relevant to social work and social care and underpin those from current users and carers (SCIE, 2004a).

The client research literature involved very detailed reviews of individual social workers' communication and helpful and (in)effective behaviour. More recent literature from service users and carers frequently addresses in more depth structural problems about social services delivery.

Helpful and effective communication from the perspective of users of services

How do the lessons from the earlier client research compare with more recent findings about users' and carers' views? The context of social work has changed with an increasing specialization in child protection, criminal justice and community care and with the concomitant rise in tension between the 'control' role of social work with involuntary clients and the 'empowerment' role with users and carers, particularly in relation to care in the community. However views from users of services continue to reflect the earlier concerns of clients, although the focus has been rather more about the 'empowerment' role of social workers (Beresford *et al.*, 1994) and less about the 'control' role where the research emphasis has been rather more on outcomes and 'what works' (Drakeford, 2002).

Users of services saw the context for communication in social work and social care as about 'providing a level playing field with those around you, to give you opportunities for interaction' (SCIE, 2005). Users of services stressed the need for better access to mainstream services, for example, education, housing, training, leisure and transport, to ensure that they enjoyed greater opportunities and fuller lives in their local communities (SCIE, 2005). Despite major contextual changes in the provision of social work and social services, there appears to be some continuity in what clients and users of services would like in terms of communication with a social worker or social care worker.

SCIE (2004c) outlines the values of user involvement. While this review is concerned with involving service users and carers in social work education, the principles outlined in relation to service user involvement are also relevant to social work practice.

There is overlap between the values of users of services' controlled organisations and those of social work and social care. Thus the values of social work and social care include the right to respect privacy and confidentiality, the right to choose, the promotion of independence and treating each person as an individual. This Code of Practice for social care workers provides the most recent and clear statement of these values, setting out in detail the conduct that is expected of these workers. (SCIE, 2004c, p. 11)

Consultation and research with service users and carers suggest that there is broad agreement in what they want from social workers and social care services across the range of different user and carer groups. Users and carers, focus on both helpfulness and effectiveness. According to SCIE (2004c):

in summary service users want social workers to be:

● physically and emotionally available;
● supportive, encouraging and reassuring;
● respectful;
● patient and attentive;
● committed to the independence of the individual;
● punctual;
● trustworthy;
● reliable;
● friendly but not frightened to tell people how they see things;
● and empathic and warm.   (p. 35)

Beresford *et al.* (2006), in relation to palliative care, stress the importance for service users of a 'genuine' professional relationship with the social worker and the need for the following qualities: kindness, warmth, respect, compassion, caring, sensitivity, empathy and thoughtfulness.

Findings about helpful and effective communication with children reinforce and add to the views of adult service users.

First the children felt that effective communication in social work had something to do with being as well as with doing. They told us how important it was for them for practitioners to be 'kind', 'friendly', 'gentle', 'fair', 'respectful', 'trustworthy', 'patient', 'reliable', 'telling the truth', and so on. They also talked about effective communication which included 'listening', 'understanding', 'explaining well', and 'getting things done'.   (SCIE, 2000, p. 5)

Major issues which emerge for users and carers are about access to social work and to social services. Beresford *et al.* (2005) provide a very detailed critique of users of services' views of social work and social care. Much of their critique is about organizational issues but these inevitably impact on how we communicate with users of services and with their satisfaction and our effectiveness.

The following quotes from Beresford *et al.* (2005) indicate problems with accessing services:

Bad assessments are service driven and disempower the user. (p. 5)

Phone access is poor and may deter people on low income. There is also little continuity in the duty process. (p. 5)

I know more about my condition that they do. (p. 8)

Service users comment on the variability of the approach they receive from staff:

Attitudes of social workers vary considerably. Their attitude depends on who they get. (p. 9)

In terms of interprofessional, interagency working, users of services comment very critically about the lack of interprofessional communication:

I have social workers, occupational therapists, district nurses and others and they never talk to each other, Every time a different worker comes they ask me what's wrong with me. I say 'Haven't other people told you?' and they say 'We don't do that'. (Beresford *et al.*, 2005, p. 11)

Beresford *et al.* summarize their findings:

There is continuing poor communication between the professions. (p. 12)

Access to services includes physical access but also provision of information and clear and accessible use of language and communication. While users of services applying for services in the community are usually visited at home for an introduction to the Single Shared Assessment other users of services are often required to attend appointments in health, social service or criminal justice departments. These buildings need, therefore, to be fully physically accessible and transport requirements need to be taken into account (Beresford *et al.*, 1994). Clear directions and large maps are necessary ahead of appointments (YIPPEE and CATS, 2002). Parking space requirements and the needs of a support worker or assistance dog also need to be considered (Shaping our Lives National User Network, 2003). Timing of meetings also needs consideration: early morning appointments may be problematic (YIPPEE and

CATS, 2002). The quality of reception areas and reception personnel may still be problematic (Hall, 1974). Access is also about language and information and communication. Language needs to be plain and jargon-free. Requirements for British Sign Language (BSL) interpreters (Shaping our Lives National User Network, 2003) and for interpreters for service users and carers who speak little English (Alexander et al., 2004) need to be carefully attended to. Accessible formats for information for people with hearing or visual impairment need to be provided (Beresford, 1994). In relation to people with hearing impairment, service users also complain that no one can use BSL (Beresford et al., 2005, p. 10). Social workers and social care workers need to give consideration to different formats for communication in writing, such as drawings, with a recognition that not all users of services can read (YIPPEE and CATS, 2002).

Clear advice about conducting consultation meetings with users is highly relevant for considering communication in social work and social care more generally. It includes:

● use of clear, plain English (with interpretation if necessary);
● avoidance of jargon;
● not interrupting a user or carer;
● making sure that a user or carer can see the worker's lips (i.e. that the worker has not covered his or her mouth) (Shaping our Lives National User Network, 2003).

Sometimes the views of users of services indicate a potential tension, for example '[t]here needs to be more confidentiality between the professions in interdisciplinary work' but 'there is continuing poor communication between the professions' (Beresford et al., 2005, p. 12). Perhaps more fundamental, in terms of communication, is the need perceived by users of services for professionals to let go of their power and listen to users and carers as potential experts in the assessment of their own needs (YIPPEE and CATS, 2002). The analysis by Barnes et al. (2000) of developing partnerships with service users in interprofessional education in community mental health also has relevance to the practice of social work. Barnes et al. trace the evolution of participation in interprofessional education, from 'consumerism' to 'empowerment' and more recently to 'partnership' which they consider to be 'a more realistic approach because it acknowledges differentials in power without demanding equality'.

Overall it is difficult to provide a comprehensive but succinct analysis of perspectives of users of services on communication in social work.

As Lindow (2000) comments, '[u]sers of personal social services are a diverse group who do not speak with one voice. Attempts to elicit service users' views often do not take this diversity into account.' Analyses based on the social model of disability (Oliver, 1996) and on a human rights model rather than a medical model in mental health (Reid and Reynolds, 1996) emphasize key areas which have already been referred to in this chapter including:

- access (both physical and to information);
- relinquishing control in areas of social work and social care where use of authority is not the primary focus;
- giving full respect and support;
- working in ways which 'de-clientize' users and do not override the wishes of users of services because the professional takes the view that he or she is the expert in judging the best interests of the user. Instead the professional acknowledges the user as an expert in his or her own life and seeks to work in partnership within inevitable resource constraints to maximize the support required by the user in ways and at times he or she needs it.

Beresford et al. (2005) emphasize the importance of training. Users of services stress the need for 'Service Workers to be encouraged to be more open to differing needs and to use their own initiative' and also 'Care Workers should learn to listen to service users' (p. 14).

However, the research reviewed so far has not addressed the views of involuntary service users. While research on users' and carers' views about social work communication has not focussed on 'involuntary' users of services, many, if not all, lessons are transferable. The research about helpful and effective communication in general found that both users and carers stressed the need for a high quality relationship with their social worker and the need for time to develop this and consistency in maintaining it. For users of services who did not perceive their engagement as voluntary this relationship was of critical importance. Millar and Corby (2006) refer to the importance of trust, sharing concerns and creating openness where children appeared to be vulnerable or at risk.

Where we are working with involuntary users of social workers we do need to pay attention to how we communicate. Overall, what are the important messages from users of services about our communication in social work and social care? We need to recognize that these are essential whether we provide services for voluntary or involuntary users even if we may not ask our involuntary service users their views in quite such a rigorous way.

Beresford *et al.* (2005) summarize the essential qualities which underpin helpful and effective communication in social work and social care:

- availability;
- reliability;
- fairness;
- flexibility;
- continuity of contact;
- honesty;
- listening;
- openness rather than an apparently patronizing attitude.

Cree and Davis (2006) further enhance what users of service value in terms of helpful and effective communication:

- responsiveness;
- building and sustaining relationships;
- a person-centred approach;
- holistic assessment and intervention;
- knowledgeable and evidence-based practice;
- enabled support which is not only practical but also emotional.

Their respondents also recognized and fully acknowledged that social work and social care has to balance individual rights, assessment of risk and protection of individuals.

Overall, therefore, what are the messages that clients (historically) and users of services (currently) tell us about how as social workers and professional social carers we need to behave and communicate? We need to be:

- respectful;
- patient and attentive;
- punctual;
- trustworthy;
- reliable;
- fair;
- flexible;
- honest;
- listening;
- responsive;
- person-centred;
- knowledgeable;
- holistic and attending to practical and emotional concerns.

(Beresford, 2005; Cree and Davis, 2006; SCIE, 2004c)

While the literature attends more to research about voluntary users of service it is important that we apply these general principles and research findings to involuntary users of services as well as voluntary ones, recognizing that the distinguishing line is a fine one and that anti-discrimination and anti-oppressive practice is a core social work value.

What implications do the views of clients and users and carers about their expectations of social work have for communication in social work and social care? Chapter 3 examines them in terms of non-verbal and verbal communication.

---

putting it into practice

This chapter drew on the views of users of services about social workers' communication.

Think about when you are a user of service e.g. visiting your GP. How does he or she meet the requirements for effective communication?

Take time to reflect on how you meet the requirements at the end of the chapter about how as social workers and social carers we need to communicate and behave.

Recommended reading

Beresford, P., Shamash, M., Forrest, V. and Turner, M. (2005) *Developing Social Care: Services Users' Vision for Adult Support*, Bristol, SCIE, Policy Press. Here detailed comments from users of services help us to think carefully and apply the previous evidence from client research about what constitutes helpful and effective communication.

Cree, V. and Davis, A. (2006) *Social Work: Voices from the Inside*, London and New York, Routledge. This book helpfully distinguishes different groups of users of services, for example, voluntary and involuntary, services users and carers. It reminds us that the boundary between service provision and service use is fluid: social workers and social carers are personally users of services.

3 | Types of communication: symbolic, non-verbal and verbal

This chapter draws, if somewhat obliquely, on communication theory defined by Randall and Parker (2000). It examines 'the selection of a means of conveying a message (language, gesture and writing), the decoding of the message by the recipient (hearing, seeing, reading) and making a response on the basis of the interpretation (reply)' (p. 69). This definition reminds us of the essentially interactive value of communication. Users of social work services interpret communication from social workers and social carers. Social workers and social care workers also interpret communication from users of services and carers. These different interpretations may not reflect the intention of the original communication but they influence, in an interactive and dynamic way (as we saw in Chapter 2), how positively or negatively further contact is perceived and how effective it is.

As we have seen, users of services historically have evaluated and interpreted social work communication, both positively and negatively.

'Well, she's 'omely. She doesn't talk posh so you can talk to her properly.'

(Cohen, 1971)

'She's easy to talk to. I just relaxed. She has a calming effect.'

(Lishman, 1985)

Such apparently simple judgements are likely to reflect a social worker's use of a complex interaction of verbal, non-verbal and symbolic communication.

Since these observations were made about social workers' communication, shifts have occurred in the way social work responds to problems presented. Coulshed and Orme (2006) identify an early contribution to these shifts. They note 'that statutory agencies were not practised in open decision making with the consumers of their services, and because of this social workers are not used to asking the opinions of the users' (p. 73). An innovative project by Marsh and Fisher (1992) 'encouraged professionals to reflect on ways they defined needs, made assessments and decisions on *behalf* of rather than in *partnership* with users' (Coulshed and Orme, 2006, p. 73).

Trevithick (2005) argues that the ensuing shift changed the philosophy of social work and social care from:

'doing things to service users' to
'doing things for service users' to
'doing things with service users' (p. 116)

While the shift has not been as clear as many users of services users have wished (SCIE, 2004a and c) and for involuntary clients may not be wholly possible, it is a part of the changing context of social work described in the Preface. For users of services in 2009, current and future judgements about how social workers convey respect, availability, support and encouragement, reliability, empathy and trustworthiness will continue to be influenced by the complex interaction of symbolic, non-verbal and verbal communications.

Symbolic communication

According to the *Shorter Oxford English Dictionary* symbolic means 'expressed, denoted or conveyed by a symbol'. Symbolic communication, therefore, involves behaviour, actions or communications which represent or denote something else. As social workers we need to be aware of the potential meaning of our presentation, actions and aspects of our work environment. For example, our punctuality, our dress, the layout of our rooms, the food we provide for users of services and the physical care we give them will have a symbolic, as well as a literal, meaning for users of services.

Davies (1994) stressed the importance in residential care of the five senses; smell, touch and taste have particular relevance to symbolic communication. For example, stale cooking smells, fresh baking smells, the smell of incontinence, rough physical handling, a gentle hug, appetizing and familiar food all have symbolic as well as literal and practical meaning to residents. Such details of our practice may symbolize love, respect, care, control, power and other significant aspects of relationships between workers and users of services.

The physical environment and symbolic care

The symbolism of the physical environment is of particular importance in residential care, since this is the daily living space of residents, not just a venue of weekly contact. Davies (1994) comments, 'the environments we provide speak directly to residents'. The experience of residential care continues to vary. Some residential homes for older people are attractively and well maintained: some are not and may smell of stale cooking or urine. The symbolic message from that is of lack of respect and of neglect. In contrast, in a day centre for families, where drug misuse is a significant problem, a welcoming building, creative murals and a kitchen dispensing cups of tea and plates of soup convey a different and much more positive, valuing message.

Basic care may be carried out in a variety of ways, each of which conveys a symbolic meaning. It may be done roughly and with haste, routinely, functionally and efficiently, or (a different message) with time, sensitivity and individualized care. Take, for example, group care for adolescent girls with severe learning difficulties. Ensuring gentle handling of bathing, showering or hair washing with appropriate toiletries symbolizes respect and value for their physical care and for their appearance.

For older people in the community, care and sensitivity in handling, bathing and returning a user of services to her bed are conveyed symbolically by gentle and respectful handling and attention to concerns about the process from both her and also her family carers.

Davies (1994) highlighted the symbolic communication involved in how a worker treats the treasured possessions of a looked-after child. Similar issues arise in terms of how older people's treasured possessions are treated by care staff when they are in residential or nursing care.

Food and its presentation is highly symbolic. A residential worker expressed surprise at the way the children in the care home where he worked became quite aggressive and disturbed when the milk ran out. They understood – and he did not – that food (and especially milk) is a symbol of basic love and care. If we are dealing with looked-after children who have been physically and emotionally deprived, the importance of an abundance of food they enjoy cannot be overemphasized. For them love must not run out. Poor quality of food or inadequate quantity conveys a lack of care for any resident. How much individual preferences are taken into account symbolizes how much attention and sensitivity is paid to the individual as opposed to the institution. Similar considerations apply to cultural preferences and requirements in food. A youth assessment centre, whose residents are all Muslim, routinely served a white, British diet of fish and chips and mince. This makes a highly symbolic statement about ethnicity and relative power. Similarly in care homes for older people, the selection, cooking and quality of food symbolizes how much attention is paid, not just to individual needs and preferences, but also to recognition of diversity, for example in relation to culture and ethnicity.

In fieldwork first contact for a user of service (statutory or voluntary) is usually the receptionist and the waiting area. Hall (1974) found that clients were often treated unsympathetically and insensitively by receptionists. My experiences of reception vary in GP surgeries as well as social work offices. A quick reception, a warm smile and the offer of a seat convey respect, concern and welcome. In contrast, being ignored for fifteen minutes while a receptionist dealt with the telephone engineer and numerous phone calls left me feeling enraged but also conveyed a lack of respect and acknowledgement of me as a person. For users of services, who may already experience profound anxiety or a sense of shame and stigma, being ignored or being rudely or abruptly treated symbolizes a devaluing lack of respect and confirmation of lack of worth. We need to think more widely about how we feel when we are waiting for the GP with an unhelpful receptionist or waiting in a call-centre queue where no-one appears interested in our particular request and then apply it to reception for users of services in social work and social care.

Waiting areas vary. Space, comfortable seating, cleanliness, fresh paint, a variety of comics, toys and magazines convey a welcome. Peeling walls, dirt, a smell of urine and broken furniture convey symbolically that the waiting user of service is worth no more than this. Oliver's survey (1990) of a small selection of social service receptions presented a depressing picture of reception and waiting areas, with few public toilets, poor access for wheelchairs, reception hatches high in the walls, making them inaccessible to wheelchair users and creating a barrier to communication, and few toys for children. While the threat of violence had influenced many social services departments' reception areas, so that some 'adopt a siege mentality', Oliver argued that respect for the user of services, conveyed by pleasant surroundings and service, may go some way to prevent anger arising, although staff should also be protected e.g. by buzzers and closed circuit television.

Interviewing rooms which are cramped, used as second-hand clothing stores, inadequately sound-proofed and uncomfortably furnished symbolically devalue the user of service, the worker and the interview process. Rooms which are attractively painted, clean and have comfortable furniture convey respect for the user of services, for the worker and for the social work process.

A major voluntary organization dealing with extremely poor and deprived users of services refurbished its waiting area. It is comfortably and attractively furnished and decorated with magazines and toys for adults and for children who are waiting. The receptionist provides a warm and courteous welcome. It conveys a symbolic message that the agency welcomes, respects and values people who use its services, and service users appreciated this refurbishment.

Breakwell and Rowett (1982) remind us that the interview room is the social worker's territory and not that of the users of services who, on entering a social worker's room, are expected to respect territorial rules, e.g. not to move chairs or sit behind or on the desk. Breakwell and Rowett noted how symbolic of power and control territory can be. We should be aware of our need for and use of these symbols such as the desk, forms and records and their meaning in terms of authority and control. It is helpful to be reflective and think about our own experience of the use of such symbols in our encounters with doctors, consultants or lawyers. If we experience discomfort in relation to them we should be aware that we may discomfort users of services in a similar way.

The way in which seats are arranged is also symbolic of territory and power. If I sit behind my desk, as lawyers, medical consultants and GPs frequently do, formality is increased, distance (emotional as well as physical) maintained and my formal authority is intensified. Without the protection of my desk I am less threatening, my power and authority less obtrusive, and physically my position lends itself to more equality. Conversely, placing a user of services in a lower chair than me as a social worker puts him or her in an inferior position and symbolizes the power differential in the relationship.

D'Ardenne and Mahtani (1989) were also concerned with symbolic aspects of physical space or territory. In particular they argued that 'the physical environment can be a powerful statement of your transcultural viewpoint'(p. 53). They suggested, for example, that pictures or photographs in an office will be 'more welcoming' to users of services from different ethnic origins if they 'depict people from different cultures or show different parts of the world'.

Dress

The way we dress communicates symbolically something of ourselves, and will have symbolic meaning for users of services and colleagues depending on age, culture, class and context. Dress may be particularly important in terms of first impressions. When we meet someone for the first time there is so much to take in that we have to be selective. Dress, hair and facial expression are immediately available to us if we are sighted, and on the basis of them we tend to make assumptions about personality, character or behaviour. So, for example, untidy dress and appearance may be interpreted as signifying carelessness or incompetence. Trevithick (2005) recalls 'a social worker being bewildered by a service user who complained when he had arrived to introduce himself wearing dirty jeans and a combat jacket' (p. 121).

A formal suit, male or female, may convey distance and power, not necessarily appropriate to a fieldwork interview, and certainly inappropriate in everyday life in residential work. In a multidisciplinary setting, where people from disciplines which may be perceived as more powerful, e.g. medicine or law, besuit themselves, the formal suit may represent the social worker's claim to equivalent authority. It may also be accepted by the users of services and other professionals as the uniform of the place. In a court setting, failure by a male worker to wear a suit and tie or by a female worker to wear a suit may be seen by magistrate, Sheriff or judge as implying a lack of respect for judicial processes, or a lack of power or authority on the part of the social worker. Such assumptions, based on appearance, can be detrimental to the user of criminal justice services, who is not a voluntary participant in criminal justice proceedings.

What messages may be conveyed by a young social worker's choice of a rather short skirt? For her it is comfortable, fashionable and attractive. For the Muslim father of the family she is visiting it may flaunt sexuality and symbolize an attack on his cultural values and his relations with women, in particular his wife and his daughter. The same skirt in a hospital ward round may equally symbolize sexuality, youth and a lack of authority, in some sense diminishing the female social worker's role and contribution in relation to the power of the male medical hierarchy. Scruffy jeans and a jumper may be comfortable for the worker and entirely appropriate in, for example, youth work or residential child care. In visiting an older person for a community care assessment they may be seen as denoting lack of respect, as Trevithick (2005) noted.

There are no fixed rules about who should dress in what way across social work and social care. However, it is important that we are aware of the symbolic importance of how we dress and are sensitive to how we may be perceived by the very different individuals and groups of people who use our services.

Punctuality and reliability

Punctuality, reliability, and attention to detail are symbolic of the worker's care, concern and competence. A couple applied to adopt a child. At the first interview the social worker arrived two hours late and then took down information on the inside of a cigarette packet. The couple, who were anxious at the prospect of assessment, experienced the lateness as insensitive, off hand and unconcerned. The cigarette packet symbolized lack of thought and preparation. Trotter (2007), in his research on criminal justice and child protection, similarly argues for the importance of the worker's reliability in terms of punctuality, as well as subsequently following up on what has been agreed. Perceived thoughtlessness continues to be criticized by users of services (unpublished research, Robert Gordon University, 2004). It may be conveyed by poor time-keeping, lack of preparation for a meeting and lack of detailed understanding of the previous contacts which users of services have had with other workers in relation to their current situation. The importance of good time management and communication with other relevant professionals is key to being prepared and not being perceived as 'thoughtless' by users of services or incompetent by other professionals with whom we work.

Unreliability ('he never does what he promises') symbolizes for many users of services a lack of 'genuine concern' (Rees and Wallace, 1982). It may also remind them or reawaken feelings about unreliability of significant people. For example, for many children in care, parents or attachment figures will have been 'unreliable' in major ways, for example by illness, separation or rejection. Bowlby (1984) suggested that 'whatever representational models of attachment figures and of self an individual builds during his childhood and adolescence, tend to persist relatively unchanged into and throughout adult life' (p. 141). Trevithick (2005) reflects, 'I can recall my own shortcomings when I have let children and young people down by cancelling appointments or failing to turn up on time. My explanation felt insignificant compared to the distress I caused' (p. 121). Unreliability, as perceived by users of services, can include lack of punctuality and preparation, failure to respond promptly to phone calls, for example, about clarification of aspects of care plans, or problems in relation to them, in general not responding quickly (unpublished research, Robert Gordon University, 2004) and not following through on action agreed. While for many social workers, time and resource constraints may make it difficult to respond as promptly as the user of a service would wish or to follow through provision of a resource agreed as needed, as social workers we need to remain aware that our lack of reliability, even in relatively minor ways, not only symbolizes a current lack of concern, but may confirm and invoke earlier problematic attachment models of unreliable care. Prompt response to correspondence is therefore essential. Beresford *et al.* (2005) note one woman's response about a promised letter, from social services: 'it went to Timbuktu, and did not come to my house' (p. 29).

Conveying concern symbolically

In Chapter 2 we saw that users of services (voluntary or involuntary) wanted respect, empathy, trustworthiness and reliability from social workers and caring professionals. Symbolic communication is an essential component of how we convey these valued aspects of our practice. In Chapter 2 we also saw that activity on the part of the social worker was seen by users of services as symbolizing concern. The following comments from clients (Sainsbury *et al.*, 1982, p. 76) illustrate satisfaction and dissatisfaction on this theme:

> He really gets down to my problems. If I had to change [my social worker] my only worry would be, would he take an active part in helping us?
> He says 'I'll see what I can do', but you never hear he's done it.

While social workers' use of activity as a means of conveying concern has to be balanced against the danger of 'taking over', and disempowering users of service, if we promise action and fail to carry it out we will inevitably convey a lack of concern and of reliability. However, we also need to be aware of how users of services may, in a symbolic way, experience economic drivers in social services as relegating them to being a cost to budgets, for example when, as care managers, we need to ration what users of services need so that demand matches supply.

> They should work around the person and their carer and not the other way round. People should be at the centre and treated individually.
>
> (Beresford *et al.*, 2005, p. 27)

Symbolic communication is an important element of how the personalization agenda for services can be enhanced (Leadbetter, 2004), although realistically, as agency employees, we also ration resources and there remains a tension between the personalization agenda and rationing.

Nevertheless, an important lesson for us is to be aware of how users of services interpret what we do symbolically and not necessarily rationally or as we intended. If we recognize and address the importance of the symbolic meaning of our values, communication, behaviour, dress and environment, this can enhance the trust and belief of users of services in our concern, reliability and competence.

Non-verbal communication

As with symbolic communication, social workers need to be aware of how they use non-verbal behaviour, including facial expression, gaze, orientation and body movement, and its potential meaning for users of services. They also need to be aware of what reciprocal non-verbal signals from users of services may be conveying.

Sutton (1994) suggested that, while spoken communication is concerned mainly with information-giving, non-verbal communication is 'the music behind the words', conveying feelings or attitudes.

How important is non-verbal communication? It is extremely important and probably rather more important and effective than verbal communication. If as professional workers our words are respectful, clear and supportive but non-verbally we convey irritation, unease or impatience, the non-verbal communication will provide the dominant message to users of services, and not our verbal communication. As Robinson (1998) suggests, non-verbal messages are 'often the best indicators of an individual's true attitudes or intentions, irrespective of what has been said' (p. 102). Argyle *et al.* (2007) found that, in relation to behaviour conveying dominance or submission, non-verbal communication had more effect than verbal, and that if the two were in conflict the verbal communication tended to be ignored.

We need therefore to be aware of and, if necessary, change what may be perceived as negative aspects of our non-verbal behaviour. Robinson (1998) argues that:

> unlike spoken language, which is used as often to conceal thought as it is to express thought and which people largely control for their own purposes, much non-verbal language seems impossible to control. (p. 102)

Non-verbal behaviour needs to be considered and analyzed and thereafter applied in terms of its relevance to quite differing and distinct ethnic groups, for example African Caribbean, Bangladeshi, Pakistani, Indian and Chinese people. Non-verbal communication also needs to be considered and analyzed in terms of its validity and application across other structural divides, including gender and social class.

Robinson makes the distinction between high and low context cultures. Low context cultures (for example the United States and Great Britain) tend to rely on verbal communication which can be elaborate and highly detailed: verbal ability is valued. According to Robinson (1998),

> high context cultures are more sensitive to non-verbal messages: hence they are more likely to provide a context and setting and let the point evolve. Black cultures have been described as high context. (p. 103)

It may be useful in examining the use of non-verbal communication to reflect on and apply this concept of high and low context cultures.

More broadly, the context of our work will affect the significance of our non-verbal communication. Children are particularly aware of and sensitive to non-verbal behaviour. In working with people with hearing impairment our posture, position and facial expression will be particularly important; with people with visual impairment our voice tone and touch are essential. In residential work our non-verbal behaviour is constantly on view.

While non-verbal communication is important, it is also difficult to interpret. For example, nodding one's head is not a single-purpose activity; it can act as a reinforcer (when one person's behaviour is followed by a head nod from the other the behaviour of the other increases) or give the other person permission to go on speaking. It can be a sign of attentive listening, but a series of rapid head nods can convey that the nodder wishes to speak (Argyle, 1975).

We need to be aware of the ambiguity of non-verbal communication (e.g. a swinging foot can convey anger, fear, boredom or energy) and of the context (e.g. the person's normal non-verbal style). Nicolson *et al.* (2006) suggest that it is changes in non-verbal behaviour or untypical behaviour which are particularly significant, for example avoiding eye contact or fidgeting more when discussing a particular issue.

Since interactions between social workers and users of services may involve mutual difficulties in interpreting such ambiguous non-verbal behaviour, it is essential that the social worker is aware of her or his non-verbal style and of how congruent her or his verbal and non-verbal communications are. Feedback from video is the most direct way to see ourselves and our non-verbal communication as others see us. While the awareness given may initially lead to self consciousness and feelings of being deskilled, there is clear potential for changing behaviour of which we were previously unaware.

Non-verbal communication can be broadly divided into two areas: *proxemics*, concerned with distance and how close people like to be to each other, and *kinesics*, referring to movements, gestures, expression and eye contact. More simply, we can consider the following areas: distance, posture and orientation, gaze and eye contact, and facial expression.

Each of these areas needs to be considered in relation to the structural issues identified earlier, which include gender, ethnicity, race and class. What follows can only be a brief introduction to what are highly complex issues.

Proxemics

We have already considered the symbolic aspects of territory and space. We must also be aware of what interpersonal distance or closeness is comfortable to ourselves and to users of our services. Preferences for closeness or distance are affected by race, gender, class, individual, and by who we are with, how well we know them, and how we feel about them. There are marked cross-cultural differences in how close people like to be to each other. For example, Swedes and Scots have tended to be most distant (Lott *et al.*, 1969); Southern Europeans tend to prefer closer interpersonal distances than northern Europeans (Hall, 1974); Halberstadt (1985) found that black Americans preferred closer interpersonal distances than Americans of European origin. Preferred interpersonal distance also depends on culture, for example, whether we come from contact cultures such as Asian or African-Caribbean (where a few inches is preferred) or non-contact cultures such as white northern Europeans where the preferred distance for most encounters is at least three or four feet for personal relationships and four to seven feet for professional and client interaction (Hall, 1966; Rozelle *et al.*, 1997). Similarly, whether we come from an individualistic culture, as promoted by the Thatcherite government and its policies in Britain in the 1980s, or a collectivist culture will affect our preferred communication distance. People from individualistic cultures 'are comparatively remote and distant proximically. Collectivist cultures are interdependent and, as a result they work, play, live and sleep in close proximity to one another' (Robinson, 1998, p. 111).

Gender also affects our preferences about what is a comfortable distance in our communication with others. Mehrabian (1972) found that women tended to tolerate greater physical closeness. Similarly Scott (1994) suggests that women require less physical space. Robinson (1998) argues that 'women seem to have become accustomed to and tolerant of invasions of their personal space' (p. 111). While the use of physical proximity may be interpreted by women as a means of promoting interpersonal engagement it can also convey dominance or aggression. As a small, female social worker working in a interdisciplinary team dealing with children with cancer and leukaemia, I became very aware of the use, by a male medical colleague, of close physical proximity, when I was questioning or challenging, (from the social perspective of the family and the child) his exclusive focus on the 'illness' and 'treatment': he used the physical proximity to try to dominate me and close down the discussion. Physical proximity used by a female social worker or care worker to convey engagement and empathy may be interpreted by a male client, service user or colleague to convey a rather different and unintended sexual message.

Finally age affects our preference for physical closeness or distance (Aiello and Jones, 1971). Children prefer and use more closeness than adults: older people may perceive close proximity as conveying a lack of respect.

So there are no fixed rules for distance: getting too close can seem intrusive and threatening, remaining too distant can seem cold and withdrawn. However we need to be aware of age, cultural and gender differences in how we, as social work and social care professionals, users of services and other professionals use and interpret distance in communication.

Proximity also needs to be considered in relation to orientation. Sommer (1965) and Cook (1968) explored different seating positions and found evidence which suggested that sitting alongside a person implies cooperation, opposite a person competition and at right angles equality of status. Thus, sitting behind a desk directly opposite someone has distancing and power implications but also may be confrontational. Seating arrangements can also influence other aspects of non-verbal behaviour including eye contact and gaze (Nicolson *et al.*, 2006).

Posture is also important, reflecting cultural and contextual conventions, status and emotions. For example, Mehrabian (1972) found that subjects were more likely to be relaxed with a low status person: such 'relaxation' involved reclining, leaning sidewards and placing arms and legs asymmetrically. As social workers we may need to consider whether our relaxed posture – intended to make users of services feel comfortable – may denote our assumption of power and status.

Posture can convey attitudes. Mehrabian (1972) found that we convey a positive attitude by reasonably relaxed open posture with uncrossed limbs, and by turning towards and slightly leaning towards users of services. Such a posture helps to convey our warmth and immediacy, openness and attentiveness. Robinson (1998) further argues that the implications of postural communication in interethnic interactions are extremely significant for social workers and social care workers: tense posture may denote vigilance and lack of trust on the part of users of services. However again, as with distance, there are no fixed rules about posture: being too relaxed may convey power and inattentiveness, being too rigid, tension, anxiety and authority.

Touch is another aspect of proxemics which may vary in meaning according to context and user of services. Like distance, there are cultural differences in the use of touch. Mehrabian (1971) found that some cultures (for example, Arab, Jewish, Mediterranean) value and use touch. In contrast, in the North of Scotland, for example, except in intimate relationships, touch can be more likely to be viewed as intrusion into personal space. In social work, individual and contextual differences also matter. For example, in working with people who are bereaved touch seems an important means of conveying concern and openness to the bereaved person's distress. A pat or brief hug can convey encouragement and support. Sometimes, however, it may be done to protect ourselves, for example, hugging to 'comfort' and thereby stop someone's extreme distress also protects us from having to share it. The use of touch in social work and social care has become more problematic. Touch may be interpreted sexually: for example for a child or woman who has been sexually abused, touch may symbolize and reawaken the abuse of power and violation of boundaries. Sadly, anxieties about sexuality in residential child care may lead to a taboo on touch at the expense of its use as a 'rewarding and undervalued way of making contact with inarticulate, distressed or emotionally isolated children and adolescents' (Davies, 1994, p. 257).

Kinesics

Kinesics includes the use of eye contact, facial expression, movements and gestures. Eye contact or gaze appears to have an important function in regulating conversation. For example, in a conversation one participant looks at the other more when he or she is listening than when speaking. A participant looks at the other when she/he finishes speaking, and away at the beginning of speaking, thus signally the beginning and end of her/his utterances (Kendon, 1973). So, when a user of service is speaking we need to keep looking at him or her, thus conveying our attention.

Eye contact can convey liking or positive attitudes, but prolonged eye contact can also signify interest in the other person, either in a friendly, sexual or aggressive way (Argyle, 2007). Eye contact therefore, has to be used with discretion.

Eye contact differs according to culture and gender. Furnham and Bochner (1986) identified cultural differences in normal eye contact: people from Arab and Latin American cultures tend to engage in higher levels of mutual gaze than people from the Western European cultures. Harper *et al.* (1978) found that Latin Americans and Southern Europeans tend to focus their gaze on the face and eyes of the person they are talking to whereas people from Asia, India and Pakistan do not. For black people, high eye contact may be seen to convey a lack of respect and over-use of power and authority (Robinson 1998). There are also gender differences in the use of gaze and eye contact. Exline (1963) found that women engaged in greater eye contact than men.

The level of appropriate eye contact cannot be specified. It has to be adjusted by the worker according to the cultural expectations of a user of services. In general, too much eye contact can be seen as staring and obtrusive. For a female social worker to engage in moderate eye contact with an Asian man may be seen as immodest, brazen and unsuitable. On the other hand, too little eye contact can be seen as 'shifty' or convey embarrassment, fear or shyness. It can also represent deep thought and withdrawal into one's inner world, or suggest respect for the other's privacy. Careful attention to cultural and gender differences in the level of eye contact we use can help us to consider how we may be perceived by users of services from varying different cultural and social backgrounds and help us to avoid making superficial inappropriate judgements about them, for example lack of eye contact denoting avoidance on the part of a Muslim Bangladeshi woman.

Facial expressions are interpreted as conveying attitudes. For example, frowning may convey criticism: a bored expression may be perceived as disinterested or devaluing. Across all cultures smiling appears to convey a non-threatening approach and a positive and friendly attitude, although it does not necessarily denote happiness (Argyle, 2007). Smiling may conceal anxiety, reflect a desire to please or represent social politeness. Women tend to smile more frequently than men (Mayo and Henley, 1981). While smiling is associated with engagement and conveying warmth it also appears to act as a social reinforcer. Greenspoon (1955) found that smiling, nodding one's head and leaning forward acted as reinforcers of the other person's behaviour, including the amount of speech and speech on selected topics. As social workers we need to be aware of such subliminal reinforcement and to use it discriminatingly. A worker who was anxious to engage with a rather withdrawn, inarticulate client found herself continuing to smile as he disclosed more and more of his anti-social behaviour until she realised she was unwittingly conveying her approval of it. Facial expression appears to be related to responsiveness. An immobile, unchanging facial expression can appear bland or withdrawn or unresponsive to another person's disclosure.

Responsiveness also appears to be conveyed by body movements such as nodding one's head, gesticulating, moving one's arms and feet and leaning forward (Mehrabian and Williams, 1969). Here there are gender differences: women are more likely to use head nodding as a way of communicating understanding and engagement (De Lange, 1995) but, as we saw with smiling (Greenspoon, 1955), nodding one's head can be interpreted as reinforcing another person's behaviour and therefore we have to use it with discrimination. In relation to body movement it is again difficult to make rules. While lack of such activity conveys a lack of responsiveness, excessive activity and movement, for example fiddling, rubbing oneself and frequently shifting position, can be distracting and convey a lack of attention (Reith, 1975). In a study of interviewing behaviour (Lishman, 1985), the level of non-verbal activity by social workers was higher than anticipated and did not appear distracting to the users of services. The one social worker who engaged in minimal bodily movement appeared rigid, immobile and rather unresponsive. The concept of 'non-verbal leakage', by which our true feelings may leak out in non-verbal behaviour (Ekman and Friesen, 1968), appeared relevant to this worker in that his only movement was of his feet. It is possible that they conveyed what the rest of his consciously controlled non-verbal behaviour concealed e.g. anxiety or irritation.

Using Robinson's (1998) distinction between high and low context cultures we need to be aware of potential differences in the perception of relative importance of non-verbal and verbal communication. Henley's (1979) reminder about the role of non-verbal feedback in relation to trans-cultural communication remains potentially relevant to all communication between social workers and users of services. We need to use non-verbal communication from users of services to inform ouselves as workers how much they feel comfortable in the interaction and how clear our communication is or is not. For example, a glazed expression, a fixed smile and frequent shifts of position are likely to convey discomfort with the interaction itself, with a specific communication, or with the purpose or structure of the interaction.

Symbolic and non-verbal behaviour represent powerful aspects of our communication. They convey messages about class, culture, ethnicity and gender, power, control and authority, and about genuineness, concern, respect and caring. As workers in social work and social care it is our responsibility to continue to increase our awareness of our own communications, by feedback from users of services, colleagues, role play, and video, and to monitor and check out our interpretations of symbolic and non-verbal communication on the part of clients, carers and users of services and their interpretations of our symbolic and non-verbal communication.

We also need to attend to symbolic and non-verbal behaviour in inter-professional communication to ensure that we convey personal and professional confidence and authority in advocating for users of services.

Verbal communication

Verbal communication means oral or spoken communication. It also involves the use of 'paralanguage', defined by Rozelle *et al.* (1997) as:

> content-free vocalizations and patterns associated with speech such as voice, pitch, volume, frequency, stuttering, filled pauses (for example, 'ah'), silent pauses, interruptions and measures of speech rate and number of words spoken in a given unit of time. (p. 72)

In considering verbal communication we need to be aware of how the underlying 'paralanguage' influences verbal communication. Verbal communication also needs to be considered in relation to symbolic communication. For example, a 94-year-old woman resented being called by her given name, Janet, rather than by her married status, Mrs Smith. We need to be sensitive in verbal communication about how we start to address users of services in relation to how they may experience our overtures, for example, in relation to age and culture.

Verbal communication in social work can be considered either in terms of its *purposes* or of the *skills* involved. Here I examine briefly the skills involved in verbal communication. Subsequent chapters examine them more fully in relation to different purposes of social work and apply them more fully to practice.

Questioning or probing

We tend to think of the exploration of issues which need to be addressed in social work or social care in terms of asking questions. As Dillon (1997) suggests:

> nothing would be seen easier or more straight forward than asking a question and getting an answer. Indeed, everyone asks and answers questions as an everyday occurrence. Yet how can we use questions skilfully in situations of professional practice? (p. 103)

Students beginning to practise interviewing skills often have the experience of falling into a question-and-answer routine in which the student feels more and more like an interrogator. Underlying this question-and-answer pattern can be an unstated assumption that the worker is the expert, the user of services has a problem which requires a solution and that once he/she has provided the information about this problem the worker/expert will provide the solution. How can we avoid this kind of unhelpful emphasis on question and answer?

First, we have to be aware whenever we are asking a question. Second, we have to think about the purpose of this question. Is the information it solicits essential? Does it help the user of services to tell his or her story? Third, is there an alternative to asking this question? Would paraphrasing what the user of services has said, or reflecting back her or his underlying feelings, more usefully explore their preoccupation or problem? Finally, if asking a question seems appropriate and essential, what types of questions might we ask?

Open and closed questions

Closed questions tend to invite a yes/no answer, or a small number of possible responses, for example:

'Are you employed?' tends to invite a yes or no reply. 'How many children do you have?', while not inviting a simple yes/no answer, will tend to be answered in a limited way. It is also problematic, for example, for an interviewee who had a child who had died or a father who has no access to a child.

Open questions invite a wider range of responses and the interviewee is free to choose how to respond, for example:

'And what about your children?'
'What did you think when he said that?
'How can I help you?'

Such questions invite the respondent to share their views, feelings or opinions.

Closed questions used too frequently tend to develop into a question-and-answer routine, but can be useful for gaining specific information. Open questions are better for helping people to tell their story or explore their problem or situation. However, Trevithick (2005) suggests that open-ended questions may feel 'threatening or overwhelming for service users who are not used to formulating their thoughts and feelings in such an open space' (p. 160).

Direct and indirect questions

Direct questions are straight questions or queries such as 'How do you manage on your current benefits?'

Indirect questions imply a question, but indirectly without a question mark at the end, for example 'It must be hard managing on your current benefits.' By making a question indirect we can make it more open and leave the other person greater choice about how to respond.

More generally in relation to the use of questions we need to think about the 'flow', that is, the frequency, rate and sequence of questions we ask. Most people do not like to be asked a lot of questions, especially at a fast rate (Dillon, 1997). Such an approach is likely to contribute to the danger of the social worker getting into an interrogative question-and-answer mode, unhelpful to both the user of service and the purpose of the interview. Other unhelpful approaches to questioning are asking very unclear questions or multiple questions caught up in what on the surface is a single question (Kadushin and Kadushin, 1997).

Appropriate and sensitive use of questioning is essential, however, in making a holistic assessment: if omitted it can lead to highly significant information about the user of services being lost to the social worker and to an inappropriate assessment. For example an energetic care manager embarked on a routine, single, shared assessment but did not ask the elderly man about his family, marriage or relationships. She therefore missed the crucial information that his wife had recently died, that he mourned her and that this loss underpinned this attempt to access relevant social services.

Probing

Egan (2007) defines prompts and probes as 'verbal tactics for helping clients talk about themselves and define their problems more concretely and specifically'. Probes can be open or indirect questions or requests to help clients talk about their concerns.

> 'You sound very upset, but I'm not quite sure what it's about.'
> 'You said that you and Jane have had several rows this week. Perhaps you could tell me a bit more what they are about.'

A probe can also be an 'accent', a one or two word restatement highlighting someone's previous response.

> 'I was a bit annoyed with her at the time'
> 'A bit annoyed?'
> 'Well, actually, I was furious'.

Reflection

Reflection involves conveying to users of services that we understand their experience and feelings by reflecting or feeding back to them what they have conveyed to us.

Reflecting may simply involve picking up a word or phrase a person has used and feeding it back, implying a request to hear more e.g. 'You felt relieved...?'. Reflecting in this way involves selection, and it is important to select on the basis of what seems important to the other person, rather than of interest to the worker.

Reflecting can take the form of paraphrasing: rephrasing or repeating what the user of services has said in different words. It is difficult to do this accurately: to find a way of saying what the other has said, using different words, but conveying exactly the same meaning. Paraphrasing can be cognitive, about understanding or content: 'You mean that...?' It can also be affective, reflecting back feelings. Again this is difficult, it involves interpreting not just what the user of services has said, but her or his tone, facial expression and body movement. Some emotions may be seen as general – 'You feel angry…? Sad? Helpless? Anxious?' but some are much more specific, for example 'Humiliated?', 'Vindicated?', 'Cheated?'.

Paraphrasing to a user of service needs to be done tentatively: it is a means of checking out whether the worker is correctly understanding how the other person feels or sees things. It indicates that the worker is attending fully to the user of service and, by checking out, it facilitates further exploration.

Paraphrasing is a useful technique to ensure that we have accurately interpreted and understood what is being said to us. In interdisciplinary work we can use it to check that we have accurately understood an assessment by a professional from a different discipline and have not filtered this, through our own professional values, language and norms, in a way that misinterprets it.

Conveying empathy

Rogers (1957, 1980, 2004) argued that empathy was a necessary and sufficient condition for personality change. Much of social work may not currently be seen to be about personality change (more the province of counselling). However, it can be in some areas such as criminal justice and child care with a focus on attitudinal and behavioural change, residential child care, and work with individuals and families where substance abuse is the problem. Here empathy remains a key component of effective professional work. Where social work is more about the provision of services than changing behaviour, feedback from users of services, e.g. care management, nevertheless indicates that empathy is still a necessary important and valued contribution to their satisfaction with the help they receive.

Conveying empathy goes beyond reflection. Egan (2002, p. 95) defines empathy as 'the ability to *enter into* and understand the world of another person and to communicate this understanding to him or her'. He suggests that responding empathically involves asking 'What is the core message being expressed at this point?' For Egan the technology of conveying basic empathy involves both identifying and reflecting back the other person's feelings – 'You feel…' – with accurate emotion and an identification of the experiences or behaviours underlying these feelings, 'You feel….. because…?':

> for example, 'You feel so angry because it's as if your father is abusing you again?'

Accurate empathic responses such as this can help a user of service experience acceptance and validation, can help them explore further problematic areas and identify and focus on key issues and feelings. Even in the current managerialist and 'what works' context of social work and social care (Butler and Drakeford, 2001; Drakeford, 2000;) it is difficult to imagine how the transition from home and community care for an older person, or the transition from a family (however problematic) or foster care (however problematic) to residential care for a child or adolescent, can be sensitively and successfully achieved if the social workers and social care workers involved do not use empathy.

In general, whether in more structured interviews or life space interviews (Keenan, 2007) we should think about the core message and not rush in with an attempted empathic response. Our responses need to be brief or they may interfere with the user of services telling their engaging story or in necessary self-exploration. Empathy is not conveyed by the following responses:

● no response – the user of services may feel the issue or feeling is not worthy of a response, or simply not understood;
● a question – again, this deflects from or ignores the core message;
● a cliché – this trivializes the uniqueness and significance of this particular person;
● immediate action – this may deflect from and ignore the feelings of the client, user or carer.

Clearly sometimes immediate action is required, when a judgement about risk is made, but sometimes we leap into immediate action without sufficiently reflecting on what the user of services would find helpful: this might be understanding, empathy, or that we contain our anxiety about our need to solve problems.

Focussing

Focussing means 'concentrating on'. Within an interview, exploration with a user of service about her or his situation can be wide-ranging, sometimes apparently tangential, and the worker may struggle to hold on to a focus, or a purpose, for the interview. The worker has to balance potentially conflicting themes:

● the need to keep the focus broad enough not to miss or ignore relevant material;
● the need to focus on some of the content at greater emotional depth;
● the need to focus discussion and guide it towards a goal.

Focussing, in this sense, links with Egan's (2002) 'finding the core message', that is, what is this person really concerned about and can I help him/her to focus on that? Sometimes what a user of services is concerned about may be what is not said, for example, anxiety about illness or death often seems too frightening to raise, and what is talked about is almost a smoke screen.

People frequently come to social services or to a social worker with multiple and complex problems, for example a combination of debt, mental health problems and difficulties with their children. These can be overwhelming for them and for the worker if some more limited focus is not agreed on. Where can we start?

Egan (2007) suggested a set of principles which may help the worker to focus:

● If the user of services is in a crisis, start with the crisis.
● Focus on what the user of services sees as important or feels as most painful.
● Focus on an issue the user of services is ready to work on even if it does not seem the most important issue.
● Focus on a sub-problem which is manageable and relatively amenable to success. This gives the user of services a sense of success and empowerment which may have a knock-on effect on other problems. For example, paying off the electricity bill may facilitate less anxious and, therefore, more patient and consistent parenting.

Summarizing

Summarizing is a means of clarifying what a user of services has been saying and it is an aid to focussing. In a sense it is like an extended paraphrase. We listen to what a user of services has said, select what seem the key issues and feed back in shortened form and different words but trying to convey the essence of what they have been saying. Again, our aim is to check that our understanding of content and feeling corresponds with theirs. Again there is a danger that, in selecting for the summary, we may omit an issue of importance to them.

Egan (2002, 2007) pointed out that, properly done, summarizing could help users of services to clarify issues from their own perspective, and then help them to develop different or alternative perspectives. 'Often when scattered elements are brought together, the client can see the "bigger picture" more clearly' (p. 173). Egan suggests that summaries can be particularly helpful at certain times:

● At the beginning of new sessions: summarizing a previous session helps a user of services to move on from where they were in a previous session.

● When an interview is unfocussed: summarizing can allow worker and user of services to consider 'Where do we go from here?'

● When a user of services gets stuck with a particular perception, a summary may help them to see an alternative one.

Summarizing, as with paraphrasing, is also particularly useful in interdisciplinary work. By summarizing we can check that we all have agreed particular outcomes (e.g. at a child protection review or at a joint health and social care meeting about discharge from hospital to the community) and agreed individual roles, responsibilities and expected outcomes.

Confrontation and challenging

Chambers Twentieth Century Dictionary (1972) defines confrontation as 'continued hostile attitudes, with hostile acts but without declaration of war' and it is in this sense that confrontation in social work is often feared – because of connotations of aggression, destructiveness and personal attack. 'When confrontation is actually an attack, it serves the purpose of helping the confronter to get a load off his or her chest rather than helping the other person live more effectively' (Egan, 2002, p. 219).

In contrast Carkhuff (1969) views confrontation as a useful skill,

whereby the helper conveys his or her understanding of discrepancies in the client's behaviour, feelings or thinking. These discrepancies can be between:

● The clients' views of how they would like to be and how they think they actually are.

● How clients say they feel and how they actually behave.

● How clients say they feel and behave and how the worker experiences them.

Confrontation does convey possible aggression and attack but social workers do need to use skills which address discrepancies between societal and legal views of the behaviour of users of services and their own perceptions: such discrepancies may be particularly marked in social work in criminal justice and in child protection.

Carkhuff (1969) and Fischer (1978) argue that a worker who is empathic will also be aware of discrepancies like these. However, any challenge about these discrepancies needs to facilitate understanding and potential change of behaviour on the part of the user of services and not be used for the worker's relief or ventilation.

Nelson-Jones (2005) uses the term 'challenging' to mean reflecting on discrepancies for example, in verbal communication or non-verbal communication or in thoughts, feelings and actions. Nelson-Jones cautions us about the *how* of challenging: 'strong challenges can create resistance' (p. 159). Egan (2002, 2007) suggests that challenging is more than confronting. It involves helping users of services to 'understand themselves, others and the world more fully and constructively.' Challenging in Egan's sense can help users of services to gain a new perspective. While challenging discrepancies is one way of doing this, giving new information or correcting misinformation can be another. For example a service user who had been suddenly bereaved expressed the anxiety that she was 'going mad'. She was greatly relieved to hear a radio programme about grief, where it was made clear that many bereaved people similarly felt they were going mad. As a result of this new information her anxiety about it was considerably lessened.

Hindrances to communication

What conditions may hinder or block symbolic, verbal or non-verbal communication between a worker and a user of services?

Environment

The physical environment can impede communication e.g. a hot stuffy room can lessen concentration. Television can be a distraction in a home visit: nevertheless, in deciding whether to request that it should be switched off, the worker has to decide how helpful it will be in terms of the purpose of the visit and how such a use of authority will be viewed.

Interruptions

Interruptions, such as telephone calls, a mobile phone, a Blackberry, a knock at the door, are distracting and interrupt the flow of communication.

Overload

There are limits to the amount of information a person can take in when it is presented verbally. Complicated information such as entitlement to benefits may be best given briefly verbally, and then reinforced by written information, in a relevant format, to be digested over time.

Unchecked assumptions

Unspoken and unchecked assumptions create misunderstanding. The 'clash in perspective' identified by Mayer and Timms (1970) is a major example of unchecked assumptions, for example, when clients needed material help, they perceived the workers as interested only in offering help with relationships.

Preoccupation

Anxiety or preoccupation with inner thoughts may limit our capacity to hear what the other person is saying. For example, a child or older person entering residential care may fail to hear introductions and relevant information because of high levels of anxiety. Similarly, a social worker, anxious about the increasing possibility of a child's or older person's need to be admitted to residential care, may find it difficult to focus on and hear what a service user or their carer is experiencing about their potential entry to care.

Stereotyping

Stereotyping can distort communications. A stereotype is a 'fixed, conventionalized representation' such as the 1970s stereotype of a social worker as long-haired, left-wing and *Guardian*-reading and the more recent stereotype of the social worker as an avenging remover of children at dawn. Stereotyping involves a process of assigning people to categories on the basis of nationality, race, class, occupation, age or appearance and then inferring general characteristics on the basis of the category.

Stereotyping can be useful in social relationships: we need quickly to be able to react differently to a six-year-old, sixteen-year-old or a sixty-year-old. However stereotyping becomes a communication block if rigidly applied and unchecked. A user of services may be unable to hear what a worker says if he or she has stereotyped the worker as too young and casual (on the basis of wearing jeans), too middle-aged and middle-class (on the basis of wearing a suit) or as a man ('all men are brutes').

Previous experience

Past experience can impede communication whether the experience is conscious and remembered or unconscious. Someone whose previous experience of social work was offhand or dismissive or who had been judged 'unworthy' of help (Rees, 1974, 1978) is likely to be more sensitive to perceived slights or rejection in a new social work encounter.

Transference, the unconscious transfer of feelings from the past by a user of services onto the worker, can also distort communication. For example, if a user of services has been consistently criticized and rejected in childhood by her parents she may unconsciously expect the worker to be similarly critical and rejecting. She may interpret positive or neutral aspects of the worker's communication as critical, and she may also even appear to elicit such criticism and rejection.

If the worker is able to see the distorted perception and communication in terms of transference (and understand where in the user of services' past it comes from) it may at the least enable the worker to understand apparently negative communication from the user of services, or at best enable the worker to explore with the user of services the feelings from the past and disentangle how they distort current communication and relationships.

Workers in social services also need to be aware of how *their* previous experiences similarly may impact on their perception of a user of services or a colleague. For example if I have had a negative relationship with my father I may find it difficult to 'hear' sensitively and accurately a father who is having difficulties with his adolescent daughter. I also need to be aware of how I may selectively interpret the behaviour of older male colleagues, both in social work and other disciplines such as education or medicine.

Translation and the use of interpreters

A final but crucial block to verbal communication is in the use of language. Users of services and workers may not share a common language and an interpreter may be required. This should be someone with 'cultural knowledge and appropriate professional background' as well as the relevant language and translation skills (Lago and Thompson, 1996, p. 61). While a family member, friend or neighbour may be willing, there are potential dangers in using an unofficial interpreter. Shackman (1985) lists some, including:

- inaccurate translation, bias or distortion;
- lack of confidentiality;
- failure of the unofficial interpreter to understand the role of interpreter.

A family member may have a particular view about the problem a user of services is bringing social work and wish to promote it. He or she may over-identify with them or the worker. Using the service user's children is particularly difficult if the discussion is of sensitive, painful issues or areas not seen by the user of services as appropriate for the child to be involved in.

For example, a male social worker was asked to see a Bangladeshi woman who was confined to her flat and appeared to be depressed. The social worker invited her teenage daughter to interpret. Although the daughter was bilingual and appeared to understand the social worker, her mother said almost nothing. Only a change of worker and of interpreter moved communication forward. The male social worker was replaced by a female, the child by a formal, non-related female interpreter. It then emerged that the mother had been suffering from gynaecological problems which she could not discuss with her male GP. She then felt it completely inappropriate to share such intimate details with either her daughter or a male social worker. Thus, gender, race, generational boundaries and language all acted as blocks to open communication.

If an official interpreter is necessary and is available what factors should be considered. Shackman (1985) provides the following advice:

● Check that the interpreter and the user of services do speak the same language or dialect.
● Use clear, simple language.
● Clarify with the interpreter the purpose and focus of the interview and ensure that she or he understands the need for a comprehensive and fairly literal translation.
● Listen to both the interpreter and the user of services, engage in eye contact with both and note their non-verbal behaviour.
● Check regularly with the interpreter that the user of services understands the dialogue.
● Take time at the end to review the interview with the interpreter.

Problems in using an official interpreter may include:

● The interpreter's difficulty in conveying rather subtle, non-verbal cues.
● Inaccurate interpretation and translation of communication by the user of service.
● Potential for breach of confidentiality: Robinson (1998) argues that 'some Asians reject interpreters who belong to the same community'.
● Finally, when a subject for discussion is perceived as taboo or embarrassing, the presence of an interpreter may compound this.

More recent research (Alexander *et al.*, 2004) suggested the following issues are important for social workers to take on board in relation to communication using interpreter services:

- interpreters need to be empathic, and trustworthiness is extremely important;
- people tend to prefer using family or friends to interpret but this may lead to complexity about what is taboo, embarrassing or confidential.

Users of services need to decide for themselves what level of English proficiency is required in an interview and therefore whether they require a family member, friend or interpreter.

A social worker or care worker working with an interpreter, therefore, requires additional communication skills including clarity and simplicity of language and sensitivity to non-verbal communication. It also requires time, concentration, patience and a readiness to slow down the pace of the interview.

Even if the user of services and worker speak English they may not share the same verbal form. D'Ardenne and Mahtani (1989) point out that:

English-speaking counsellors expect their clients to share their manner of speech. When they do not, counsellors may devalue their clients, either by believing they are intellectually slow or that they are uneducated. (p. 64)

They argue that:

black clients who speak another form of English, for example, are even less likely to be understood by their counsellors than those who speak another language and require interpreters. (p. 64)

Conclusion

The communication skills involved in working with users of services, whether voluntary or involuntary, for example in child protection (Platt, 2006) and criminal justice (McIvor and Raynor, 2007), are relevant to effective communication with other professionals, for example, in health, education, housing and the police. Use of questioning and challenging is essential with other professionals but needs to be undertaken with respect for their different professional roles and empathy for their own particular professional issues, including accountability, time and resources. The use of focussing, paraphrasing and summarizing in interprofessional work is crucial to ensuring that we do – in spite of hindrances to communication such as different professional values and assumptions or stereotyping – agree on a shared focus for specific interventions. These situations might include child protection or for an integrated approach to work with a child in residential care, or a single shared assessment for older people and more broadly an integrated approach to the provision of integrated service delivery, for example, the Joint Future agenda for people with mental health problems or learning disabilities or older people.

However, if, in relation to service provision, undue emphasis is placed on verbal communication, users of services who are less articulate or lack complex verbal skills, including some people with learning difficulties, or children and adolescents will be disadvantaged.

---

putting it into practice

Consider and reflect on an appointment you have had with your general practitioner. How did the physical environment affect you including the receptionist, the waiting room and the general practitioner's room? Did they convey approachability? Did they convey power differentials? What trans-cultural viewpoint did they convey?

Re-read this chapter and consider and reflect on a recent personal experience with a professional you consulted. How did you experience their kinesics behaviour, for example eye contact and facial expressions? Did you feel that this helped or hindered in your consultation?

Again in terms of verbal communication, re-read this chapter and consider and reflect on a recent personal experience with a professional you consulted. How did you experience their questioning, concern and empathy?

What were any hindrances you experienced in this interaction?

Now consider how users of services might experience you as the professional: you might want to compare your experience as a user of service with how a user of service may perceive you as a professional.

Recommended reading

Hargie, O.D.W. (ed.) (1997) *The Handbook of Communication Skills*, 2nd edn, London, Routledge. This is a comprehensive, research-based, edited survey of communication skills particularly relevant to people working in social and health care.

Nelson-Jones, R. (2005) *Introduction to Counselling Skills*, 2nd edn, London, Sage. This contains a wealth of information and guidance about counselling skills and the different types of communication used which are highly relevant to social work and social care.

Egan, G. (2007) *The Skilled Helper: A Systematic Approach to Effective Helping*, Pacific Grove, CA, Thomson/Brookes-Cole. A long-standing and detailed textbook about how professionals may best help clients in a skilled manner which includes attention to different types of communication and their use.

4 | Types of communication: written and information technology

Chapter 3 explored symbolic, non-verbal and verbal communication with users of services and drew analogies from this to helpful communication with colleagues, both in social work and social care, and with interprofessional colleagues.

This chapter explores the use of written communication and of information technology as a means of communication. Again the focus of the chapter is mainly on direct communication with users of services but the lessons can usefully be applied to our communication with colleagues, both in social services and interprofessionally.

Written communication: reports and records

While social workers are frequently required to use different kinds of written communication, for example letters, reports and records, discussion of written communication skills in social work literature has been neglected. It is an area of social work practice which is frequently criticized, anecdotally by employers and in a more evidenced way in reports of enquiries into social work tragedies (see, for example, O'Brien, 2003).

This chapter runs a risk of failing to do justice to the complexity of the written communication skills required in social work. Only general guidelines can be given and, as argued in Chapter 3, while a written analysis may provide useful pointers, skills are learned in action with practice and feedback.

Thompson (2003) importantly points out that, while 'putting it in writing' may add weight to what is perceived as a more minor verbal communication and therefore may make it more influential, 'putting it in writing' also gives it a longer 'shelf life'. So when we write we need to think about how what we have written might be perceived in the future if it were to involve formal procedures. We should also remember this in relation to email communication.

I will address specific issues in relation to written communication in letters, emails, reports and records. However, there are general principles which underpin written communication in social work and social care. Thompson (2003) has a useful chapter on 'Putting it in Writing' (pp. 145–68) which addresses these issues.

Very broadly we need to think about why we are using written communication. For example is it to avoid a challenging and complex face-to-face interaction, or is it to make a clear and permanent record of what has been discussed and agreed between a user of service and a social worker? Is it necessary? Thompson (2003) argues that we need to be clear about agency policy and procedures in relation to what should be recorded in writing:

> Without clarity about such criteria, you may find that some things which should have been committed to writing are not while a lot of time and energy are wasted recording things that did not need to be in writing. (pp. 147–8)

Whether we are writing letters to users of services or other professionals, emails to colleagues, recording for our agency, responding to complaints, or writing reports for the court, juvenile justice system or children's hearings, we need to write fluently, clearly, briefly, use appropriate language for the recipient, and keep to the purpose we intended when we began the written communication. We also need to remember that what we write may subsequently be part of more formal proceedings as a result of complaints or formal enquiries. The management of this tension between clarity and responsiveness to users of services in our written communication, and the potential, longer-term implications of what we write, is a complex process.

Letters

Perhaps nowhere is this tension more clearly illustrated than in how we write letters to users of services. In Chapter 2 users of services identified their wish for accessible formats, plain language and supportive, respectful, friendly and empathic communication from social workers. We need to be careful about both clarity and tone in our letters to users of services: we also need to remember that they may rightly be used in a complaints procedure. For example, to write in a letter to a carer that the service user has increasing behavioural problems rather than physical deterioration, when (as a result of chronic illness) their need for increased support in physical care has increased, will be perceived as insensitive and inaccurate both by the carer and in an investigation of the subsequent complaint.

Letters to other professionals are also part of the public record: they include equivalent assessments to those discussed in report writing. Emails should be seen as having equivalent formal status to written letters.

Report-writing

Criticism of social work records and reports has been about their lengthy, unclear and frequently un-evidenced style, and written reports clearly need to be concise, focussed and relevant to the important features of the case. This is sensible to prescribe but more difficult to carry out. Brevity is important and social work reports, in common with other reports, need short paragraphs and sub-headings to break up the text and key the reader into the main points.

Let us take a Social Enquiry Report as an example. In Scotland these are undertaken by local authority social workers. Although this is not the case in England, the considerations involved in preparing and presenting such a report are also relevant to all other formal reports and can be applied throughout the United Kingdom.

First we need to consider the purpose of a report since that will define not only the content but also the structure and presentation. In Scotland a Social Enquiry Report is compiled 'with a view to assisting the Court in determining the most suitable method of dealing with any person in respect of an offence' (Criminal Justice (Scotland) Act 1999).

The Social Enquiry Report is intended as a means of providing information to the Court to assist it to deal with the accused person. It is an aid to sentencing and should provide the court with background information and a critical and succinct analysis of it in relation to offending behaviour. It should not suggest guilt or innocence but is used by the Judge or Sheriff to decide what sentence to pass. It is not a confidential document. It becomes the property of the court and may be made public in a court hearing. It needs to be copied to the accused person and to her or his solicitor.

What qualities of the report will best achieve this purpose? It needs to be written in clear, straightforward language. It should avoid professional jargon. The use of such phrases as 'structural factors', 'deviant sub-culture' or 'material deprivation' alienate the non-social work reader. The report must contain accurate information, carefully checked and scrutinized. It must distinguish between evidence and, indeed, professional judgement.

At the beginning the report needs identifying details, including age and details of the offender. Thereafter the writer has to balance the relative advantages of using a consistent structure for all reports, and the need to individualize each report. Consistency of headings across reports helps the Court familiarize itself quickly with the contents of an individual report, but a stereotyped presentation may fail to present important information early and thereby highlight it. For example, a recent family death, conflict with a step parent, or changes in drinking or drug-use patterns presented late in a report in accordance with the standard format, will fail to highlight the significance of such factors. Such a failure undermines the purpose of the report: to give the Court the necessary information to deal with the accused.

The report writer therefore needs to combine a broad, consistent structure with a need to be flexible according to the requirements of presenting information about this particular offender.

Using Social Enquiry Reports as an exemplar of report writing, how might a report in general be structured? In Scotland the National Objectives and Standards (Scottish Executive, 2003) help us by setting clear requirements for Social Enquiry Reports. These are:

(a) To inform and advise the courts by:
   ● putting subjects' offending behaviour into a personal and social context;
   ● examining the subject's views of that behaviour;
   ● considering the likelihood of and scope for minimizing future offending;
   ● assessing the possible effects of the range of disposals available to the court on the subject and on any dependants.
(b) To offer an assessment of the subject's willingness, motivation and ability to address problems and issues associated with their offending behaviour.
(c) To provide, if social work assistance is recommended, action plans making clear what services will be made available, and linking them clearly to the aim of helping offenders to reduce the risk of future offending.
(d) To ensure that reports are of a consistently high quality.

These requirements are not confined to criminal justice in Scotland, but address more broadly reports about assessment in social work and risk assessment and management (Kelmshall, 2007; Lishman, 2007; McIvor, 2007).

The general structure of such a report can be seen as beginning with, for example, the subject's family life and relationships and narrowing to consideration of the particular offence.

Headings could then be as follows:

- Family details and relationships
- The offender in relation to his family
- Work, finance
- Associates, leisure, drink patterns
- Personality assessment
- Previous offending behaviour
- Characteristics of present offence
- Social work possibilities inherent in the court's decision, if applicable

The report does have to be concluded. While it must not judge guilt or innocence or appear to usurp the Court's function of deciding appropriate disposal, it is now accepted that a report may contain a recommendation and the Streatfield Committee (1961) argued that the expression of an 'opinion' was an integral part of the report. However the writer should not feel compelled to submit a view in every report. If he or she feels in doubt, for example because of inadequate knowledge of this offender or the likely consequences of a particular disposal, a recommendation should be left out. Any expression of opinion, like any conclusion, has to follow from the evidence in the report. A final paragraph, even without a recommendation, needs to identify and summarize key factors relevant to the Court's decision about disposal.

Similar considerations would apply to reports to the Children's Hearings in Scotland, where, in youth justice, the Children's Hearing system takes a welfare approach to children who offend as well as those in need of care and protection (Buckley, 2007).

Here a front sheet contains 'hard' basic information about child and family. The body of the report concentrates on areas not dissimilar to the Social Enquiry Report including:

- Family relationships – relationship between parents, parental roles and authority
- Social habits of the parents, relationships between child and parents and between child and siblings
- Criminality in the family
- Finance
- Leisure
- School
- Previous contacts with social work, the police or the Hearing
- Personality

Again the writer needs to use simple, clear language and avoid jargon to ensure that family members and the lay Hearing members clearly understand it. The writer has to balance the advantages of a common structure for reports with the need to present and highlight individual factors and issues relevant to this particular child. The writer has also to consider the purpose of the report: to provide an assessment which is a tool for the Hearing members to arrive at suitable ways of intervening on the child's behalf.

The report has to contain not just factual evidence but the worker's assessment of the reasons underlying this particular referral. For example, in stealing, investigation of group involvement, family poverty, family attitudes to crime, disposal of the goods or money will provide clues to understanding patterns of behaviour, the needs of the child and therefore the most appropriate disposal.

The report requires a conclusion and again, while it is for the Hearing to decide on how the referral is to be dealt with, the social worker has to indicate the possible range of disposals meeting both the interests of the child, and the concerns of the public about safety and control.

Both these examples, Social Enquiry Reports and reports for the Hearings, highlight more general but essential skills and requirements in report-writing including clarity, simplicity, brevity, and the use of structure and flexibility. These skills and requirements apply to reports in social work and social care including those to Adoption and Fostering panels, to Child Protection Reviews, and also to reports to managers or panels responsible for allocating packages of care for older people, people with learning disabilities or physical disabilities. They are also crucial to report-writing about people with mental health problems where the balancing of care and risk is complex.

Recording

Social workers spend a considerable amount of time engaged in recording but, like report writing, this is a neglected area in social work education and literature.

Before identifying the skills required to record clearly, accurately and appropriately it is necessary to examine the purpose of recording. The purposes are multiple, may be in conflict and legislation gives users of services the right of access to files held on them by housing and social services departments (Data Protection Act 1998, Access to Personal Files Act 1987). The Gaskin case (Prince, 1996) led to legislation to allow clients access to information about them kept by local authorities. The context of social work involves an increasing emphasis on citizen participation, partnership and advocacy.

Prince (1996) describes social workers' ambivalence about 'open records' as beginning with initial scepticism and resistance and then gradually moving to a recognition and shared agreement that the record of social contact was valued by users of services. They help them to correct inaccuracies and help both worker and users of service to deal with a potential clash in perspective (Doel and Lawson, 1989).

Drawing on Payne's (1978) framework of analysis of the purpose of written records for the agency and the worker, I explore the different and potentially conflicting purposes. Then the implications of the emphasis on the purpose of records for users of services (as opposed to agency or worker records) are considered.

Agency records

Here I examine the various purposes for social work agencies of written records, including legislative requirements, financial accountability, and accountability for service delivery and its evaluation.

Legal records

Social service/work departments are specifically required by legislation to keep some records, e.g. the requirement to keep a register of people with visual impairment. Records may also be used as evidence in formal proceedings, e.g. complaints procedures or legal proceedings in child care.

In cases of alleged child abuse, records provide evidence which may be used in legal proceedings – both court proceedings concerned with the protection and welfare of a child and public inquiries investigating the practice of social workers and other professionals. Here accurate records of dates and times of contact (with parents, but particularly with the child) and detailed observation of his/her physical, cognitive, developmental and emotional development, current behaviour and current physical and emotional state are crucial.

Financial records

The financial position of users of services may have to be recorded as it has increasingly become part of the assessment of their entitlement to services, particularly in relation to care management for older people. There may be inherent conflict: therapeutic intervention aimed at empowering and increasing coping strengths in an older person may conflict with what is available based on a financial assessment of their means. Similar tensions may arise in relation to child care. For example, checking parental contributions for children in residential care (with its implications of debt collection) involves a different purpose from the therapeutic intervention aimed at empowering and increasing coping strengths in a family.

Management control

Records can be used by management and workers to show that workers are complying with legal, agency or management requirements. Such records are used as part of hierarchical accountability procedures in senior management. A rise in manageralism in social work and social services has increased the emphasis on the purpose of records as part of managerial control and as part of meeting wider agendas of national standards, target-setting, monitoring and audit. The context of social service work provision has greatly increased the requirement for accountability on the part of social workers and social care workers.

Accountability

Both recording and supervision involving verbal accounts of practice (Pithouse, 1987) have been the main means by which social workers fulfil their accountability to management and to wider society. Davies (1994) argues that it was the Colwell Inquiry (DHSS, 1974) which 'marked a watershed in pinpointing the accountability of social service departments in areas of public concern' (p. 180).

The concept of accountability, applied to child care, child safety and child abuse has extended to other areas of social work practice so that as social workers, rightly, we have to account for decisions, assessments and work done. However accountability in social work is complex and involves tensions. We are professionally accountable to the users of service: we are also accountable to our employing agency. We may be accountable to other agencies, e.g. the court. To take an example of tension: in care management we are accountable to the agency for financial management and assessments which concur with an available budget; we are also accountable to the user of services to make professional assessment of need. The dual accountability may not coincide.

A further major concern about accountability arises if, in practice or recording, it leads us to a defensive, no-risk, 'covering ourselves' strategy, with, for example, a meticulous record of contact but an unwillingness in practice to consider any risk at all, even where positive probabilities outweigh negative, to the detriment of the user of services.

Information storage

Organizations may keep information for which there may have been no immediate use if it has potential as a data bank of needs, agency resources and take-up of services. Reith (1984) argued with continuing relevance that few information systems:

collect the kind of information about service processes and outcomes that would be useful to practitioners. Categories of client problems and agency responses tend to be crude, and the data elicited may not be very reliable.

(p. 31)

While information collection and storage has become more sophisticated, and is used for example to underpin strategic planning in the integrated children's services and Joint Futures agenda, it is still not clear how this affects service provision on the ground and therefore the work of the individual social worker or social care worker.

Agency evaluation

Information storage is closely linked with research and evaluation since agency records allow for a statistical analysis of work done. Particularly in voluntary organizations or short-term innovatory projects renewed funding is contingent upon a favourable evaluation. Such a requirement may appear to threaten the traditional 'neutrality' of research, and it may be difficult to separate such evaluation (complex as it is) from a political context. Increasingly, however, independent researchers are involved in the evaluation of new initiatives, while recognizing the funding and political implications of their research. It is crucial that agencies and individual workers recognize the need to evaluate the effectiveness of the services and practice they provide. As we saw in Chapter 2, we need to focus much more on how best to achieve desirable outcomes for users of services. Clear, comprehensive, focussed agency recording can contribute to the necessary evaluation of how effective we are. Apart from the requirement for evaluation of services for the practitioner, some purposes for the agency of recording, outlined above, may seem rather remote. What are the significant purposes of records for the worker? How do they relate to agency recording? Evaluation is key (Shaw and Lishman, 1999).

Worker records

For the worker, as for the agency, records have multiple purposes including a record of work done (accountability), evaluation and the basis for ongoing supervision and development of practice.

Record of work done

The record a social worker or, in group care, a team keeps 'covers' the individual or team and is the means by which they are accountable to their agency and even to society. For example, accurate records of visits made and of direct observations of children and the care they are receiving are essential evidence in child protection work, but may also provide evidence and justification for worker action and decisions in a subsequent enquiry.

There is, however, an equal professional responsibility that we use recording not just to 'mind our backs' but also to monitor and, as discussed earlier, evaluate what we do. We should not just describe *what* we did, but *why*, *how* and *how effective* it could/would be.

Personal evaluation

Reith (1984), Shaw (1996) and Shaw and Lishman (1999) argued that evaluation should be a function of practice. However, many social workers record their work to comply with agency statistical requirements but do not analyze their work systematically in an evaluative way where practice *and* outcomes are recorded. Too often we record *what* we did ('visited X') but not *how* we did it or *why* (in order to achieve a desired outcome). Reith (1984) argued that our failure to evaluate our practice means that we may perpetuate unhelpful interventions without any check and we lose opportunities to improve our practice. (This remains true, see Macdonald, 2007.)

In one evaluation (Lishman, 1978) I compared retrospectively my perceptions of my practice (as I had recorded them) with the views of users of services about what I had offered. This exercise revealed the inadequacy of my records in terms of their vagueness about aims and intervention, the 'clash in perspective' between myself (vague as my recording was) and users of services, and my failure to check whether we actually shared a purpose. The existence of written records made some evaluation possible but threw into question the use of unsystematized recording which was not shared with or checked out against the view of users of services. While standards for recording social work practice in a more systematic way have been developed, as Trevithick (2005) argues, 'record keeping is an area most criticised in the findings of the 45 public inquiries into child deaths held in Britain between 1973 and 1994' (p. 248). While this calls into account agency practice and requirements, it also raises issues for individual social workers about how they record and evaluate what they do in practice.

Historically, we have not been critically evaluative about the outcomes of our contact with users of services, but we cannot and should not *assume* our intervention is helpful although it may be provided with the best intentions. Evaluation of effectiveness is an essential part of professional social work practice (Macdonald, 2007; Shaw and Lishman, 1999).

As social workers and social care workers we do need to monitor and evaluate how effective a specific service is, but also how effective we are. We need individually and professionally to build evaluation into how we practise (Shaw, 1996).

In order to engage in such practice evaluation as well as agency evaluation and accountability we need to keep high standard records. Trevithick (2005) quotes Munro (1998) about poor record-keeping in relation to child deaths: 'Lack of information was particularly demonstrated by the poverty of social work records' (p. 94). Trevithick (2005) draws attention to the need for initial baseline information in records in order to monitor whether intervention actually attended to and addressed the initial problems, and whether there was any evidence that this was effective – not just 'I visited' but 'what was the purpose and what was achieved?'.

Evaluation, at a personal level, can be seen as reflection 'on action', i.e. retrospectively, rather than 'in action', i.e. at the time (Schon, 1987).

Reflecting 'on' action includes the following questions:

● How did I engage with that person?
● What did I do?
● Why did I do it?

Analyzing these questions and our responses should improve our critical evaluation of how effective we are and help us to develop recording practices which address both the need for the record to be agreed and valued by a user of services and, in the longer term, potentially to stand up in a court of law.

Overall it is our responsibility to be systematic in what we record and to evaluate how far our aims are achieved. We can also use such records to press for increased resources for users of service, but our recording needs to be shared and agreed with users of services.

Supervision and worker support

Currently supervision is often a vehicle for management control of accountability and efficiency. It can also be used to enhance professional development and, as a consequence, our practice and service provision (Lishman, 2002). In this sense supervision is related to consultation and is a professional-to-professional relationship rather than a superior-to-subordinate one (Payne, 1978). Here records are a basis for extended discussion about professional development. As an element of this O'Hagan (1986) suggests that recording is 'a crucial learning tool'. He argues that after a crisis, detailed scrutiny is essential 'although the temptation to walk away ... is difficult to resist'. Such recording facilitates learning and self-awareness by a review of the behaviour, feelings and interaction of all participants including the worker. O'Hagan suggests that this can lead to 'the most uncomfortable realisation that one's actions are on behalf of one's (harassed) self rather than the client' (p. 127).

Records potentially can enable the worker to do a better job. Nicolson *et al.* (2006) argued that writing a record after an interview 'helps clarify thinking' (p. 73). They suggested a structure for recording which includes the following:

- a list of problems;
- the interviewer's thoughts, hypotheses, new perspectives, possible ways of resolving them;
- a note of agreed action.

Coulshed and Orme (2006) suggested that records can be an 'aide-memoire' for the individual worker, particularly as a means of clarifying and recording the worker's thoughts and hypotheses.

There have been increasing problems inherent in the use of such recording as an aid to the worker's personal development and self-evaluation of their own responsiveness and effectiveness with users of services. 'Personal' (to the worker) records are illegal under more recent legislation (Data Protection Act 1998, Freedom of Information Act 2004). What we write as social workers about users of services in general should be available to be accessed by them. Therefore, even our supervision notes should be written with a careful recognition that they may be accessed by users of services and used for more formal proceedings. We need to remember that, while a hypothesis may be helpful in clarifying our thinking, it needs to be checked out with the user of services. If put in writing it may lose its tentative, hypothetical quality and stand as a recorded, but possibly assumed, judgement of the personality and behaviour of a user of services.

Similar concerns apply to recording in group-care settings. Here recordings, logs or day notes are intended to share information or feedback on key incidents between staff, particularly on different shifts. Again, however, comments which may be selective and subjective, when written down, achieve unwarranted objectivity and power. For example, a written observation about a resident swearing may reflect a worker's values about swearing but be taken to imply that the resident is behaving aggressively. This selective focus on particular behaviour may begin or reinforce labelling by other staff of the resident as 'difficult'.

There is a problem of confidentiality: who has access to such a day book? What access do residents have to what is recorded by staff about them? What opportunity do they have to challenge staff perceptions and judgements? Similarly, where a personal record is kept for each resident, what access does the resident have to such records? Again recent legislation has rightly ensured that residents do have access to information recorded by workers who are employed to provide a service to meet their needs.

The legal context of social work and social care has changed dramatically with an increased emphasis on access to information recorded about them for users of services. Social workers' apparent belief in the crucial importance of gathering (and recording) information about users of services has been criticized (Gurney, 1990) who suggested:

> Most social workers seem to operate on the basis that the more they know the more likely they are to be good social workers, to know what they are doing and to retain some control and power over what they do and who they do it to.

He warns that:

> if knowledge is power the more information they have about a user the more likely they are to be in control of their work and the greater becomes the power gap between 'us' and 'them'. (p. 18)

Gurney argues that such information gathering may be at the expense of assessment and analysis: we should ask, 'Is this information relevant to my work? Does it help progress the task?' If not, he suggested, we should consider why we are collecting it?

I have argued that recording (and information collection) has several purposes and that these may conflict. It is important for us to consider always the following questions about recording:

- Who is this record for?
- Who has access to it?
- What purpose does it serve?
- Is the information contained relevant to the purpose?
- Is the information fact, opinion or speculation?

Gurney (1990) argues that open access disciplines our use of recording:

> It is a lot harder to collect extensive and useless information in a case file if that file is regularly being read by the user. (p. 19)

The following section explores the implications for our recording when it is a part of our communication with users of services rather than as a worker or agency record.

Records for users of services

The Data Protection Act (1984) originally gave people statutory right of access to files held about them on computer. This right of access was extended by the Access to Personal Files Act (1987) to records held manually in housing and social service departments. Since April 1989 people have had the right to see their manual records. The Data Protection Act (1998) has updated these requirements.

Anyone wanting to see their files has to give notice and authorities have up to forty days to respond. Information about third parties (except professionals) cannot be divulged without their consent (Neville and Beak, 1990).

The legislation reflected public concern about computerization of records, access to personal files and accuracy and quality of personal records. What values in social work might open access reflect? It implies an open, shared approach with users of services where as little as possible is hidden from them. It promotes the rights of users of services. It involves shared assessment and checked and agreed actions, decisions and records. It was suggested earlier that agency and worker records, where information is not shared with users of services, reflect a position of power and control by the worker and agency over the user of services. Open access, with its implications of shared planning and decision making, enhances the empowerment of users of services. Clearly this right of access to records is obligatory. What difficulties might there be in such a policy?

Initially, a major anxiety was whether social workers' judgements at times needed protection and confidentiality. Doel and Lawson (1986) usefully distinguished the different kinds of judgements we have to make. 'The first concerns the decision about whether to begin to accumulate information in an investigative manner in order to make a case for legal action' (p. 425). Suspicion of abuse would fall into this category and the worker's need to record in terms of accountability and legal evidence has already been discussed. Doel and Lawson accept this limitation to access.

A second kind of judgement is about eligibility for a service or resource, and a third about tentative 'diagnostic' judgements about individual or family functioning. Here Doel and Lawson challenge any need for secrecy or restricted access. 'If you can't confront the client with what you think about them you certainly shouldn't be hiding it away on a record' (p. 425).

In Doel and Lawson's study, users of services were understanding about a worker's need to record, e.g. as an aide memoire:

> I agree with clients being able to see their files but I also think the worker should have his own personal file, what only he can see like a top secret file, in effect, that only he sees, no other worker, no other body.

Another service user, while accepting the worker's need to record said:

> I don't mind if other people's views or facts be put in as long as I've got the right to see them and the right to have my views expressed as well, or have it altered. (p. 425)

This person's comments again symbolize the issue of power. As Neville and Beak (1990) warn:

> the instinctive approach of 'doing to' rather than 'doing with' service users, which has for so long underpinned workers' attitudes, will be a tough mould to break. (p. 17)

In summary open access means records have to be clear, not jargonistic, well evidenced, and open to discussion with users of services. Social workers have to distinguish evidence from speculation. Records should be used to negotiate a shared purpose with users of services. Workers should see recording as a means of communication and intervention and not as residual to their work. Recording should promote partnership between worker and user of services and promote empowerment in a way that can enhance integrated interdisciplinary and inter-professional assessment.

These recommendations, although difficult to achieve, are hardly controversial. Difficulties may occur in judging when limited access is required because of the need to accumulate legal evidence, or because some confidentiality between different family members is required. Agencies and workers need to identify purposes of recording in order to be aware of when they may be seen as incompatible. They then need fully to understand and adopt a policy of open access, using this as an enhancement of good practice and being aware of when its implementation has to be restricted. The Bichard Report (2003) has major implications, both practically and legally, about the necessity for interprofessional and inter-profession information sharing where potential risk and vulnerability has been identified (for example in physical or sexual abuse of children).

Information technology

The next section in this chapter examines the use of information technology (ICT) in communication in social work and social care. The use of email has already been briefly addressed. Since the late 1990s, the application of information technology to social work and social care has vastly increased and now underpins the organization and management of local authority social services. It has been applied, in particular, in relation to maintaining information, financial and human resource management about service provision e.g. the number of people receiving home care services and what specific services are provided, and about maintaining records of contact with users of services. Its use in the voluntary sector remains more patchy. Small projects with short-term funding may have minimal access to information technology. A more recent focus has been on how to use information technology to improve communication between social workers and users of services.

Historically, the use of information technology was predominantly focussed on broad overall information needs, for example, about legal information, central government statistics and records and referrals. That is, the perspective was about information needs of social work professionals, but there was limited recognition of the potential use of information technology in direct work with users of services (Horobin and Montgomery, 1986).

In a brief overview of the use of information and communication technologies in social work, Rafferty (2000) suggests that ICT can 'support the social work processes of communication, information sharing, recording, retrieval, processing and exchange through computers' (p. 169). In general, she refers to the application of ICT to agency information systems rather than as a means of communication between users of services and social workers and social care staff.

In a national study assessing the communication, information and training needs of Approved Social Workers, Fakhoury and Wright (2004) focussed on their needs and not their communication with users of services. Their findings are highly relevant to interprofessional communication. For example, Approved Social Workers had most contact with community psychiatric nurses and psychiatrists. In terms of helpfulness in communication, while contact with other Approved Social Workers and community psychiatric nurses was rated as extremely helpful, access to GPs and their helpfulness was rated rather more poorly. Interestingly, in this study information technology and its relevance to interdisciplinary communication did not seem to feature.

How may ICT be incorporated more clearly into the range of communication skills that social workers need to use in their work with users of services? Rafferty (2000) stresses its value for users of services in terms of improved provision of information (see also Chapter 6). Discussion of other uses of ICT as a means of direct communication with service users, carers and clients will, inevitably, be somewhat limited (detailed analysis probably requires a separate book) and will focus on general principles and specific examples of the use of ICT as a means of direct communication.

Thurlow *et al.* (2004) outline useful core concepts in relation to Computer Mediated Communication. Their focus is on human communication and social interaction and they outline our key concepts:

(i)   *Communication is dynamic*: it is not simply about the words we use but is dependent on context. As an example they give 'the word "kiwi" where, without contextual information, it is impossible to know whether this is meant to mean a bird, a fruit or a New Zealander' (p. 17).

(ii) *Communication is transactional*: it is about the meaning of what we say and want to convey and how that is perceived by the recipient.

(iii) *Communication is multi-functional*: we use words not just to convey information but also at the same time to engage in relationships with, for example, connotations of power, approval, befriending or control.

(iv) *Communication is multi-modal* and includes non-verbal communication.

All these factors need to be considered when we use online communication as when we use more traditional written or email communication. What elements of face-to-face communication which are useful in negotiating shared understanding and meaning may get lost and how do we compensate for this?

Joinson (2003) raises questions about how emotions, positive and negative, are communicated and dealt with online, e.g. positively in relation to empathy or negatively in relation to flame wars (see below). Preece (1999) found that online support was used to provide empathy:

After lurking on medical support groups for several months, it became clear to me that similar questions were being asked again and again by different people. What amazed me was the tolerance of the community. (p. 64)

Preece (1999) realized that people were not simply looking for facts about their illness: they wanted to communicate with other sufferers and share empathy. Winzelberg (1997) also found that electronic social support was used in relation to people suffering from eating disorders, for personal disclosure, providing information and providing emotional support.

A particular danger of use of the internet and specifically email is 'flame wars' or 'flaming' in which a simple factual question – 'Has anyone got the departmental internal telephone directory or video camera?' – becomes interpreted as an accusation and recipients respond as if they feel accused of stealing whatever valuable commodity has been lost or mislaid. It is clear that the use of the internet does not always facilitate the principles outlined by Thurlow *et al.* (2004) about dynamic, transactional, multi-functional and multi-model communication. Thompson and Foulger (1996) found that, where a flame war was perceived, the inclusion of 'emoticons', such as a smiley face, i.e. an attempt at non-verbal communication, relieved tension unless the messages were perceived as antagonistic where 'ending your attachment with a smile is not perceived as credible friendliness and may fan the flames rather than douse them' (Joinson, 2003, p. 71).

In terms of the specific use of online communication as a direct communication tool with users of services, examples from mental health and child care and protection provide a useful analysis of potential advantages. For the user of services it is seen as highly confidential. It can be interactive and non-judgemental. It has the advantage that it does not mean facing a social worker who may be perceived to be judgemental. In 2001, the NSPCC introduced an innovative interactive online advice, information and support service for young people which was evaluated in 2004 (http://www.sws.soton.ac.uk/t4mstudy). This service used qualified and trainee social work staff to provide information, support and counselling anonymously to twelve- to sixteen-year-olds via the web. The evaluation found that young people valued being able to talk in confidence about issues which concerned them and that social workers adapted their skills effectively to offer appropriate support in a virtual medium.

However, while there has been a rise in internet access to households in recent years, internet access remains strongly related to income, class and region. We need therefore to recognize that the use of online direct communication tools may not be accessible to some of our most vulnerable users of services, e.g. children and young people from very deprived areas and families, people who are homeless and older people for whom this new technology may seem inaccessible.

The provision of online services for people with mental health problems (Suler, 2004) demonstrates a number of positive ways in which they are used:

letter writing and the creation of postal systems enabled more people to interact more personally via text. Online text communication offers unprecedented opportunities to create numerous psychology 'spaces in which human interactions can unfold'. (p. 19)

In addressing online therapy for people with mental health problems, Suler also raises a number of issues about communication defects, e.g. symbolic and non-verbal, and then suggests potential online solutions. He acknowledges the lack of nuances in online communication, i.e. the lack of non-verbal communication, and suggests that for different individuals this may have different meanings. Some people will experience the lack of physical presence as reducing intimacy and trust. Others, for example, people suffering from social anxiety, guilt or shame, may find the lack of intimacy helpful. A useful aspect of online communication is that users of services and workers do not necessarily have to respond immediately and, therefore, have time for reflection (this facility is known as asynchronous communication). Suler (2004) reviews disinhibition in relation to online communication and suggests that it arises in the main from anonymity and invisibility, both of which can be seen as extremely positive for users of services.

Suler (2004) does suggest some potentially useful techniques to overcome some of the limitations of typed text to increase the vocal, kinaesthetic and non-verbal element of the communication. These include:

- Emoticons like the smiley, winky and frown. However, as we have seen, these need careful monitoring. In a flame war the smiley may exacerbate irritation.
- Trailers to indicate a pause in thinking.

As with young people in the NSPCC study, people with mental health problems have valued online counselling. It can provide anonymity, privacy, time for reflection as well as clear and regular support.

Summary

In this and the previous chapter many general principles apply to the different types of communication. They include respect for and courtesy to all users of services and to other professionals, accountability, careful attention to legal obligations and the need for careful crafting of written communication, including online and email communication.

Written communication has been considered in this chapter in only a limited sense. Written communication as a means of direct work is also considered in subsequent chapters in more detail, particularly in relation to sharing information, to making contracts and engaging in intervention (Chapters 6, 7, 8 and 9).

Chapter 3 and 4 have referred both to research based on client views in the 1980s and key current messages from users of services (Diggins, 2004) about effective communication. All stress the need to be courteous, to speak directly to service users, not to use jargon, not to over-promise and to say when and why you cannot help in a particular way, that is, to use clear, responsive communication.

I think if we can consider and apply the principles outlined in these chapters – the need to be genuine, responsive and sensitive, warm, empathic, and convey acceptance, encouragement and approval with users of services – this should help us address the requirements of improved communication in social care. Such principles also usefully underpin our communication and partnership working with other professionals.

---

putting it into practice

Consider your preferred personal written methods of communication. Are they IT-based, e.g. email or Facebook? What can you see as their strengths and weaknesses? Are they paper-based e.g. letters? What do you consider the strengths and weaknesses of paper-based written communication?

Now think about your professional life and do the same.

What are the similarities and the differences in how we use written communication and information technology personally and professionally?

In relation to your professional life what are the challenges of written communication and information technology? Brainstorm how you might address these.

Recommended reading

Prince, K. (1996) *Boring Records? Communication, Speech and Writing in Social Work*, London, Jessica Kingsley. A useful research-based text about the neglected subject of social work and social care reading.

Joinson, A.A. (2003) *Understanding the Psychology of Internet Behaviour: Virtual Worlds, Real Lives*, Basingstoke, Palgrave Macmillan. A general text to help us understand how online and web-based communication is likely to be interpreted, understood and received. Worth reading in order to understand the application to social work and social care.

Thompson, N. (2003) *Communication and Language: A Handbook of Theory and Practice*, Basingstoke, Palgrave Macmillan. A broad analysis of communication in social work and social care. Chapter 7, 'Putting it in writing', adds to the discussion of written communication in this chapter.

Trevithick (2005) and Coulshed and Orme (2006) discuss written communication briefly but helpfully in relation to skills, assessment and intervention in social work and social care.

5 | Building and maintaining relationships

The previous two chapters examined different kinds of communication, and this chapter draws on their findings. In Chapter 5 we begin to explore how communication skills may be used for different purposes in social work and social care. Building and maintaining relationships underpin any intervention in social work or social care, whether psychosocial, behavioural, advocacy or group care. Partnership working with users of services or interprofessionally requires building and maintaining a relationship.

The historical emphasis on the worker–client relationship has been challenged because of its inherent lack of purpose, and excessive preoccupation with the *process* of helping at the expense of the evaluation of *outcomes* (Macdonald and Sheldon, 1998). More recently there has been a necessary shift of emphasis in social work to achieving successful *outcomes* in community care, care management, child care and child protection and, in Scotland, criminal justice with a focus on evidence-based practice. Lishman (2007) has addressed the tension between the importance of achieving successful outcomes and the usefulness and relevance of ensuring that social workers need to employ the relationship skills discussed in this chapter. There is evidence from counselling and psychotherapy, from social work users of services, and from the research basis for a cognitive behavioural approach in social work (Macdonald, 2007) of the importance of the relationship as a means of engaging in collaborative problem-solving and achieving shared positive outcomes. It is in this sense – as a necessary base for carrying out social work and social care tasks and improving outcomes for users of services – that this chapter explores the communication skills required for building and maintaining helping relationships.

It is crucial that social workers have the necessary case management and outcome orientation in child care, community care and, in Scotland, criminal justice (Porporino and Fabiano, 2007), but this still needs to be underpinned by relationship building and maintaining. How can one provide residential child care for children and young people, for older people or for people with severe learning disabilities without skilful use of relationship building and maintenance? How can one provide a relevant community-care or child-care assessment without them?

The skills examined are those involved in conveying:

- genuineness
- warmth and acceptance
- encouragement and approval
- empathy
- responsiveness and sensitivity

Genuineness

Genuineness is one of the three core conditions or characteristics found to be necessary (although not sufficient) for a counsellor or therapist to help clients effectively (Truax and Carkhuff, 1957). The three core characteristics are genuineness, warmth and empathy. The studies of perceptions of clients and users of services, reviewed in Chapter 2, reinforced the findings of Truax and Carkhuff (Rogers, 2004). Further, user perceptions reviewed in Chapter 2, while at times using different language, e.g. about trustworthiness and reliability, also reinforced the need for genuineness (SCIE, 2004c). It is difficult to describe genuineness adequately, but essentially it means being oneself. Rogers and Truax (1967) define it as involving the worker in 'direct personal encounter with the client, meeting him [sic] on a person to person basis'.

I find it difficult to envisage how we can be engaged in social work or social care if we are not ourselves and do not use ourselves in direct personal encounter whatever our role.

Although an essential element of skilled communication in the helping professions, genuineness is not simply a skill to be learned and practised since it involves our whole self, awareness of self and ease with self. It is particularly important in showing respect to a user of services and, as such, it crosses barriers of class, gender, race and age. What does it involve?

First, it involves being oneself, without relying on one's role or hiding behind it, expressed by one client as 'I thought they'd be uppity – they were right friendly, as though it were your relation instead of a social worker' (Sainsbury, 1975, p. 86). It involves being open and spontaneous although, as Rogers points out (1980), that does not mean saying everything we feel.

Behaviourally, genuineness involves consistency between verbal and non-verbal messages. Showing verbal interest while tapping my foot suggests my interest is not genuine. As Chapter 3 discussed, in a conflict between verbal and non-verbal messages, it is the non-verbal which is usually authentic. Genuineness also involves consistency over time and willingness to recognise one's own inconsistency. For example, I had to acknowledge to a female user of services whose self-esteem had been low and who had problems in asserting herself: 'We've been working on your being more assertive, and now you've just challenged me I've put you down.' Better that I hadn't put her down in the first place, but given that I had, genuineness involves willingness to acknowledge a mistake or inconsistency!

Genuine responses require confidence in the worker's ability to be in touch both with her own feelings and with those of others, and to feel comfortable with them. If I am embarrassed by tears, for example, my responses will be stilted, and I will give a message to the user of services that I cannot handle his distress. If I have enough confidence to say, 'I feel very sad with you', I convey a message that it is appropriate to have these feelings, and that I can cope with them. One user of service spoke about how much she appreciated a worker who cried with her when her son was dying. The worker was not out of control, but confident enough to respond genuinely to her grief.

Genuine responses require confidence to say 'I don't know' to a user of services and then say 'I'll find out' and do so!

If I find a user of services difficult to understand, I need to be able to say so. 'I feel quite confused' is a genuine response to their apparent confusion. It may also clarify that the situation is confusing, thus beginning the possibility of trying to disentangle it. Recently, in dealing with a user of services who I found difficult to understand in what was her second language, I did not try to clarify what she had said and what I had understood. Subsequently we both agreed that it would be more useful for her if I had been honest and checked when I did not entirely understand her use of English.

Genuine responses are not defensive. If a user of services is critical of me or angry with me, I need to feel secure enough not to counter attack or retreat into self-justification or my professional role. Instead I need to be able to listen, and, if necessary, acknowledge my responsibility. For example, if a user of service is angry because I have misunderstood her or him, have not responded to something important or have appeared critical, I would need to listen, to acknowledge her or his anger and, if it is valid, to say 'I can see that was not helpful on my part.'

Genuineness is an essential component of all helping relationships, but it is particularly important with children and adolescents who, as in *The Emperor's New Clothes*, see only too clearly our inauthentic behaviours: 'She's just putting it on', 'She's just a fake.'

In residential work, too, genuine responses are essential: as Clough (2000) points out, residential work embraces many of the complexities of family living. Because it is concerned with the whole of an individual's life, it will encompass all the emotions which are part of living – joy, sorrow, fulfilment and despair. It constantly tests the worker's capacity for genuine responses, which may include exasperation, irritation and despondency. Again, genuineness does not involve showing all our natural responses: for example, as Clough (2000) argues, residential workers should not reveal all their feelings, for example, disgust. However, while it is possible to hide behind roles or tasks (and may be necessary sometimes for self preservation), the strain of maintaining a false self would be untenable, clearly perceived by the residents, and render the worker impotent to engage in purposeful work.

Genuineness is clearly linked with self-disclosure. Traditionally social workers were trained to reveal little or nothing of themselves. To users of services this lack of response frequently felt defensive. We need, however, to think about the purpose of self-disclosure. It should only be used when it seems likely to help the recipient, and not to meet our own needs. 'I am a bit lost – can you go over that again' is self-disclosure which can help the user of services clarify his or her situation or feelings. Sharing current feelings we have had, for example, sadness or anger, may also help them to 'normalize' emotions which may not otherwise feel bearable.

Sharing details of personal life can be more difficult. 'How many children have you?' can be a straightforward request to get to know me as a person, it can be a challenge ('What experience have you had of child rearing?'), it can be an avoidance (changing from a difficult topic) and sometimes it can feel like an intrusion into my privacy. My responses therefore will vary according to my assessment of the underlying meaning.

We should never disclose pain and distress because of our own needs. This is where we need to monitor closely whether we are disclosing what remains for us painful or distressing, or what has been processed, accepted and integrated. Several years ago my brother committed suicide. Only now with time and healing do I feel it is safe to disclose and that I might be able to use the experience in a helpful way where appropriate and relevant with users of services.

Genuineness is difficult to describe and difficult to learn or, at least, if it is too obviously learned it isn't genuine. For me it involves self-awareness and self-monitoring, reasonable self-acceptance, self-confidence and a willingness to risk trying out authentic responses, but always within my professional role boundaries.

Warmth

Non-possessive warmth, also called unconditional positive regard, is another attribute found by Rogers and his client-centred school (1957) to be a core condition for helping. More recent evidence from users of services (SCIE, 2004a and c) found that they valued both warmth and empathy highly.

Warmth is linked with acceptance, and, like genuineness, conveys respect. It involves the worker accepting the experience of the user of services as part of that person without imposing conditions, and can be thought of as almost a physical way of showing caring and understanding. It is mainly expressed non-verbally, and for that reason is difficult to define in writing. I know when I experience warmth from someone, but have difficulty putting that into words.

Reece and Whitman (1962) found warmth to be conveyed by frequent smiling, eye contact, leaning forward and absence of finger tapping, Mehrabian (1972) uses the term immediacy to describe a group of non-verbal behaviours conveying warmth, affiliation and liking. They include physical proximity, leaning towards and turning towards the user of services, sitting in a relaxed position (although not so relaxed as to appear asleep), maintaining eye contact and smiling.

Immediacy involves physical proximity but, as was discussed in Chapter 3, we vary in how close we like to be to each other and how comfortable closeness feels. We need to be sensitive to the meaning of closeness for users of services. If I stand too close to someone I may seem pushy and intrusive and he will back off. If I stand or sit too far away he may see me as cold and unfriendly. Leaning slightly towards someone conveys immediacy: it indicates attentiveness, and lets him know I am with him. Sitting in a relaxed open position conveys immediacy, but being too relaxed, laid back or slouched may convey lack of interest, boredom or lack of respect.

Eye contact is a component of immediacy or warmth, although, as was discussed in Chapter 3, it is also part of regulating interaction and conversation. Low eye contact can indicate lack of warmth, embarrassment, shyness or fear, and is often interpreted as shiftiness or failure to engage.

Looking away, in the sense of out of the window or at the clock, conveys inattention or boredom. Users of services notice it and dislike it. Eye contact, like proximity and position, is subtle, involving a balance between conveying interest, concern and warmth but not becoming intrusive and uncomfortable. As we examined in Chapter 3, smiling is an important means of conveying warmth or immediacy. Smiling is also a social reinforcer, conveying acceptance or approval of what it follows. So when we smile to convey warmth and a desire to relate to a user of services, we also have to be aware that we are likely to be seen to be rewarding and approving their actions and words.

As discussed in Chapter 3, we need to be aware of cultural differences in the expression of warmth. While smiling appears to be universally interpreted as warmth, eye contact is more problematic and, in some cultures, may be interpreted as non-respectful and intrusive.

Touch is another extremely complex area of communication in social work and social care. Touch is a means of conveying warmth and, of course, empathy. It means being comfortable oneself with physical closeness, and then being aware of what that means to users of services. So, again, using touch is a matter of complex judgement. For a sexually- or physically-abused child or adult, touch may be dangerous and intrusive, at least without prior discussion about the child's or adult's ability to control the interaction and what happens to their body.

For a bereaved person physical contact and holding is often comforting. I found that in working with bereaved clients some physical touch, shoulder or hand, seems important in beginning and getting 'in touch', although I am not sure why. It may be that it makes contact when the person feels isolated and conveys a physical warmth when the person is feeling the cold chill of bereavement.

For children with severe learning disabilities and adults, touch and physical proximity may be essential means of communication where verbal communication skills and understanding are limited. Touch expresses warmth, affection, reassurance and containment.

For children and young people in residential care, how we deal with touch and physical contact is complex. In family life, where children and young people feel safe and enjoy healthy relationships with a parent, grandparent or other adult family members, children snuggle close to them when watching television, give and get a bear hug, have a goodnight kiss and cuddle. Adolescents will have different physical contact with parents and family, recognizing their developing separate identity from the family, but nevertheless involving touch and hugs. In residential child care, where children are looked after by the state, in local authority or voluntary sector provision, we need to think carefully about how we mirror 'safe parenting' when we are not the parents but know that children and young people will need touch in a responsive and sensitive way, as an integral part of a caring, trusting and therapeutic relationship.

As we saw in Chapter 3, the use of touch has become increasingly complex in social work and social care. It involves recognition and application of professional boundaries, appropriateness and judgement in terms of age, gender and culture. It also requires judgements about context and setting: what might be appropriate in residential child care in terms of a physical pat on the shoulder for an adolescent young man might not be appropriate in a fieldwork local authority criminal justice setting.

Similarly, touching a user of services of the same age and opposite sex may be construed as having sexual connotations, as may touch between a young female worker and an adolescent boy. However, to avoid physical contact or to have fixed and defined rules about it, while helping the worker to feel less vulnerable to potential allegations, is probably at the expense of normal human communication.

A student in a residential unit for disturbed adolescents became uncomfortable with the attempts of one boy to make physical contact with her. She felt there was a sexual component in his touch, and she withdrew from him. She was also aware that he was a child who had been constantly rejected, and that she was repeating this pattern. She used this awareness to feed back to him her discomfort at the way he touched her. She requested that he stop and respect her boundaries, but at the same time said that she did not want to reject him. After this discussion she and the boy had a closer relationship in which she did not feel uncomfortable and so did not reject him, and in which he was increasingly able to trust her but keep to the boundaries she had set.

Smiling, eye contact, proximity and touch are all essential in conveying warmth, as is spontaneity. However the worker has to be aware of the complex interpretation of these non-verbal behaviours, differing according to culture, context, gender and individual, and to be sensitive to the meaning of her or his behaviour for each individual user of services. Sadly, as acknowledged earlier, because of concerns about potential abuse or harassment, physical proximity and touch has become much more problematic, in particular in work with children and young people. While touch may be used abusively we need to remember and, where appropriate, use its much more positive connotations of empathy, sympathy, concern and approval.

Encouragement and approval

'I think it sounds as if you've done very well.'

'You know I think all of us can find bits we feel badly about and lose sight of the good bits. Clearly there are lots of good bits in your family.'

(Lishman, 1985)

Both these statements from a social worker to a user of services convey a clear and explicit positive message of approval or encouragement. Surprisingly, in a study of social worker–client interaction (1985), I found social workers made little use of explicit verbal statements conveying support, encouragement or approval. Mullen (1968) and Reid (1967) in their American studies of worker–client communications found similarly low use of reassuring verbal comments, and they suggested that this was because it was conveyed non-verbally. However it may not be conveyed enough.

There seems general hesitancy or ambivalence in social work about the value of explicitly conveying approval or positive encouragement. This may reflect in part a cultural bias against giving or accepting positive feedback or an anxiety that giving approval can be patronizing. It may also reflect underlying traditional values in social work, for example, acceptance and taking a non-judgemental approach (Biestek, 1965) which may have been interpreted to mean not only that workers should refrain from conveying their disapproval to users of services but also their approval, since to approve is also to judge. We need to re-examine this. For example to convey encouragement and approval to a hard-pressed carer is an important component of a care-management package to provide additional support.

In social learning theory terms, conveying approval is giving positive reinforcement, defined by Macdonald (2007) when:

● the consequence presented is contingent on the behaviour;
● that behaviour becomes more likely to occur because, and only because, the consequence is presented when the 'behaviour occurs' (p. 171).

Positive reinforcements include tangible rewards, such as money or sweets, or social rewards, such as thanks, praise or appreciation.

Criticisms of the use of social learning and behavioural techniques in social work and social care have focussed on dealing with external symptoms without understanding their meaning for the user of services, treating the user of services as an object and not a whole person, the approach being seen as manipulative, and for giving power to the worker and disempowering the user of services. Consciously and explicitly using positive reinforcement may therefore be tinged with anxieties about control and manipulation associated with behaviour modification. Views from users of services confirm these anxieties: users of services want social workers to be more person-centred and less forceful and in control (Beresford *et al.*, 2005). However, in criminal justice, for example, in relation to a motivational framework for the case management of offenders and motivational interviewing, use of influence and reinforcement can be helpful and effective (McIvor and Raynor, 2007).

In reality, regardless of whether we consciously use behavioural techniques in subtle ways, as we saw in Chapter 3, we may manipulate and modify the views and behaviour of users of services in particular by our non-verbal behaviour. We therefore need to be aware of the reinforcers we use. Smiling, nodding one's head and leaning forward act as reinforcers in verbal conditioning experiments, increasing, for example, the amount of speech or the amount of speech on selected topics. Brief verbal recognitions (e.g. um um) with smiles and positive head nods also act as reinforcers.

In general, users of services historically came to social workers because of needs or problems and therefore, as Nicolson *et al.* (2006) point out, there was a tendency for workers to focus on problems and not strengths. Currently many users of services do not see themselves as having problems, but as requiring social work, social care and interdisciplinary services to ensure they can maintain an independent life (see Chapter 2). A potential danger is that we may then be selectively responding to problem behaviour and negative circumstances, thus reinforcing their importance in people's lives.

However many (although by no means all) users of services have low self-esteem, and are worn down by poverty, ill health and poor housing. If we continue to focus predominantly on problem areas for users of services we may be in danger of reinforcing their sense of powerlessness.

In contrast, the conscious use of encouragement and approval reinforces positive action and behaviour. In common with showing respect, unconditional regard and empathy for users of services it challenges their potential negative self-belief or poor self-concept by giving them information which is discrepant with their own beliefs about themselves. This kind of 'attribution method' appears to be a more effective way of promoting change than simple reinforcement. The argument is that the worker's belief in the user of services is discrepant with their view of themselves, and one way of dealing with the discrepancy is for them to change their self-image. The discrepancy and consequent challenge is conveyed graphically in the response of one user of services: 'And you can take a cup of tea even in this dirty house.' I did, conveying non-verbal acceptance and encouragement, and then we set to work jointly on how better to manage her child care.

If a user of child care services who is having difficulties with her toddler manages on one occasion not to slap her but stays relatively calm, and brings this to the worker, why not praise, approve and say 'That's good. Well done', and acknowledge that achievement. We need to be constantly aware of positive behaviours and change on the part of users of services and give verbal feedback and recognition of them, i.e. appreciate their endeavours and successes. Keeping an appointment, losing two kilograms, paying an instalment on the electricity bill, getting to mother and toddler groups can be major achievements for a woman contending with poverty, poor housing, motherhood and depression.

Many other users of services, for example, in relation to care in the community, come to social work services as an expert by experience, requiring services and wishing to negotiate for them in partnership with the social worker. Encouragement and appreciation of their expertise is equally relevant for them.

Empathy

'She had the gift of putting things into words. I came feeling mixed. I came out feeling eased and understood.'   (Lishman, 1985)

This person experienced the value of empathy, the worker's sensitivity to her feelings and her verbal ability to communicate this back. Empathy is the third core condition or characteristic found to be necessary (but not sufficient) for a counsellor or therapist to help clients effectively (Truax and Carkhuff, 1957).

In order to be empathic, the worker has to be able to enter into the subjective world of the user of services, to feel what it might be like for them, to understand what they might be thinking, and to convey this understanding back to them. The worker has to be able to do this without taking on the internal world of the user of services as her or his own. This means that I, as the worker, have to be able to understand the confusion without becoming lost in it.

Why should empathy for a user of services be such an important part of a helping relationship? Frequently users of services experience powerful and overwhelming feelings of chaos and muddle, of anxiety, of anger and rage, of grief and loss. These feelings seem overwhelming not just to them but to their family and friends, who may then react by avoidance, rejection or criticism. If the worker can convey that she or he understands the power of such feelings, but is not overwhelmed by them, then the user of services can be reassured that they can be managed and contained.

A woman whose husband died suddenly in an industrial accident was so overwhelmed with feelings of worthlessness, pointlessness and despair that she frequently felt suicidal. For her family this was terrifying, and they could not bear to listen to her distress, instead reassuring her of her importance to them.

My task, as an empathic worker, was to convey to her that I understood that it felt, at this time, as if there was no meaning or purpose for her, that her pain felt unbearable, and that therefore the possibility of suicide offered relief from suffering. However empathy did not mean that I took on her inner world as my own. While I was in touch with her despair, I did not confirm her perception of suicide as the only solution, but held on to my inner reality of the possibility of change for her. Subsequently she stressed the value of a place where she could safely bring any emotion, without fear that it would be avoided or rejected; my acceptance and understanding of the depth of her feelings, without being overwhelmed by them, was part of a process by which she chose to continue living.

Empathic responses can help a user of services make sense of what may feel a jumble of thoughts and feelings. They may be reassured that there is some meaning in what has felt incoherent, irrational or even crazy. Egan (2007) suggests that to respond empathically we need to ask, 'What is the core message this client is expressing?'.

Often users of services approach us with anxiety and even suspicion, unsure what to expect, sometimes feeling shame at needing help. By conveying some understanding of how they may feel, we may help them begin to develop some trust and free them to work on the problems they have brought.

Where a user of services feels shame or stigma at asking for help, for example, that she or he should be able to cope with caring for a spouse with dementia, conveying understanding of how difficult it is to ask for help and how important she or he has felt it to be able to cope, may enable her or him to think more constructively or appropriately of what she or he can or cannot offer and therefore what services are required. Similarly for a parent with drug problems to approach a social service agency involves anxiety about their inadequacies in child care and how these might be viewed. An empathic response can then help reduce the anxiety and engage in shared and realistic problem formulation.

When I worked in child care, a client whose son had been stealing and soiling told me much later how terrified she had been that I would simply remove him. For her, most of our early contact was taken up with that preoccupying anxiety. Had I been sensitive and empathic enough to acknowledge that anxiety and her feelings of responsibility and blame, our early contact might have been more effective.

Many families faced with a report for a Children's Hearing will have similar anxieties. Even where these are realistic, conveying understanding of how the family might feel at this point may enable them to share more freely necessary and relevant information and, possibly, even become more involved and accepting of the decision-making.

In working with children, accurate empathy may be an essential tool. A child or adolescent entering residential care may be overwhelmed by the size, noise and the group of adolescents. For the key worker to acknowledge these feelings – the strangeness and loneliness and the loss of his familiar home and family – will not change these feelings but may make the transition more bearable.

I am not suggesting that empathy will always create open trusting relationships with all users of services, but for shared work and problem-solving, a user of services has to develop some trust in the social worker, relevant also in criminal justice (McIvor and Raynor, 2007), and some part of that will come from a sense of being understood. How many users of services fail to engage with social services because they do not experience a worker as understanding their predicament? How many adults and children in residential care feel isolated and withdraw because they do not experience an empathic response from their carers?

Responsiveness and sensitivity

> 'She listened; she checked out and was fair, so we felt her judgements were sound.'
> 'Very perceptive. He gave evidence of how much he had taken in and how open he is to correction about his mistakes.'   (Lishman, 1985)

These social workers engaged in checking out their perceptions with people, and were open to the possibility of getting things wrong. They were not arrogant or insensitive in their interactions, but showed an ability to be sensitive and responsive to users of services.

Responsiveness can be conveyed non-verbally and verbally. Mehrabian (1972) found that it was communicated non-verbally by activity, by movement – head nods, gesticulation, leg and foot movements, and by facial expression – pleasantness and changes in expression.

In a study of social worker–client interaction (Lishman, 1985), I found that social workers engaged in surprisingly high levels of non-verbal movement, in particular of hands and feet, fiddling and rubbing themselves. In general this behaviour did not appear distracting or inattentive, but rather seemed to convey alertness and responsiveness. As Chapter 3 notes, the social worker in the study who used few non-verbal movements, in contrast, appeared rather wooden, rigid and unresponsive.

Facial expression conveys mood e.g. licking or biting one's lips conveys anxiety. Small facial movements have a big impact on the onlooker; e.g. drooping eyelids convey weariness. Facial movement conveys alertness and responsiveness, so that I need to be aware of how I respond visually to what a user of services tells me, e.g. smiling at his achievements, looking grave at his problems. Again, in my study of social worker–client interaction, the workers with very few changes of facial expression looked rather like a wax model, immobile and unresponsive to clients (Lishman, 1985).

What is involved in verbal responsiveness and sensitivity? Clearly they are linked to empathy and understanding, but also involve openness, checking out and an ability to seek and receive feedback.

There is a world of difference between:

'I wondered if you felt a bit that he was taking you for a ride.'
'I thought you were saying you were tired of him?'
'Have I got that right?'

and:

'Obviously you felt he was taking you for a ride and you are tired of him.'

The first, more tentative statement gives the user of services the opportunity to rephrase or correct a faulty impression, and actively checks out the worker's perceptions. The second assumes the worker's view is right.

A social worker has to be aware of the power difference between herself and a user of services. How can someone challenge a worker's perception if the worker appears arrogant and shows no respect for and sensitivity to their views? How can a user of services engage with and trust a worker who appears to be unaware of her or his perspective, who makes untested assumptions about it or who appears unwilling to explore it and negotiate some kind of shared perception.

In social work and social care we work with users of services who are of a different gender, who are from different ethnic groups, class or culture and different ages and stages to our own. We must be aware of this: I need to recognize that my perspective – female, middle-class, middle-aged and eurocentric – is clearly not shared by all users of services I encounter. I must constantly check, question and negotiate about my understanding and interpretation of the perspective of the user of services.

If I fail to do this I will be perceived as arrogant and insensitive. Further, I will be ineffective. Lack of sensitivity and responsiveness affects agreement between users of services and the worker about the nature of the problem and the purpose of contact and contributes to the clash in perspective identified in Chapter 2. As Chapter 8 will discuss, failure to achieve agreement about the purpose of social work contact is linked to poor outcomes.

Clearly this discussion of sensitivity and responsiveness is linked with earlier discussion in this chapter, particularly of empathy, and with subsequent chapters on listening skills, purpose of contact and reflection. Being responsive helps to build and maintain a relationship, is a core skill in listening and questioning and is involved in techniques of change as a component of persuasiveness or social influence.

Skills in building relationships, particular genuineness, warmth, and responsiveness and sensitivity are also necessary skills in working with colleagues in social work, social care and in interdisciplinary settings.

Conclusion

The skills of conveying genuineness, warmth, acceptance, encouragement and approval, empathy and responsiveness and sensitivity have in general been discussed in relation to users of services who are *not* involuntary, unwilling or resistant. These skills are also involved in building relationships with involuntary users of services to engage with them in joint work on cognitive behavioural change and, with interprofessional colleagues, to engage in effective working relationship and partnerships, whether with health, education, housing or the police or prison service.

---

putting it into practice

Using the content of this chapter reflect on and evaluate – you could use a Likert scale – how well you exhibit genuineness, warmth, encouragement and approval, empathy and responsiveness and sensitivity with users of services.

Reflect on and evaluate how well you use or exhibit these characteristics with fellow professionals.

Consider/reflect on the tensions you may have found in relation to users of services.

Consider/reflect on the tensions you may have found in relation to interprofessional colleagues.

Recommended reading

Egan, G. (2007) *The Skilled Helper: A Problem Management and Opportunity Development Approach to Helping*, Pacific Grove, CA, Thompson/Brooks Cole. A classic text which examines in detail the skills required in relationship building and how these underpin helpfulness in achieved desired outcomes for users of services.

Trevithick, P. (2005) *Social Work Skills: A Practice Handbook*, Maidenhead, Open University Press. A useful summary of communication skills involved in building and maintaining relationships.

Trevithick, P., Richard, S., Ruch, G. and Moss, B. (2004) *Teaching and Learning Communication Skills in Social Work Education*, London, SCIE. A comprehensive survey of communication skills needed in social work and social care with a strong emphasis on perceptions of users of services.

6 | Attending and listening

As with building and maintaining relationships, attending and listening is part of the core skills (introduced in Chapter 3) which are essential to underpin assessment and the range of methods of intervention used in social work and social care (Coulshed and Orme, 2006; Trevithick, 2005).

In order to understand users of services and their needs, requirements and problems we must be able to attend and listen to them. In order to work effectively and in collaboration to provide integrated services for all users of services, we need both to attend to and listen to colleagues in interdisciplinary teams whose purpose is to provide integrated services. We need to listen not just to acquire information, but also to empathize, and understand the other person's perspective, whether she or he is a colleague or user of services.

This chapter examines how we may most effectively listen to users of services and colleagues in the active way which the early client studies have shown are necessary. These earlier findings from client studies are reinforced by the literature on user views (Diggins, 2004; SCIE, 2004a and c) and on interprofessional working (Barrett *et al.*, 2005; McLean, 2007).

Preparing for attending: context

'She was friendly but I got the impression sometimes she was trying to think what was on a notepad in her head, an imaginary one, like to bring out from last week, and not fully listening to us.'   (Lishman, 1985)

Users of services stress the importance of the worker (from whatever interprofessional discipline) being attentive to them as an individual and they are sensitive to inattention and critical of behaviours which convey it. So, we should usefully remember, are our colleagues, whether from social work, social care or an interdisciplinary team or agency context.

Attending and listening carefully are important ways in which we convey respect and concern for both users of services and colleagues. How can we convey that we are actively paying attention? First, we need to prepare to attend to each interaction. Clearly the context we work in influences what kind of and how much preparation we have the opportunity to make. In a residential or group-care setting a user or resident may begin to share important facts or feelings and require active attention without warning, e.g. in the middle of household tasks, while watching the television or while going to bed.

A care worker in a residential home for older people was saying goodnight to a resident who was reading her bible and said, 'There have been a lot of deaths recently'. This was the opening for the resident to share feelings of loss at the death of fellow residents and anxiety at the prospect of her own death. For the worker, this remark came out of the blue, and required him to attend immediately to the core message. However, responding to this resident required him to delay attending to others. Decisions to attend to one individual in group care have to be taken in the context of the impact on other group members.

In health settings such preparation is important. For example, a doctor needs to have carefully attended to and noted meticulous assessment and treatment from other previous health and social work professionals in order to avoid unilaterally prescribing a new treatment regime which may not fit easily with treatment for the patient's other medical conditions or his social circumstances.

In fieldwork settings preparation includes place and purpose. Where is the interview to be carried out: the worker's office, the home of the user of services or some neutral territory? For some users of services a visit at home is necessary: for example, a parent with pre-school children or an older person with difficulties in mobility may find getting to a city-centre office impossible. If we are concerned about child care or a child's development, direct observation of the child within the home is essential. The tragic outcomes for Victoria Climbié (Laming, 2003) and Caleb Ness (O'Brien, 2003) both highlight the need, when working with vulnerable children who may be at risk, for the worker, whether from social work or health, to have access to the child on a regular basis at home for observational and assessment (including risk) purposes.

However, a home visit may not always be appropriate, and if undertaken may inhibit our full attention because of anxiety about personal risk. Violence against social workers has increased. Balloch *et al.* (1999) found that 75% of the social services work-force had experienced verbal abuse at work, 33% had been threatened with violence and 33% had actually been attacked. Workers in residential care are most at risk.

Twenty-five per cent of all social workers had been physically attacked in their current job. If we are planning a home visit we need to make a risk assessment. We should always leave a record in the office of where we are and when we expect to come back. If we have any indication that any user of services is potentially violent, making a home visit alone may be dangerous and we should involve a colleague.

For some users of services, an office interview, with its anonymity, may be preferred as being less intrusive than a home visit. For some users of services who are attending on a voluntary basis, attendance for office appointments may act as a gauge of their commitment to contact. For others, who are seen on a statutory basis, attendance at an office interview is a condition of, for example, a probation order.

If an office interview is chosen, preparation means securing a room and then arranging it, taking into consideration proximity and orientation, discussed earlier in Chapter 3. Putting chairs too close can be oppressive and overwhelming to a user of services; too great a distance symbolically conveys just that. Remaining behind a desk is distancing and conveys a power differential, not conducive to the enabling and empowering elements of social work inherent even where the authority of the role predominates. Preparation means ensuring privacy and minimal interruptions, even by phone. In undertaking a home visit we may have little control over these arrangements, although we can ask for the television to be turned off or for an unexpected visitor to give us some time in order to complete the interview.

We need to consider general areas to explore and be aware of sensitive areas which may be difficult to discuss, for example our concern about whether child care is adequate is likely to be met with defensiveness if not anger and hostility. We need always to be aware of the possibility that feelings and issues which we did not predict may arise and, while we may try tentatively to plan an interview, we have to be sufficiently flexible to discard our agenda if necessary and respond to pressing concerns of the user of services. While we need to be purposeful in interviews – Davies (1994) argues that interviews are conversations with a purpose – we also need to be flexible and responsive.

We do need to be clear about the purpose of contact, for example to prepare an initial enquiry report or to assess an older person's needs for home-care services. We have to be prepared for other agendas: a family's wish for an older person to go into residential care may not be shared by the older person or even have been discussed with her or him. We need to be prepared about the kind of information we are likely to need, 'a checklist of areas and topics' (Nicolson *et al.* 2006), but this should not too obviously dominate the interview as the opening quotation about the imaginary notepad indicates. For example, the very thorough application of a single shared assessment questionnaire irritated my mother who was nearly ninety because to her much of it seemed irrelevant to what she perceived she needed, i.e. a community care alarm. For a variety of reasons she never got one.

Preparing for attending: ourselves

We also need to be prepared in ourselves. Nelson-Jones (2005) stresses the need for self-awareness; in particular, awareness of which situations and topics generate most personal anxiety for the worker, since intense anxiety is likely to lead to inattention, poor listening and inappropriate responses and action. Such anxiety may be realistic, e.g. when a user of services is drunk and/or aggressive, but it may also be influenced by the worker's own personal history or experience with previous users of services. A student was working with a user of services who had problems with alcohol and was aware of a feeling of intense anxiety and a wish to get out of the situation which she realized was not appropriate to the current situation. In supervision she saw that her anxiety belonged to a previous, but similar contact, where the person had committed suicide. The student had 'forgotten' this very distressing experience until it was reawakened by this user of services with almost identical problems.

Our own family histories will affect our responses to current families and situations we work with. For example, experience in childhood of violence by parents may generate intense anxiety and feelings of helplessness, as adults and social workers, when confronted with potential violence. Bereavement in childhood is never talked about, but may leave us with intense anxieties about dealing directly with loss.

In order to be prepared to attend and to listen we need to be clear about areas we personally find difficult. My experience has been that by acknowledging and understanding the personal origins of my difficulty, I have been able to attend to and work with users of services with similar problems to my own with empathy. Awareness of difficulty, however, can also mean realistic recognition of problems one is ill-equipped to work with. For example, if I had recently lost a child by a cot death, illness or an accident, the loss might be too immediate for me to work with others in that situation. In the future, however, it may enable me to be more attentive, sensitive and empathic to users of services who face such a loss. It is my professional responsibility to be aware of how functional or dysfunctional I am likely to be.

Attending

Initially being punctual is an indication to users of services of attentiveness: if we are late it is important to apologize. Lack of punctuality can denote lack of concern (Trevithick, 2005). Once engaged in an interview how do we convey attentiveness?

Egan (2007) stresses the importance of our values and attitudes in attending to the particular user of services, for example:

> 'What are my attitudes to this particular user of services?'
> 'How are my values and attitudes being expressed in my non-verbal and verbal behaviour?'

Such self-monitoring is an essential component of our ability to attend fully and openly to all users of services, voluntary or involuntary.

Egan (2007) used the acronym SOLER for the non-verbal behaviour necessary to convey attention:

Straight position facing the interviewee
Open position
Leaning towards the interviewee
Eye contact
Relaxed position (p.76)

These components of attending behaviour are now examined in more detail. The evidence on which Egan drew was examined in Chapter 3 in the section on non-verbal behaviour.

First we need to think about our position. The worker should face the user of services, as Egan (2007) says 'squarely'. Turning towards or facing them conveys that we are ready or prepared to be involved. We should lean towards users of services at times, again to convey interest and involvement. Leaning back tends to convey boredom or lack of interest, although leaning too far forward may be intrusive or intimidating. We need to adopt an open and alert posture. Crossed arms and legs can be perceived as closed or defensive, not open to or attentive to the other's communication.

Being too 'laid back' can appear as if we are not interested and not involved. However we also need to appear relatively relaxed. This means neither fidgeting too much nor being so stiff and controlled that we appear to be totally unresponsive. Excessive fidgeting or restlessness can convey nervousness or boredom. Too little bodily movement, in contrast, can convey rigidity and lack of responsiveness (Lishman, 1985).

Some movement, e.g. occasional shifting of position or leaning towards a user of services, conveys attentiveness and alertness. Similarly our facial expression can convey responsiveness or lack of interest. We need to consider what our normal facial expression conveys – friendliness, anxiety, tension, fear, aloofness or disapproval – and how much it changes in response to communication from users of services or colleagues. Complete immobility of body or face is likely to be interpreted as disinterest or even rejection. One user of services said angrily, 'I was pouring out my heart: he never moved and his face never flickered'.

We need to smile; as Priestley and McGuire (1983) suggest:

> Not all the time, like a Cheshire cat and not so rarely as a sunny day in November but enough to show that you are awake and listening and also what an essentially nice person you are. (p. 36)

Eye contact or looking at the user of services is important. It conveys that we are attending to the other: it is a way of saying, 'I am interested in what you say and feel'. Clearly we do look away at times, for example when we start a long utterance or sometimes if the material is intensely personal. However, repeatedly looking away can indicate a general difficulty in getting involved or a specific reluctance to getting involved with this person. Either of these responses needs to be explored. Why, if we are in social work, is it difficult to get involved with others? If this is not a general problem, why am I having difficulty in engaging in eye contact with this person? The difficulty may reflect anxieties on our own part, e.g. about anger, abuse or loss, or alternatively problems on the part of the user of services about sharing, disclosure or intimacy.

Defining, as I have just done, general principles about eye contact, raises issues about general applicability of communication in terms of culture and gender as we saw in Chapter 3.

Nelson-Jones (2005) provides a useful exploration of the distinction between culture deficit and culture-sensitive approaches to communication: 'The culture deficit approach assumes that the rules of the dominant culture are normal…..The culture sensitive approach avoids the assumption that dominant group practices are proper and superior' (p79).

So what for me, as a white, middle-class female, seems the appropriate level of eye contact to convey attentiveness may be perceived as an overuse of power and authority or as immodest and unsuitable by users of services from another culture. All the principles about attending need to be reviewed in relation to how appropriate they are in terms of gender, culture, ethnicity, religion and age.

Attentiveness is conveyed by nodding our heads. Again Priestley and McGuire (1983) put it succinctly and humorously:

> No need to outdo Noddy, but gentle, affirmative movements of the head will show that you are following the train of an argument and will encourage further speech. (p. 36)

As we saw in Chapter 3, we do however have to be careful that in our use of nodding our heads we do not reinforce potential anti-social or criminal behaviour.

Manner also can convey attentiveness or distance and boredom. It can convey arrogance and power which signal unwillingness really to listen.

Each of these lessons about careful attending, while essential in working with users of services, is also crucial for our work with interprofessional colleagues. For example, in relation to punctuality, lack of punctuality for users of drug services may well reflect their chaotic life style and we need to work with this. In relation to interprofessional colleagues, lack of punctuality on our part may be seen as unprofessional. Equally, while keeping people waiting may appear to reflect higher status, it is not consistent with a social-work value base or with maintaining relationships interprofessionally and with users of services. In working with users of services we need to think reciprocally about interpretation of body language in listening and attending: does their body language signify for example that they are defensive, nervous, or unprepared to be involved. As we saw in Chapter 3, body movement and eye contact are particularly important in how we interpret, in attending and listening, behaviour and responses from users of services. We also need to pay the same attention to our colleagues from other disciplines: how much are they attending and how much are they displaying non-verbal behaviour which indicates they are not and if not why? Are we contributing to this and if so how?

In relation to our own behaviour, it is important, as Sutton (1994) suggests, to consider how 'confident, over-confident, tentative, condescending, cold, aggressive, distant or anxious' we appear. Feedback, if we are open to it, comes from users of services, colleagues, videos and simulation. Feedback from video indicates that I look anxious whether I am role playing worker or user of services. I have had to use this feedback to practise appearing more relaxed than I feel: specifically breathing deeply, relaxing my facial muscles, and consciously adopting a more relaxed posture, including not tensing my hands and fingers. Other feedback from colleagues has indicated that, when I know I feel extremely anxious, they perceive me as highly confident and potentially undermining. Again I have had to practise appearing relaxed but not over-confident.

Listening

Non-verbal attending behaviour is an essential ingredient of listening. Semi-verbal 'following' behaviour (Rozelle *et al.*, 1997) is another important component. Priestley and McGuire (1983) suggested that we need to 'grunt'. Like smiling, nodding one's head and leaning forward, brief 'semi-verbal recognitions' like 'a ha', 'mm mm' and 'uh uh' have been found to act as reinforcers in experiments on verbal conditioning (Greenspoon, 1955).

We have, of course, to be aware of the reinforcing element of such 'grunts' and not reinforce behaviour which is destructive to the user of services or others. Here our own values are important. I am not advocating that we take a narrow, judgemental, moralistic position or that we simply reflect the prevalent social morality and values. Nevertheless it is not helpful to a user of services if, unintentionally we reinforce racist, sexist or other discriminatory views or behaviour or potential violence and aggression, and we need to be aware of when our non-verbal or semi-verbal behaviour is in danger of doing so.

Attending behaviour and semi-verbal prompts are necessary components of listening but they are not enough. We also have to follow and understand the user of services, and convey that we are doing so. Listening actively in this way is complex and demanding: we have to observe and then listen to the non-verbal behaviour of users of services.

Like the worker, a user of services conveys attitudes and feelings non-verbally. As we saw in Chapter 3, where there is a conflict between verbal and non-verbal messages the non-verbal messages are generally more important (Mehrabian, 1972). As Coulshed and Orme (2006) argue:

> Only by listening and observing the way that people seek help can there be an effective interpersonal exchange which correctly receives overt and covert messages, decodes them and responds to the various levels of communication there in. People can say one thing but their behaviour may indicate the opposite. (p. 85)

In Chapter 3, we discussed the difficulties of interpreting non-verbal behaviour. In particular, we need to be aware of non-verbal behaviour 'leaking' otherwise forbidden communication, e.g. anxiety, anger or hostility. Egan (2007) usefully summarizes the following meanings of non-verbal behaviour in overall communication by users of services, by us as social work and social care professionals, and also by our colleagues in other disciplines, e.g. health, education or police.

Confirming or repeating: non-verbal behaviour can confirm what is said.

Denying or confusing: non-verbal behaviour may be in contrast to verbal utterances: for example, a user of services or a colleague from social services or another discipline may deny anger while her or his face flushes and her or his body assumes a tense, hostile posture. *Strengthening or emphasizing*: non-verbal behaviour can emphasize as well as confirm what is being said. For example if a user of services says that she finds a worker's questioning critical and intrusive, and then remains frowning and silent, her non-verbal behaviour adds intensity to the verbal message. *Controlling or regulating:* non-verbal behaviour can be used to control interaction. For example, if a user of services becomes distressed whenever a worker begins to challenge her, the worker needs to be aware of this pattern of behaviour and consider what it might mean. There are no simple rules for interpreting individual non-verbal signals. It is unhelpful to focus on one single behaviour at the expense of listening to and understanding the whole person. Non-verbal signals have to be understood within the context of an individual's normal non-verbal behaviour, their gender, their age, their ethnicity and their culture.

Trevithick (2005) usefully introduces the concept of 'non-selective listening' where 'listening occurs at several levels: to what people say, how they say it; at what point they say certain things, whether certain themes recur and also what people do not say. This is sometimes described as "listening with the third ear"' (p. 123). This idea usefully ties symbolic, non-verbal behaviour and verbal behaviour in their interlinked contribution to how, as social workers and carers, we need to attend to listening.

As well as attending and listening to non-verbal behaviour we have to listen to and understand verbal communication. We can broadly distinguish between communication of factual information, and communication of feelings (which may be non-verbal as well as verbal). If we are writing a social enquiry report, a report for the Children's Hearing, a single shared assessment or an assessment for residential care, we have to absorb a considerable amount of factual information. Absorbing such information can be very difficult: to absorb large amounts we need to condense it and organize it into key components. We may need to note down in writing certain factual information but will need to rely on our capacity to absorb and memorize information in order to fill out such notes.

Even where predominantly factual information is being given, e.g. about income and resources, if a service user is asking for Welfare Rights advice, feelings such as depression or anger at poverty and lack of help can emerge. The expression of feeling demands more of the listener than just an ability to absorb, memorize and feedback what is said. It involves the listener's ability to get in touch with the other person's world at a feeling level and then respond on that basis, i.e. empathically.

Perhaps more useful than a distinction between facts and feelings is Egan's (2007) distinction in verbal communication between experiences, behaviours and affect or feelings.

Listening to experiences

Users of services often describe their *experiences* to us:

'She got mad at me'
'He's staying out too late for a boy of his age'
'His mother is driving me mad with her forgetfulness'
'She is so demanding. I am not sure how long I can go on coping'.

These are experiences of personal problematic situations.

Egan (2007) argues that attentive listening to these experiences and feelings of users of services is critical for further work: these experiences help us to understand where they are starting from and their frame of reference. While we may wish to challenge this later we have to start there.

Users of services will also want to tell us about their experiences of gaps and inadequacies in service provision. Beresford *et al.* (2005) suggest that users of services frequently felt, for example, that the model on which social care was based was still primarily medical. 'Professionals don't understand the social models of disability' (p. 8). Beresford *et al.*'s respondents also emphasized that social care should be needs-led not budget-led or service-led.

We need to listen carefully to these experiences rather than reacting defensively. However they raise a major tension for us. We need to consider whether a social model of disability (Oliver, 1996) or a medical model (Shakespeare, 2006) is appropriate: if we use a social model it may be problematic for us to influence service delivery because, in needs-led social care, there is a considerable tension between the financial resources available and the needs of users of services with whom we work. We need to attend and listen very carefully to experiences of gaps in service provision. There is some anecdotal evidence that if we do and explain why we cannot provide a required resource, users of services will still feel attended to and listened to properly.

Listening to accounts of behaviours

Following Egan's model we need also to listen to users of services' accounts of their behaviour. Egan (2007) suggests that describing our behaviour is more difficult than describing our experience because we are aware of more responsibility for it. Behaviour can be overt or covert. Overt behaviour is that which can be seen by others:

'When he is late I shout at him.'
'Sometimes I am rough when she gets up again to go to the toilet in the night'
'When he asks me the same thing for the 30th time I ignore him'.

Covert behaviour is about thoughts, attitudes, decisions, memories over which people feel they have some control, e.g. planning to stop smoking, deciding to change jobs. As Coulshed and Orme (2006) suggest:

Advanced practitioners such as those who are expert in family therapy are able to use the literal message, alongside what is known as the 'meta-message' (that is messages about the message) as part of their interviewing. (p. 85)

They use the examples of adolescents leaving home where the literal message is of support and approval from parents, but the meta-message is much more doubtful, 'Will you be able to manage without us?' or 'Will we be able to manage without you?'.

Listening attentively to accounts of behaviour from users of services is critical: such behaviour may have patterns or triggers of which users of services are unaware: equally such behaviour may perhaps become the focus of quite specific planned change.

For example, if we begin to see a sustained pattern or trigger in how a child irritates a parent, this may be a potential beginning for them to consider changes in how they respond. Similarly if we perceive that carers find particular behaviours of the person they care for problematic we may jointly begin with the carer to examine the pattern, what it means to them and how they might helpfully change their response.

Listening to feelings and affect

Finally we need to listen to the feelings or affect of users of services. Sometimes these will be expressed non-verbally, by a defeated posture, by tears or by angry silence. Sometimes they are expressed verbally, 'I feel so down, what is the point of going on?', 'I felt so angry with him, I wanted to kill him'.

Listening and an empathic response are important components in enabling the user of services to feel that such emotions can be accepted, expressed and lived with, and do not have to be hidden or feared. Such acceptance may be the starting point for them to learn to live with and manage previously disabling emotions.

If our listening is partial or distracted, for example because the feelings of a user of services trigger off our own (about abuse, loss or victimization), we may convey to her or him that such feeling is unmanageable or has to be avoided or is dangerous and unsafe. Such a message, from our poor listening, can only compound feelings of being overwhelmed by and out of control of her or his emotions.

Listening attentively and the acceptance conveyed, however, should be carefully and critically reviewed. Is this person a potential risk? Might she be at risk of suicide? Might she harm someone else? Listening is a complicated process. We need to engage in it fully and not be distracted. However 'listening with the third ear' also involves listening to the potential risks a user of services is conveying.

We need to learn the microskills involved in attending to and listening to the experiences, behaviours and feelings of users of services, but we also have to listen in a more holistic way. As Egan (2007) has suggested, we are all more than the sum of our verbal and non-verbal messages. Listening genuinely and attentively therefore means learning deeply and holistically about the other person as they are influenced by the contexts in which they live and pursue their own lives. Such listening involves empathic understanding (considered previously in more detail in Chapter 5). To be empathic we have to put aside our own prejudices and ways of seeing and interpreting the world in order to enter the world of the service user or colleague, and to see things from their perspective.

Such listening also involves listening 'for recurrent dominant themes rather than focussing on detail' (Kadushin and Kadushin, 1997, p. 250). Such an ability involves, as suggested earlier, 'listening with the third ear' (Trevithick, 2005) or, as Freud suggested, with 'free floating attention'. I have previously argued that having a purpose in an interview aids preparation and attention. However there is a tension between a clear purpose and 'listening with the third ear'. We need to be aware of it and prepare to relinquish the original purpose. Otherwise we may fail to listen and be like the social worker in the quotation at the beginning of this chapter, with a mental notebook or checklist with which we are preoccupied.

Problems in listening

Problems in listening can arise from the setting, the speaker or the listener. A room which is poorly soundproofed allows for outside noise which is distracting, but also renders a user of services and worker anxious about the possibility of confidentiality. Interruptions by phone or person distract both speaker and listener. Poor acoustics make the task of listening more difficult.

While it is the worker's responsibility to listen attentively sometimes this may not be easy if the user of services presents communication problems, for example, by slurring speech because of drink or drugs. Here, explaining to the user of services that I am unable to hear him or her properly also conveys a message that I wish to listen attentively but the influence of their drink or drugs is impeding me. It may be appropriate to stop the interview and require him or her to return when not under the influence of drink or drugs.

This may not, however, be an option if we are in a home visit undertaking a risk assessment about parents' ability to provide safe parenting for their children: here we may have to continue despite the problems in effective listening and hearing.

Sometimes a user of services may have a speech defect: this means we have to practise and perfect accurate listening, checking with them to ensure we have properly understood. Users of services who speak very softly also present challenges to effective listening. I worked with a woman who initially spoke almost inaudibly. I strained to listen and even wondered if I was beginning to suffer hearing impairment. Eventually I explained to her my difficulty: she was surprised that I thought she spoke softly but then acknowledged that other people had difficulty in hearing her. In time it emerged that her presentation reflected her low self-esteem and feelings that what she had to say was not worthwhile. In a sense I was challenging this belief and conveying that I did wish to hear what she had to say.

Users of services may appear rather monotonous: if I find myself bored I begin to feel alarmed. What does my boredom mean? It may reflect the other person's low self-esteem, feelings of not being worthy of attention, or depression. Difficulty in listening attentively or boredom signal to me concern: I then have to examine whether the difficulty belongs with the user of services (low self-esteem, withdrawal, depression) or with me (distraction, defensiveness or, for example, personal difficulty about dealing with depression). With colleagues from social work and social care or interdisciplinary professions we also need to reflect and consider if we feel bored. For example, does this reflect a colleague's lack of engagement or feeling of professional superiority, or my own stereotyping of that individual or professional discipline?

Users of services may be involved in an interview where the language used is not their first language and may therefore need to use an interpreter (see Chapter 3). Listening to an interpreter involves further challenges to attending and listening. How do I ensure that my interpretation of the interpreter's communication is exactly what the anxious parent would have wanted to convey if she and I both spoke fluent English or Urdu? Similar issues arise for people with hearing impairment where we need to use a skilled signer in order to conduct an interview. How do we check that we have listened with the 'third ear' to the signer and that key messages have not got lost in the interpretation process?

What problems may the worker bring to listening? We have already identified difficulties in being distracted, preoccupied with a previous encounter, stereotyping or finding ourselves with a user of services who triggers a painful or unbearable aspect of our experience.

Egan (2007) examines in detail problems in listening: inadequate listening, evaluative listening, filtered listening and sympathetic listening. Trevithick (2005) and Coulshed and Orme (2006) talk about 'selective' listening.

Inadequate listening

Inadequate listening involves being distracted and we have already examined some factors which may distract us. Egan (2007) lists the following additional possibilities:

- *Physical condition:* if we are ill or over-tired our listening skills will be reduced.
- *Overeagerness/anxiety about performance:* if we are too anxious about responding properly we may concentrate on our responses rather than listening.
- *Attraction:* if we find a user of services attractive or unattractive this may distract from our full ability to listen.
- *Similarity of problems:* if the problems of a user of services are very similar to our own we may think about our own situation at the expense of hers or his.
- *Differences:* if her or his experience is very different from our own this may also be distracting.

Evaluative listening

It is difficult to listen without evaluating what the speaker is saying in terms, for example, of good or bad, right or wrong. Such evaluation makes it difficult to empathize and may distract our listening: we need to be aware, therefore, of our tendency to evaluate while listening. For example, a student working in group care for adolescents found their swearing so offensive that it prevented her from listening to their very real pain and anger. Egan (2007) further distinguishes stereotyped listening by which we listen and interpret someone as a stereotype, e.g. neurotic, psychopath or hysteric. Stereotypical listening is a form of filtered listening.

Filtered listening

Filters are ways in which we screen information we receive from the world: what we pay attention to and what we ignore.

Filters can be culturally based on class, gender, race, nationality, religion, politics, sexual orientation or lifestyle. Positively they enable us to classify, generalize and predict. Negatively cultural filters are likely to lead to prejudice and bias. For example, my experience as a woman, and therefore structurally more likely to be discriminated against and oppressed, can render me less able to listen to and understand a middle-class man, who appears structurally to be powerful and potentially oppressive, although privately feels depressed and inadequate following the break-up of a long-term relationship.

As workers, we need to be aware of our potential prejudices: e.g. a student who had felt quite confident in his lack of racism was confronted by his prejudice, the result of years of socialization, against travelling people.

Finally psychological and social models can act as dysfunctional filters. If I see problems in living as entirely structurally induced, or entirely resulting from interpersonal problems, such a rigid framework will limit my listening to the range of influences (structural and interpersonal) on the life of a user of services and will lead to me artificially imposing my model on his or her world. Individual psychological and social models may help us integrate the information we receive, for example in terms of attachment or loss, but we should be aware that they can also have a potential to distort it.

Sympathetic listening

Sometimes in listening to the experiences of users of services, e.g. of abuse or bereavement, we can become overwhelmed with sympathy. However, sympathy, like bias, can distort: it can lead us to over-identify with the difficulties of service users at the expense of helping them examine their own responsibility and part in the difficulties – the area that Egan (2007) would argue potentially can be changed.

So, for example, if we over-identify with the structural problems a user of service confronts, we may be unable to help her or him solve immediate issues of budgeting and child care. Similarly if we over-identify with her or him about personal issues in relation to loss and attachment we may be unable to help her or him constructively to engage more positively in current parenting.

Silence

Silence can be one of the most difficult challenges to a listener. Silence, socially, generates anxiety and even embarrassment. Kadushin and Kadushin (1997) point out that a social worker may feel anxiety that continued silence implies a failure in his or her interviewing ability. We can as professionals, therefore, feel uncomfortable with silences and try to interpret them, but silence can be very productive and helpful.

Silence can have different meanings. The user of services may:

- have said enough on this particular topic;
- need time to think;
- have remembered something and withdrawn;
- have shared highly emotional material and need time to reflect on and deal with it;
- be feeling angry;
- be engaging in resistance or self-protection;
- be not saying something which would be very anxiety-provoking.

So, for example, I have experienced users of services who were silent because they were overwhelmed with a sudden realization of feelings from the past, because they were intensely angry with me, or because they became aware of intense vulnerability and dependency on me.

Silence can also be controlling: 'You must do something about my pain/problem'. Used in this way it raises anxiety and can be hurtful or discomforting to the worker.

Faced with a prolonged silence we need to interpret what it might be about. If a user of services is needing time to reflect, premature intervention is unhelpful, so we need to decide whether he or she needs the silence to be broken. If we are clear that this is so (and not that we are responding to our own anxieties), we can use the following interventions (Kadushin and Kadushin, 1997). The responses are intended to be tried in the following order:

- Say 'mm' or 'I see' and then wait a moment.
- Repeat and emphasize the last word or few words of the user of services.

- Repeat and emphasize their last sentence, or rephrase it as a question.
- Summarize or rephrase their last utterances.
- Say 'It's hard to talk' or 'You find it difficult to talk'.
- Say 'Perhaps you're trying to think out what to say'.
- Say 'Perhaps you are afraid to say what is on your mind'.

However even if none of these responses elicits a reply we still need to respect the silence and remain engaged with the user of services.

Conclusion

This chapter has examined effective listening between social workers and users of services. Effective listening skills are relevant to social work with involuntary users of services as well as users of services who require and wish for a service. How might the lessons be applied to effective listening with colleagues in social work and social care, and also in interprofessional work?

We need to remember, observe and interpret how other professionals use non-verbal language (e.g. in leaking anxiety or anger). We really also need to be aware of how much we use the skills delineated in this chapter in relation to listening and how much we apply this to our work with other professionals, both in how we behave and listen and how they communicate and we interpret. For example, how do I as a social worker or care worker deal with what I perceive to be filtered listening or evaluative listening from a colleague from another discipline? I need to recognize this and then think how skills discussed later in this book, for example in terms of sharing information and challenging, may be used to encourage my colleague to engage in more active listening.

Attending and active listening are essential for engaging with users of services, understanding them (and therefore as a basis for assessment) and getting information from them. They are also absolutely essential skills in interprofessional practice. In social work and social care we should ask and review:

- how well we prepare for attending to our colleagues from other professions (including rooms, space, layout and absence of interruptions);
- how well we pay attention to listening to colleagues including symbolic, non-verbal and verbal messages and 'listening with the third ear'. If we think attending and listening are essential for effective interaction with users of services they are also so for effective interdisciplinary collaboration.

The next chapter considers more specific techniques for getting information and for giving information.

putting it into practice

Consider and reflect on a recent experience in which you were the user of service, for example the GP. Examine whether you experienced full attending and listening skills or not. In doing this, list the reasons you felt positively or otherwise.

Now consider yourself as the professional. What lessons can you learn from your own experience as a user of services?

Recommended reading

Nelson-Jones, R. (2005) *Introduction to Counselling Skills*, London, Sage. Relevant and useful analysis of communication skills in counselling applied to social work and social care.

Kadushin, A. and Kadushin, G. (1997) *The Social Work Interview*, New York, Columbia. Clear and detailed information about how we best listen and attend in interviews.

Egan, G. (2007) *The Skilled Helper*, Pacific Grove, CA, Thompson/ Brooks Cole. Again clear and detailed information about how we may best listen and attend in interviews.

7 | Sharing information

Sharing information involves both gaining information and giving it. As we have seen, users of services appreciate both; specifically they appreciate active listening, are critical of intrusive questioning and value advice and information.

Gaining information is an essential task in social work (including criminal justice) in order, for example, to make an assessment of need or risk, to write a report, to plan an intervention, or to justify obtaining a resource. It involves attending, listening, exploration, questioning, probing and accurate recording, whether paper-based or online.

Giving information is also an essential task, e.g. about benefits, resources, or rights of users of service. It is difficult to do this in such a way that any recipient can absorb the information. Again we should reflect on our own visits to other professionals. How much do I absorb when my GP is telling me about my blood pressure or eyesight problems? How easy is it for a very anxious parent to hear what the GP is saying about a sick child? How much more difficult for me if English is not my first language?

An important concept in information sharing between users of services and between professional workers who, we should remember, have access to resources and authority to recommend restriction of freedom (e.g. in criminal justice, a jail sentence; in child protection, the removal of a child from the family; in mental health, compulsory admission to a psychiatric hospital) is the idea of information 'trading' (personal communication, Peter Ashe). Put simply, if I, as a service user, need a resource, how much personal information and loss of privacy am I willing to share to improve my case? Similarly how much am I prepared to share, as an involuntary user of services, in order to reduce my 'punishment'?

We need to be sensitive to this implicit bargaining and aware that users of services are reluctant to give up privacy. Again, consider a visit to the GP and how much we are actually prepared to reveal about our lifestyles, worries and problems.

Gaining and giving information are interlinked. They may be achieved by face-to-face interaction, in writing or online. How to share information needs to be considered in relation to the following:

● users and professionals gaining and giving information;
● interdisciplinary (e.g. social work, health and education) or interagency professionals accessing, gaining and giving information, i.e. sharing information, while ensuring that legislation in relation to human rights, privacy, data protection and freedom of information legislation is properly adhered to;
● practitioners accessing information to ensure that their practice is informed by up-to-date evidence and research.

We need to think very carefully in relation to information sharing about what kind of communication is most appropriate: is it face-to-face, written or online, who is it for and in what circumstances? This chapter focuses predominantly on information sharing directly between a user of services and a worker, but also addresses, albeit more briefly, interdisciplinary and interagency information sharing. Finally, the need for practitioners to access information about relevant research and evidence in order to update their practice in an evidence-based way is briefly addressed.

Gaining information

Attending and listening, in the ways discussed in Chapter 6, are necessary for a user of services to feel properly listened to and understood, but do not adequately convey our understanding of more complex material. Similar issues arise in interprofessional communication. As Barrett *et al.* (2005, p. 41) argue, '[a]ctive listening skills can enable professionals to demonstrate they can "respect the validity of differing perspectives and seek constructive ways of reconciling different viewpoints" (DfES, 2001, p. 17)'.

These differing perspectives and different viewpoints may be between social workers and users of services or between professionals from different disciplines including social work and social care. In order to properly understand someone else and convey to them that we do really understand them, 'sophisticated' verbal responses such as clarification, paraphrasing, making linking statements, questioning and summarizing are necessary. In terms of our gaining information as social workers or care workers, I focus here on communication between social workers or social care workers and users of services and colleagues from social services and from other disciplines.

For the increasing number of users of services who have access to the internet, gaining information may usefully and confidentially be achieved from user- or carer group-specific websites. In Chapter 4 we saw the usefulness of online communication for vulnerable children and mental health service users, for example.

However, when we consider *effective* information gaining, whether between social worker and user of services, between interagency and interdisciplinary professionals or by users of services from service providers, we need to be aware of the potential dangers of a 'clash in perspective' (Mayer and Timms, 1970) in which the participants do not achieve a shared meaning. Paraphrasing, reflection and clarification can all contribute to more effectively gaining a shared meaning. We also need to recognize the relevance to online communication where similar skills and principles from face-to-face interaction need to be applied to online dialogue with users of services, other social work and social care colleagues and other professionals.

Paraphrasing and reflection

Paraphrasing and reflection were described in Chapter 3. A useful distinction is also provided by Dickson *et al.* (2003) in a text for health professionals. Paraphrasing is concerned with showing an attempt to understand *what* the user of services is saying while reflection of feeling involves trying to demonstrate an understanding of *how* the person *now feels or has felt.*

Paraphrasing involves selecting an important issue from what the user of services is saying but then rephrasing it in some detail and feeding it back. Paraphrasing is hard work and cannot be feigned. As discussed in Chapter 3, it is a crucial skill which any social work student or practitioner concerned with continuing professional development (CPD) needs to practise and engage in. The discipline of actually hearing and accurately translating what a user of services or professional from another discipline said and intended to say is necessary and sometimes difficult. If a user of services says, 'That's what I really meant' we really have understood what was said. Parrotting, as opposed to paraphrasing, does not convey active listening or understanding.

Reflection often involves selecting or repeating a word or phrase a user of services has used but less specifically than in paraphrasing. Using reflection in this way implicitly conveys an invitation: 'Tell me more about ...' We need to be careful to select something which the user of services sees as relevant or important rather than something we ourselves find interesting but which seems irrelevant to them. We can also use reflection to convey back to a user of services what they had said earlier and link it with something they are saying now: 'So you feel ashamed now and you felt ashamed when...?'

Reflection, used with a colleague, involves reflecting on and inviting expansion of what they have said, for example, 'You said you thought he was both angry and depressed. Could you expand a little on your reasons for saying this?'

Such techniques are important for conveying understanding but also for checking that we accurately understand what someone is saying. Given the prevalence of clashes in perspective between workers and users of services (discussed in Chapter 2), such checking out is essential to ensure that they do not occur either with users of services or, in an increasingly interprofessional service delivery, with our interdisciplinary colleagues.

Reflection and paraphrasing need to be expressed tentatively. Consider the difference between:

'I wondered if you felt a bit that he wasn't being entirely straight with you. Have I got that right?'

and:

'You *obviously* were furious.'

In the first quotation the worker reflects her understanding back to the user of services in such a way as to leave room for them to disagree or to rephrase what she has said. In the second quotation the worker does not check that she is accurately understanding and she leaves no room for them to disagree. Tentative reflection is more likely to facilitate further communication and exploration. The almost dogmatic quality of the second quotation is more likely to close down communication.

Clarification

Clarification also means making things clearer; this is essential for communication between ourselves and users of services, with other social services colleagues, and with colleagues from other disciplines, e.g. the police, health and education. Like paraphrasing and reflection, it is a means by which the worker can check out and convey their understanding to the other person. However it is more than simply restating: if a worker successfully uses clarification the other person may also see a situation more clearly or in a different light.

Clarification also means helping a user of services to be more specific. For example, a carer says, 'I've been feeling rather down recently.' and the worker clarifies, 'In what ways have you been feeling down? When did you begin to feel like this?'.

Clarification can be about making clearer rather vague communication. Interviewer responses which begin with 'It sounds as if ...', 'Do you mean that ...?' are intended to reflect back to a user of services what he or she is saying and in doing so to clarify any vagueness. As an example, a user of services talked at length in a rambling and disconnected way about different aspects of her life, conveying a vague sense of dissatisfaction. The worker responded by saying, 'It sounds as if nothing in your life is very satisfying at the moment: your children seem thoughtless, your husband preoccupied with his work and your boss critical. Life doesn't sound too good.' Here the worker drew together the apparently vague and disconnected negatives and fed back more clearly to the user of services her current unhappiness and the factors contributing to this. By such clarification the worker checked out whether she was understanding accurately, but she also helped the user of services to see more clearly that her current mood was depressed and to begin to examine reasons for this and subsequently areas for potential change. Clarification also needs to be used with colleagues, in both social services and other disciplines, so that again we really are clear what is being said and, therefore, often decided, for example in a child protection review or an interdisciplinary risk assessment for someone with mental health problems.

Thus clarification, like reflection and paraphrasing, involves the worker checking out the accuracy of her or his understanding. Reflection, paraphrasing and clarification are linked but represent increasingly detailed and complex ways of checking, conveying and increasing shared understanding of the worker or the user of services and of other professionals of what should be a shared assessment and subsequently agreed intervention into what has been presented as a problematic issue. Reflection, paraphrasing and communication focus on expressed and conscious perceptions and do not attempt to interpret any underlying meaning. Used appropriately and sensitively they are likely to elicit further information. Probing and questioning, used appropriately and sensitively, are also techniques by which we seek to elicit information.

Questioning and probing

Chapter 3 examined the appropriateness of questioning as a technique and highlighted the danger of the worker becoming drawn into an interrogatory question-and-answer routine. It suggested that other techniques, for example, paraphrasing and clarification are equally useful as means of eliciting information. Such techniques may be essential in work with involuntary service users in child care and protection.

However, in terms of gaining information, questions can help the respondent to tell his or her story, to elaborate or clarify it, and to explore both facts and feelings. The kinds of questions asked can help the respondent to understand what information is relevant to the interview: for example, questions about feelings convey the message that these are important, as well as facts. The interviewer's use of questions may help the respondent to some clearer understanding of what he or she is describing. Questions can help to structure an interview and to focus attention on particular aspects of the respondent's story. Finally questions can help the respondent to consider alternatives, in terms of understanding problems, and of responding to them and agreeing ways forward, which may lead into contract setting and problem solving, examined in subsequent chapters.

Chapter 3 also examined the appropriateness of using different types of questions, open or closed, direct or indirect. While these distinctions are useful, it is important to realize that, rather than a dichotomy, there is a continuum of how open or closed, or how direct or indirect questions are.

What are the advantages and disadvantages of different kinds of questions? Open questions tend more clearly to invite the respondent to share his or her perceptions, views, opinions or feelings openly. Open questions allow the respondent to choose what response he or she will make, and to focus, therefore, on what he or she considers of greatest concern. Open questions communicate that the interviewee carries responsibility for the conduct and direction of the interview as well as the worker: they set a model of a mutual approach to problem solving. Open questions are also more likely to elicit information about the interviewee's feelings and attitudes and behaviour. Open questions tend to help people to feel that their perceptions have been sought and attended to. We saw in Chapter 2 that users of services appreciated an unhurried approach, attentiveness, concern and being listened to. Purposeful open questions are more likely to convey these qualities than a rather rigid checklist of closed questions. Respondents who valued such an open-ended approach said:

'There was a need to question ourselves, a reappraisal'
'You've got to realise your whole life is being laid open and this is correct.'
(Lishman, 1985)

There are also disadvantages in the use of open-ended questions. They may be puzzling or even threatening to interviewees who have had little experience of interviews or who have rigid expectations of structure and guidance. One user expressed this:

'I didn't know what he was after, he wouldn't say. I didn't want to be analysed.'   (Lishman, 1985)

In response to these anxieties, Trevithick (2005) suggests:

> Some individuals try to address their confusion and anxiety by trying to guess the response we are looking for. This kind of mind-reading can seriously detract from the purpose of the interview unless it is addressed. (p. 160)

If a user of services is unclear about the focus of their need, concern or problem an open question, 'Can you tell me what brings you here?' may be too vague and more specific questioning may be necessary to clarify what the problem is. Closed questions can help to structure and focus an interview and to elicit further information about specific areas the user of services has already raised.

Trevithick (2005) suggests that initially, until trust is established:

> closed questions can be particularly valuable when working with people who do not have a great deal of confidence, perhaps because they feel reticent or mistrustful or find it difficult to formulate their thoughts and feelings. (p. 161)

However, in a sense, closed questions can be a means whereby the interviewer exercises control of what is discussed. As a consequence of the use of a structured questionnaire, often for assessment purposes, whether as a prompt in face-to-face interaction, e.g. the Looked After Children materials (Ward, 2001), or as a written form, e.g. Single Shared assessment in community care (Scottish Executive, 2004), the control involved in what are often closed questions can lead the user of services to feel disempowered: 'Too many questions. There isn't enough attention to what I need'. We have to be aware of the use of power and control in interviews which closed questions (for example, in order to underpin an assessment of need) can represent, rather than enabling a service user or carer to share their experiences and expertise about their life and situation. As Trevithick (2005) suggests:

> The main disadvantage when using closed questions is that they may steer the interview in the wrong direction by being too focussed. This can lead to a sense of frustration on the part of the interviewee, who can easily feel their experiences are being disregarded or categorised and squeezed into little boxes. (p. 161)

In contrast, however, for example with reluctant or involuntary users of services, open questions may allow them to avoid problematic areas, e.g. about current offences, difficulties about child care or domestic violence, and the worker may need to use direct questions to focus on these problematic areas about which she or he has concerns.

Similar considerations apply to the use of direct and indirect questions. As suggested in Chapter 3, by using an indirect question we leave a user of services greater choice of focus and response. Total reliance on direct questions may be intrusive and lead to a closing down of interaction and communication on their part. However direct questions may be necessary to elicit specific information or focus on particular areas. Direct or closed questions may sometimes be useful in opening up a particularly sensitive area which the user of services is struggling to raise, for example, a disclosure that she has been previously abused either physically or sexually, or that her partner is violent to her.

Probing, which often involves questioning but also includes paraphrasing and reflection (see Chapter 3), is used to elicit more specific information when someone has been unclear or ambiguous, or where a user of services has made a rather general or global statement. So, for example, if a user of services has been complaining about her child's 'difficult' behaviour the worker might ask, 'Difficult?' (i.e. using an accent to probe) 'In what sort of ways?'. If the reply is, 'He's always having temper tantrums', the worker might continue, 'How often do these occur? Every day, more than once a day?' and then 'What started the most recent one?'. Here the worker is engaged in gaining much more specific and detailed understanding about the child's behaviour. Such detailed probing is highly relevant to understanding what triggers problem behaviour and is necessary before the worker and user of services can move on to identifying possible means by which such behaviour can be changed. Probes can also help users of services to identify what aspects of a situation or what specific feelings they find most difficult and to clarify the extent of a problem. For example, if a woman says, 'I get quite depressed', it is not clear what 'quite depressed' means. It could range from 'fed up' to 'suicidal' and the worker needs to probe to understand the nature and depth of such an expressed feeling. In work with carers of people with dementia or with brain damage, for example from a tumour, probing may help to elicit more specific triggers for problematic behaviour, e.g. irritation or anger, and therefore how best to manage these potential triggers.

We have discussed previously how questioning which becomes a question-and-answer routine can impede communication. In what other ways may questioning be unhelpful? Overuse of questions can seem like an interrogation and lead a user of services to feel threatened and hostile: 'It was like the hot seat, friendly enough, but questions, questions, questions. I was made to feel it was my fault. Others might not go back' (Lishman, 1985).

Kadushin and Kadushin (1997, pp. 248–58) identify the following kinds of questions as unhelpful:

- leading questions
- yes/no questions
- 'garbled' questions
- double or multiple questions
- 'why' questions

A leading question is one which is worded in such a way as to elicit the answer the questioner expects or requires. For example, 'You must feel pretty angry about it, don't you?' implies an affirmative answer, as does 'You are feeling better, aren't you?'. The use of leading questions can be particularly damaging where a service user is considering alternative possibilities and the worker's question suggests or emphasizes one particular view, e.g. 'Do you *really* think you'll be happy in Oaktree Care Home?'.

Children may be particularly vulnerable to the use of leading questions. 'Your dad hits you pretty hard, doesn't he?' or 'Your dad really loves you, doesn't he?' may each be inaccurate, and equally hard (phrased as they are) for the child to disagree with.

Leading questions are least helpful with users of services who are likely to agree with what the worker says either because of their need to please and agree or because it is the line of least resistance. Children who have already been subject to abuse of power may have particular difficulty in challenging leading questions from an adult in authority, a further abuse of power.

The use of leading questions has been particularly critically reviewed in relation to social work investigations of alleged child sexual and ritual abuse (see, for example, the Clyde Report, 1992). Here, social workers appeared to have used leading questions with some of the vulnerable children to confirm their hypothesis that all the children involved had been abused. Evidence gained by social workers from vulnerable children by the use of leading questions is rightly viewed in legal proceedings as potentially unsound. For the sake of the children who have been abused, we need to be extremely careful that our inappropriate questioning of them does not lead to their evidence being perceived as invalid in legal proceedings.

Yes/no questions are those where the respondent can only answer yes or no. Closed questions are more likely to be yes/no questions. 'Do you play with your children at all?' or 'Are you employed?' imply a yes or no answer. Sometimes this may be appropriate, for example to gain specific information about employment. Often, however, questions beginning with 'What?' or 'How?' will elicit more detailed information and open communication, e.g. 'What kinds of things do you do with your children?'.

Garbled questions are unclear. They arise from our having a rather complicated or unfocussed set of interlinked questions in our minds and blurting out the confusion or complexity, rather than clarifying and focussing a set of simpler questions to present. For example, how can a service user respond in the following situation? A baby had required 'special nursery' care following a difficult birth and the worker asked the mother, 'You didn't blame yourself you said. You thought your husband blamed himself, you know. Did he say that to you? Did you blame him secretly? You might not have said yes, maybe it is?'(Lishman, 1985). The worker's utterance is confused, includes several questions and it is not clear what the focus is (the mother or her husband), i.e. it is garbled. It also includes a leading question, 'Did you blame him secretly?'.

Multiple questions within one utterance, or 'double questions' as Kadushin and Kadushin (1997) call them, are likely to mean that the user of services is unsure which question to respond to. For example the worker and a user of services were discussing a baby coming home from hospital and the way in which the mother included the older daughter to try to prevent jealousy. The worker asked, 'So feeding was something she shared in and your husband was still at home, he hadn't yet actually gone?'. How would I know which of these multiple questions I should respond to?.

Finally Kadushin and Kadushin (1997) counsel against excessive use of 'why' questions. I was struck when someone pointed out that we only use 'why' questions with children in a negative way: 'Why did you do/ steal/lose that?' We do not ask: 'Why did you do so well?' 'Why' questions, even to adults, may often carry a sense of accusation or at least apparently require the person to justify his/her actions. 'What' questions may be more useful: they probe and require a user of services to reflect on and analyze behaviour but are less likely to elicit defensive justification. So, for example, rather than saying, 'Why did you get angry with your husband?', we might ask 'What was going on just before you got angry with your husband?'.

In summary, questions are an important tool in gaining information and in understanding the issues users of services bring to us but they should not be overused. Overuse can close communication, make people feel interrogated or make them feel they are not getting anywhere.

When questions are appropriate they need to be put simply and clearly, and we need to consider what kind of a question is appropriate; open, closed, direct or indirect.

However, we may need to be careful that our questions are not perceived as critical. This will depend partly on how well we convey the qualities of empathy, warmth and acceptance discussed earlier: how much a user of services trusts us may also depend on a sparing and judicious use of questions and an ability to make use of the alternative techniques identified in this chapter.

In relation to interprofessional communication we need to reflect on how we use questioning and probing with colleagues, whether in social services or in other disciplines. Do we use questioning with colleagues as readily as with users of services? Does our differential use of questioning reflect our authority in relation to users of services and our recognition that we do not have the same authority in relation to fellow professionals?

Open questions allow colleagues to put forward their professional perspective and judgement but we also may need to use closed and direct questions if we are eliciting factual information (Koprowska, 2006). We need to avoid the kinds of unhelpful questions that Kadushin and Kadushin (1997) identify, in particular 'garbled questions', leading questions and double or multiple questions. As well as being confusing to the recipient they may lead colleagues, particularly from other disciplines, to question our ability and expertise. Barrett *et al.* (2005) stress the importance of confidence and competence in inter-professional working. The use of garbled, or multiple questions can convey a lack of professional confidence; the use of leading questions a lack of professional competence.

Giving information

Giving information and gaining information are two sides to the same coin.

Users of services are frequently in need of information, for example about resources such as entitlement to welfare benefits or to services, about legal rights and about social and support networks and how to access them. Users of services value being given accurate and relevant information when they need it. In social work and in the social work literature, historically its importance has sometimes been underestimated.

For users of services, having accurate information about rights, resources, services and networks is one means of empowerment, i.e. having control over their own lives. As Croft and Beresford (2000) argue, service users 'see a role for professional workers and allies in *supporting* them to empower *themselves*, for example, by providing information and support and increasing people's expectations and by valuing, supporting and involving service users' organizations' (p. 117). A particular tension, for example in care management, is between giving information about entitlement, and thereby raising expectations, and limited or insufficient availability of appropriate resources.

Users of services need to understand what our role as social workers is and what our agency's remit and responsibility is, but without information about resources, benefits and rights, users of services are relatively powerless. With it and ongoing support they may demand and work for rights, benefits and resources to improve their lives. Giving information is an empowering activity. Withholding it or failing to provide it is frustrating and disempowering. Contrast, for example, the experience of the users of services in Chapter 2 – where a social worker said she did not know anything about the information they requested – with the following experience of a social worker: 'He's got a lot of knowledge ready at hand that it would take me ages to find out and he knows right away because he's come up against it before' (Lishman, 1985).

Giving information is a means of helping people to problem solve. For example, information about normal development and behaviour in childhood may help a parent become less anxious, and reduce their over-high expectations of the child. Information about dementia may help carers to see problem behaviour as part of the deterioration of dementia rather than in terms of voluntary wilfulness or difficult behaviour on the part of the older person.

Giving information to users of services can help them to challenge depressing or self-defeating beliefs by offering a new perspective or frame of reference. Parents who have suffered a cot death may be freed from some feelings of personal responsibility by understanding the general features of 'sudden infant-death syndrome'.

Giving information is an important skill but it needs to be done with care. Ley (1977) found that between 40 and 50 per cent of patients did not understand or remember the information given to them by their doctor. This is unsurprising given the short duration of the encounter (five minutes on average (Byrne and Long, 1976)), the anxiety of the patient, and the perceived authority of the doctor. The information we give needs to be accurate and we may need to refer users of services to more specialized sources of information, e.g. about housing, welfare benefits or legal rights. Trevithick (2005) warns:

It is alarming how many service users are given incorrect information at this stage: for some it must feel like being sent on wild goose chase, where only the most charmed or most determined get through. (p. 195)

An analogy might be with the banking system. An older woman described how devalued and disempowered she felt as she was passed through a maze of wrong information and contacts when she was trying to sort out an error in the issue of her cheque book which meant that her cheques bounced. Do we think enough about these issues in relation to involuntary users of services, for example in criminal justice and child protection?

Effective information giving

How can social workers ensure that their information giving is more effective? It needs to be done in a context of trust, it needs to be relevant to a specific user of services, it needs to be presented clearly and it needs to be timely.

Information is more likely to be retained if it is given in the context of a trustworthy encounter so that the skills of engaging and relationship building (Chapter 5) are highly relevant to effective sharing of information.

We need to be sure that the information we are giving is relevant and that the user of services wants it or needs to have it. For example, a service user who is disabled will want and need information about benefits such as the Disability Living Allowance. However, a parent may need (although he or she may not want) to know the implications of a diagnosis of a child's learning disabilities.

As social workers, we should not give information simply to make ourselves feel better: we should always question who the information is for. Nor should we use information to fill an uncomfortable silence or to avoid a painful area like death or separation. For example, talking about funeral arrangements may be useful and necessary but it can also be used by a worker to avoid confronting raw feelings of shock, anger and pain. Nor should we use information to impose our own values on users of services.

Timing is important: we need to give information at the point the user of services is most ready to hear it. By using attending and listening skills explored in Chapter 6, we can explore the current and pressing preoccupations and expectations of users of services and thereby give information more responsively, both at the appropriate time and with relevance to their needs.

Information needs to be provided in a simple form: we need to use short sentences and simple, clear words. We need to be explicit, specific and detailed and to give examples wherever possible. We should present information gradually, giving time for it to be digested. We may need to repeat it more than once in order to emphasize and clarify it. It can be helpful to ask a user of services to paraphrase the information just given in order to ensure it is really understood. I also find it helpful to check out frequently with the other person whether what I have said is clear and understandable.

It is important to check with users of services how the information we have given applies to their specific situation and how it may be used to solve their particular problem. For example, if an older person is requesting information about residential care it is essential to provide information about the range of options, that is, to include the services which can be provided to support and maintain the older person in their own home as well as the information about residential care initially requested. It may then be useful to consider how each of these services would apply to this person and what costs and benefits they would involve. From such information about a range of choices applied specifically to this person's situation, he or she may be better able to choose appropriate care, based on cost, suitability and quality.

Presentation of information

Finally, we need to think about how we present information. Diagrams, flow charts or cartoons can be helpful to people who find it easier to take in information or concepts visually rather than verbally.

Information about services, resources or benefits is difficult to retain if it is only given verbally. Such verbal information can usefully be followed by clear, simple, written information which can then be referred to at more leisure. If this is a general leaflet it may be helpful if the worker discusses with the user of services which specific parts apply to her or his situation and highlights them so that they can easily be re-found.

We should remember that people differ in what helps them to take in information. I prefer information from the written word: others may find it easier to take it in the course of a verbal discussion. As a worker I need to be aware of such differences, and attempt to check out with users of services the most useful way of presenting information to them. In general, though, presenting information in different ways offers users of services the opportunity of taking it in the best way for them and is likely to reinforce their ability to take in and retain the information.

Information as 'bad' news

Particular consideration needs to be given if the information is 'bad news'. The importance of trust and a trustworthy relationship as a basis for giving information has already been noted but may be particularly important where the information to be given is unwelcome or hurtful or threatening. Here the 'news' may be so disturbing that the recipient finds it difficult to take in, or explicitly rejects it, or is hostile to or blames the information giver.

In order to give such information effectively we need to understand these potential reactions as normal responses to any loss or change which threatens the current meaning of life for the recipients. Parkes (1975) identified shock, denial and anger as normal responses to the loss of a loved person. Marris (1974) suggests that responses may apply to loss in a wider sense, when a change imposed represents a loss of the previous meaning of life or existence to the person involved. 'Bad news' can represent just this. For example, if an older person is faced with the diagnosis that a recent fall is likely to impair her or his mobility to such an extent that continued independent living is no longer possible, that information represents the loss of their previous way of coping and living and the need for an enormous change. It is small wonder they may not understand or reject that news, however clearly, sympathetically and skilfully it is given.

Given the normality of denial, anger or rejection of the news, how may our information giving best aid people to take in unpleasant information? The skills identified so far – timing, clarity and application – are important. Understanding resistance to the information is helpful. It prevents us from responding impatiently. We can be prepared to take time over several interviews in order that the information is reasonably understood and accepted. Finally, if the information is the diagnosis of an illness (e.g. that the recipient is HIV positive) written information about the likely implications may also be useful.

Written information

We have already noted the value of written information in reinforcing verbal information. Written information, simply and clearly presented, allows the other person, as long as he or she is able to read easily, to take in information at an individual pace. It can be a basis for further interviews where discussion and clarification can take place. A further advantage of written information is that it can be translated into the first language of the user of services, thereby supplementing an interview using an interpreter, or clarifying an interview conducted in English but not fully understood because English was not the first language of the user of services. Social work and social service departments and voluntary agencies have a duty to provide written information in all the languages used by the community they serve. Trevithick (2005) notes, for example, that 'the current Attendance Allowance leaflet (DS702) is available in several other languages: Bengali, Chinese, Greek, Gujarat, Hindu, Periyali, Turkish, Urdia, Vietnamese and Welsh' (p. 196). In working with asylum seekers it is crucial that written information is provided in their own language. Koprowska (2007), however, warns us about potential problems in the use of written communication:

> Some service users have poor literacy skills, and these may not be evident. People are usually ashamed of poor literacy and develop ingenious ways of concealing it: 'I haven't got my glasses, could you read it to me?' (p. 79)

The skills involved in providing written information are similar to those involved in clear report writing and recording: we need to think of the needs and perspective of the user of our information, whether social work colleagues, colleagues from health, education or the police, or users of services. Written communication should be clear, concise and relevant. We need to read carefully the information leaflets we hand out to users of services. Do they make sense, not just to us? Have we piloted them with users of services? Are they clearly written? Do they rely on jargon? Can we more clearly reword them?

What kind of information might usefully be presented to users of services in written form to supplement verbal discussion? The following are examples:

- Information about legal rights, processes and procedures, e.g. about a children's hearing or juvenile court, the compilation of a social enquiry report, a magistrate's court or a sheriff court.
- Information about legal rights in relation to care proceedings for children.
- Information about different kinds of services for older people, people with disabilities or people with learning disabilities, e.g. home-based respite care, direct payments, day care, lunch clubs, user groups such as Hearing Voices groups and single care homes (including prospectuses about the establishments).
- Information about residents' rights while in care.
- Information about agency procedures, e.g. about intake processes, the use of videoing or of one-way screens used in family psychiatry and some child care teams.
- Information about appeals procedures.
- Information about rights and resources in community care.

In a positive inspection report (SWIA, 2006) the inspectors found that the users of services they met reported that they 'found it easy to get clear information about services that might help them' (p. 19). They also commented positively that 'there was a comprehensive range of leaflets. In common with the web pages, the leaflets were clearly written in plain English with a range of other languages and formats available'. These leaflets did appear to provide people with the information they needed in an accessible way.

Information giving: other techniques

Not everybody finds written information easy to digest. DVDs can provide information orally, but with the advantage that the user of services can control the speed of information giving and replay it. They can be used to present information. They can be used to present a range of basic information rather similar to written techniques, e.g. about tenants' rights, child care rights and resources, supplementary benefits, job opportunities. They can also be used to present more complex information about processes, procedures or skills such as:

● Introducing people to their rights, e.g. in tribunals or in mental health law.
● Introducing people to procedures involved in tribunals.
● Introducing users of services to procedures and skills involved in job interviews and selection.
● Introducing users of services to means of empowerment, e.g. challenging poor or damp housing or inadequate child care facilities, or challenging poor practice in residential child care.

Finally, DVD recording can be used to give information to users of services about how they behave and relate to each other in their family, marriage or partnership. Such direct feedback is information, although it may also provide a means of change, e.g. in relationship counselling or family therapy or negotiating compromise settlements in mediation or family group conferencing.

The use of DVDs can be helpful in enhancing the range of modes in which information can be given and accessed. However we need to offer these modes with sensitivity: does this particular user of services have access to a DVD player?

Information can be given by telephone. Help lines, such as Senior Line, provide information about eligibility for welfare benefits: Senior Line is concerned that £2.5 billion of pensioners' benefits is unclaimed each year.

Information can be given via the media: the local paper, radio or news. This may be particularly useful for people who would not have access to verbal or written information direct from a Social Work Department, who would be eligible for rights or resources but might not see themselves as potentially eligible. Information can be given through computer information packages. In the North of Scotland, Grampian Care Data has been a database of local information about services and resources and is available at advice centres, libraries and community-based IT centres (learning centres). Information can also be given via the internet. For example, Senior Line uses Help the Aged's website (www.hta.org.uk) and the National Perceptions Forum (www.voicesforum.org.uk), 'run *by* mad people *for* mad people' (as it describes itself), gives support and valuable information about how people manage to live with schizophrenia. Best Treatments (http://besttreatments.bmj.com/btuk/home.jsp) presents patients with friendly information about clinical evidence from medical research. Its aim is empowering, 'we can help you understand how treatments work and help you decide which is best for you'.

Social service organizations need to give information by providing their own websites. These need to be easily accessible and clear. In the positive SWIA report (2006) referred to earlier the inspectors comment that 'We found the Council information clearly laid out and accessible' (p. 19), and they reported positive views from people who used services about finding out about and accessing them.

As with giving information via DVDs, we need to be sensitive about whether users of services and, indeed, colleagues actually have access to the internet. A recent report by the Office of National Statistics (ONS) found that access to the internet is now an indicator of inequality between high- and low-income groups: while 80% of highest-income households had online access only 10% of homes in the lowest-income bracket did. While libraries, local learning centres and community centres do provide internet access it takes confidence, an ability to develop IT skills, and a recognition that they are needed to engage with the process. If I am coping with a grossly inadequate income and children who are becoming anti-social, developing IT skills may not be top of my priority list and I may therefore not have information which would be extremely useful, e.g. about welfare benefits and problem solving techniques with difficult adolescents.

Similarly, we cannot assume our colleagues in social services currently have access to the internet via their work. Agencies vary considerably in access to and use of IT. For example, some small voluntary organizations may still have very limited IT resources. Some local authorities may restrict employees' access to the internet.

In making sure that we effectively engage in giving information we need to think creatively about using a wide range of alternative means.

The proposals in the Grampian Community Care Plan (1991) for dissemination of information remain a useful conclusion to this section on giving information:

> Information dissemination may be by word of mouth, via leaflets and brochures, directories of services, television and radio, newspapers, computer databases, etc. The format which suits one individual may not be appropriate for another... Account will be taken of the particular needs of visually impaired and hearing impaired people, people with learning difficulties and those whose first language is not English.

Sharing information with colleagues from other disciplines

In relation to giving information to colleagues from other disciplines, making sure it is clear, accurate and accessible remains important:

> Successful sharing of knowledge and information between professions and agencies requires the ability to communicate complex knowledge in simple terms. The avoidance of jargon and discipline specific language can aid understanding. (Tarr, 2005, p. 45)

However, other issues, particularly in relation to confidentiality (Data Protection Act 1998), arise when we give information to colleagues from other professions or in other agencies. As Trevithick (2005) says, 'The general rule is that no information will be disclosed without the service user's consent' (p. 247). The need to share information, however, has become increasingly apparent (Bichard, 2003). Clarification of our professional boundaries and the tension involved between data protection, human rights and information sharing requirements needs to be addressed. We do need to make our 'confidentiality policy available, in written form, as a guide for practitioners and service users' (Trevithick, 2005, p. 49). We need also to think carefully about where information needs to be shared across disciplines and agencies in order to manage risk and safety (Bichard, 2003).

Giving advice

Traditionally, giving advice has not been particularly valued by social workers as an activity. Rees and Wallace (1982) quoted a probation officer in a study by Rodgers and Dixon (1960): 'We don't *tell* people to do things like that – we'd arrange things if they asked us but we don't tell them what to do' (p. 103).

As we saw in Chapter 2, clients traditionally valued activity such as advice giving on the part of social workers as denoting concern and, indeed, construed lack of advice as social workers 'not bothering'. They could also construe failure to give advice as incompetence.

Trevithick (2005) distinguishes advice from guidance: she suggests that guidance seems less prescriptive than advice but argues that 'advice is often sought either to help identify the problem clearly or to help identify possible solutions, but should be offered with the greatest care because we can be inaccurate or simply wrong in the advice we offer' (p. 193).

For users of services, relevant advice is necessary providing that it does not reflect a professional assumption of knowledge and expertise as power and is used in a way that is responsive to the needs of users of services in order to promote empowerment and mutual equal relations based on trust, honesty, respect, reliability and openness. For involuntary users of services the social worker does have authority and power. However, the broad principles of trying to establish trust, respect and reliability will influence how useful the advice is perceived to be.

Why should social workers appear to be so wary about doing what users of services clearly expect and value? Giving advice may be seen to conflict with self-determination (Biestek, 1965) although, in reality, this principle is of limited application in certain social work settings, e.g. child care or court settings. Maluccio (1979) found that workers in a casework-oriented agency working with clients with emotional problems were unsure of the value of advice giving. They found it difficult to reconcile with the counselling aspect of their work whose aim, they saw, was to help clients solve their own problems. From this perspective, advice giving might increase dependency on the worker and undermine client independence and self-determination. However failure to give advice may also reflect the worker's lack of confidence in giving it. I found it difficult to give advice on getting a toddler to bed when I was a newly qualified worker: with my own experience of being a parent I would now feel more confident about exploring strategies and if necessary offering advice.

A worker may be reluctant to give advice because of uncertainty about whether it will be useful or acted upon. However as Kadushin and Kadushin (1997) point out, even if advice is not acted upon, it can have 'the effect of actively engaging the client in problem solving if only by giving her something specific to react against'. We may, in the current litigious climate, be reluctant to give advice in case, with the best and most considered intentions, in retrospect it is judged as wrong.

We should not, however, overestimate the influence of our advice giving or underestimate the ability of users of services to evaluate it and reject it if it is not perceived as useful. Mayer and Timms (1970) found that advice was appreciated if it was similar to that given by friends, relatives or other professionals, i.e. it was evaluated in a social context. As Trevithick (2005) suggests:

> It is important for service users to decide for themselves whether or not they want to hear advice that is on offer, rather than deciding for themselves. Most service users weigh up the advice they are given quite carefully and will tend to ignore advice that seems inappropriate. (p. 194)

Effective giving of advice

Rather than rejecting advice giving out of hand, how may we use it appropriately? Some considerations are rather similar to those involved in giving information. We should not use it as a means of imposing our values or morals: it is unethical to advise someone either to have an abortion or not to have one because of our own beliefs. The basis for giving advice has to be the request or requirement for it from a user of services and not as a response to the worker's needs, for example to be seen to be 'doing' something or to be seen to be competent or knowledgeable. We should make sure that our advice is soundly backed by professional knowledge, whether of legislation, child development, welfare rights or community facilities and support groups.

Kadushin and Kadushin (1997) suggest that:

- Giving advice has to be based on professional knowledge and expertise. For example, if it is advice about child care it needs to be based on knowledge, from research or practice, about techniques of child care which are likely to ameliorate this situation.
- Advice has to be given in relation to the context in which the user of services lives including the social norms of his or her group and how much the advice would be supported or rejected by significant others in their life.
- We should only give advice after a user of service has explored his or her own suggestions, strategies or solutions, and again only if they have indicated advice would be useful.

How may we best give advice? Again there are similarities to giving information. Advice is more likely to be taken if it is given in the context of a good relationship, so it is better given later rather than earlier in an interview or series of interviews. Advice needs to be given clearly and simply and the worker needs to check that it has been understood. Finally, Kadushin and Kadushin (1997) suggest it should best be given tentatively so that the user of services does not feel forced to accept it. Given in this way it can be rejected but it can also be a basis for discussion, clarification and even reformulation: the user of services is then more likely to consider the 'advised' action positively and use it as his or her own.

On a cautionary note, giving advice to interdisciplinary professionals does not feature in the literature about collaborative and interprofessional working (Barrett et al., 2005). We need to consider again whether this reflects the use of advice as conveying power and authority rather than useful information. We may however need to seek advice from colleagues in other disciplines about how a particular medical or educational problem might be best handled. Perhaps they also need to think more carefully when looking to seek advice from social work and social care professionals in interdisciplinary assessment and intervention.

When we try to gain information or when we give information or advice it is crucial that we try to explain ourselves and to check that the other person understands the purpose of what we are doing. Otherwise our need for information will be seen as inquisitory and rejected and any information or advice we give is likely to be seen as useless and also rejected. All the skills discussed in this chapter – reflection, paraphrasing, questioning, clarification and giving information and advice – are essential to the process of sharing information whether verbally, in writing, by telephone or online. The chapter has focussed on communication between social workers and social carers and users of services but is clearly relevant to interprofessional and interagency information sharing.

Sharing information in interprofessional working

Sharing information needs to be undertaken between colleagues in social services and in other disciplines. The general principles and skills involved of effective information sharing are relevant to interdisciplinary work, where issues of power, privacy and confidentiality have to be negotiated if the user of services is to benefit from the purpose of interdisciplinary interprofessional work, i.e. to receive an integrated service. In the context of successful information sharing in interprofessional working and communication it is helpful to reflect on underlying principles (Barrett and Keeping, 2005).

'The first is willing participation: an individual's commitment to interprofessional working is likely to be linked to a viewpoint that values the ideologies of user-centred services and holistic care' (Freeth, 2001) and recognizing that 'no one discipline can help people reach their full potential and optimal level of well being' (Russell and Hymans, 1999, p. 255).

The second is confidence aligned with competence: to work interprofessionally we need to be sufficiently confident and competent to be flexible in engaging in cross boundary, interprofessional working (*Changing Lives*, 2006). The third is trust and mutual respect (Barrett and Keeping, 2005; McLean, 2007). As with users of services, trust, integrity and mutual respect are essential, underpinning components of working with interprofessional colleagues:

> An atmosphere of mutual support is required to enable individuals to feel sufficiently confident and safe to express their opinions without fear of ridicule or reprisal. Active listening, together with the explicit acknowledgement of each professions' unique contribution and distinct body of knowledge conveys an acceptance of different perspectives.   (Barrett and Keeping, 2005)

The essential components of information sharing with interprofessional colleagues mirror those with users of services.

Accessing information for social workers

The need to access relevant research information to underpin our practice is another essential component of sharing information. Trevithick (2005) and Lishman (2007) both examine evidence-based practice as defined by Macdonald (2000, p. 123):

> Evidence based practice denotes an approach to decision making which is transparent, accountable and based on current best evidence about the effects of particular interventions on the welfare of individuals, groups and communities'.

We need to use the best and most up-to-date information which comes from a range of sources. Here I can only suggest a few sources but not promote them. Books remain useful in updating social work practice. SCIE (www.scie.org.uk) has developed a range of useful texts on users' and carers' views of social work and social services practice. The Joseph Rowntree Foundation has useful summaries in its 'Findings: Informing Change' series. *Research Highlights in Social Work* addresses topical issues, for example, personalization and provides a summary and critique of relevant research findings.

As a social worker or social care worker it is crucial that you use and apply current relevant research: a major source for you is the web. As part of your continuing professional development you need to think whenever you are unsure in practice, how might I access useful information to move forward, whether from books, reports or the web?

Conclusion

This chapter has focussed on sharing information with users of services and shown that the principles and tensions involved also apply to information sharing between colleagues from different disciplines.

The next chapter explores how we may better ensure that 'clashes in perspective' are minimized and shared perspectives achieved.

---

putting it into practice

Reflect on when you have been given information, for example, by your GP. How was this done: simply, clearly, sympathetically?

● Verbally, in writing or by reference to the web?
● Did the provider assume English was your first language?

Now consider the implications for how you give information in social work and social care and how you might do this more sensitively and effectively.

Now reflect on when you have been giving information to a professional. How much was paraphrasing, clarification and probing used? What kinds of questions were used? Did you feel they helped you tell your story? If so, why? If not, why?

In this chapter on sharing information, I address *gaining* information before *giving* information: perhaps we should reflect on our experience of information sharing where professional information giving may be at the expense of eliciting information which is essential and relevant to the user of service.

Recommended reading

Kadushin, A. and Kadushin, G. (1997) *The Social Work Interview: The Guide for Professionals*, 4th edn, New York, Columbia University

Press. A detailed guide to communication in therapeutic interviews, whether non-verbal, verbal or written.

Barrett, G. Sellman, D. and Thomas, J. (2005) *Inter-professional Working in Health and Social Care: Professional Perspectives*, Basingstoke, Palgrave Macmillan. This book explores fully the requirements, dilemmas and pitfalls of interprofessional communication.

Joinson, A.A. (2003) *Understanding the Psychology of Internet Behaviour: Virtual Worlds, Real Lives*, Basingstoke, Palgrave Macmillan. A very useful discussion of how best we can use the internet in communication, including its use in sharing information.

8 | Shared purpose and assessment

Introduction

As we have seen, differences in perception between social workers and users of services about what was happening in their encounter appear to be common. More worryingly, lack of agreement between the worker and the user of services about the nature of the problem and how it should be tackled was historically an important factor associated with poor outcomes from the perspective of the user of services, for example in terms of improved child care or child behaviour (Fisher *et al.*, 1986; Lishman, 1985; Maluccio, 1979). This issue has continued to be problematic in social work and social care. Beresford *et al.* (2005) found that poor assessments which are service- or resource-driven disempower users of services. Users of services, for example in mental health or caring for children with learning disabilities, are 'experts by experience' (Reid and Reynolds, 1996) and will know more about the problems they encounter and need to be solved than a professional entering their lives for the first time. For the involuntary user of services, for example in criminal justice or child care, it is difficult to see how positive outcomes can be achieved if there is not some minimal agreement about shared purpose (Buckley, 2007; McIvor, 2007).

Communication in social work and social care must always be undertaken with a specific purpose. It is not simply a social conversation. As we have seen, it needs to ensure that trust and engagement is established whether with users of services or colleagues. However the engagement needs also to be purposeful and lead to shared, agreed and, if possible, positive outcomes.

Clashes in perspective

What lessons can we learn from the numerous examples in the research literature of misunderstanding between a worker and a user of services about the purpose of contact? Mayer and Timms (1970) identified two which more recent research has confirmed: a lack of attention to the need for financial help, and a difference about where the responsibility for family or interactional problems lies. A further area identified by Beresford *et al.* (2005) is about who in the encounter between user of services and social worker has relevant expertise.

Chapter 2 described Mayer and Timms' finding that where users of services required financial or material help they perceived that they were offered psychological or interpersonal help and thought that workers were completely unaware of their desperate financial circumstances. How did this apparently fundamental lack of awareness come about? While the users of services might not have been clear and specific about their need for financial help because of feelings of humiliation and stigma, it should have been the worker's responsibility to clarify the nature of the problem from the perspective of the user of services, and the workers involved failed to do this. As social workers we still need to be very attuned to the situation of users of services in relation to basic needs and deficits, for example poverty, housing and employment.

Currently we may need to exercise caution about assessment of financial needs at the expense of a more holistic assessment of the user of services.

In care management, for example, there is some concern from users of services and social workers that an initial focus on assessment of needs, resource requirements and financial details can be at the expense of attention to, for example, potential feelings of despair, loss or anger of the user of services around the problems which have brought them to care management. A social worker was interviewing an older man about his care needs. She was so detailed in her questions about these that she failed to understand that his main distress was about loss and grief: his wife had recently died.

Mayer and Timms' second area of apparent misunderstanding and disagreement about purpose of contact was where users of services were dissatisfied with the help they received with interpersonal problems. Here the worker appeared to offer psychological insight with a particular focus on understanding how the user of services had contributed to the problem, whereas the user of services tended to locate it in another person, e.g. partner or child, or to want very specific advice and guidance on what to do about it.

This disagreement about the 'cause' of the problem was relatively widespread where users of services were seeking help with interpersonal problems. The belief that the problem lay with someone else and, therefore, the intervention should be directed at that someone else was particularly prevalent in child-centred problems (Fisher *et al.*, 1986; Lishman, 1978). It continues to have relevance, for example, in child protection services (Dale, 2004), in complex work with families around mental health problems (Stanbridge *et al.*, 2003) and in working with older people and their partners or families about problems arising from ageing, disability or loss or transitions from one type of appropriate care to another (Foote and Stanners, 2002).

As Fisher *et al.* (1986) found, 'social workers took as a fundamental tenet that the genesis of child care problems lay in family relationships, rather than in the intrinsic qualities of individuals, and sought solutions in "talking things through"' (p. 48). If parents were unwilling to consider relationships, social workers interpreted this as 'defensive refusal' and did not explore alternative interpretations, e.g. that the parents felt out of control, unable to influence their children or the situation, and therefore in need of someone else to do so.

Here an assumption was made about the parents' motivation but there was no communication about it or attempt to test it out. Sadly the focus was often on the discrepancy of perception at the expense of areas where the worker and user of services agreed. Dale's (2004) research confirms these concerns (see also Platt, 2006).

However, a social worker who understands family dynamics in systems terms will need to question whether a child is solely responsible for problematic behaviour although she or he will also understand that the parents may perceive the problem in this way (Coulshed and Orme, 2006). Where an assessment indicates that the child's behavioural problems do not have an organic origin and are not as a result of autism or Asperger's Syndrome, for example, it is the responsibility of the social worker to convince the family of the need for a family approach.

A third particular clash of perspective between users of services and social workers is where users of services see themselves as 'experts by experience' and social workers disregard or do not respect this. A young man with severe learning disabilities was being assessed by an inexperienced social worker in order to develop a care plan. The social worker started by making her assumption that she was the expert in care planning. The carer, the young man's mother, knew very much more about her son than the social worker did and challenged her perspective: 'I am the expert in my son's care'. She could see how the social worker struggled with this perspective but a shared perspective was negotiated and she and her son are pleased with the outcomes for him and have a positive trusting relationship with the social worker.

Lessons from the literature about clashes in perspective

How may we better address these clashes in perspective? They are less likely to occur if we:

- have been able to engage with the user of services;
- have shown understanding and empathy;
- have listened attentively;
- if required, have given advice and guidance;
- have explained clearly the purpose of contact, and in such a way that the user of services understands it in order to challenge or accept it.

We need to avoid the following:

- initially failing to accept and deal with presenting problems, particularly financial ones;
- making assumptions about hidden problems;
- making assumptions which are untested and not explained about motivation or behaviour on the part of the users of services;
- subscribing to a rigid model of understanding or solving a problem;
- failing to communicate, check out and test with the users of services our assumptions and models, and theirs.

Effective social practice needs to include careful attention to the perspectives of users of services and a clear shared purpose for engagement between users of services and social workers or social care workers. This clear purpose needs to underpin a shared and transparent assessment and regular review of progression towards achieving identified goals. Therefore social workers and social care workers need to continue to develop a value base with an emphasis on openness, mutuality, reciprocity and partnership, and on clarity of communication about expectations and means of achieving them. This value base must also include a much greater acknowledgement of the strengths of users of services in finding, with skilled help, solutions to their own problems. An example of this is in the use of family group conferences in which extended family members join together to make a safe plan for a child at risk and ensure that 'local' and 'family' knowledge and expertise informs decision-making by professionals (Tunnard and Atherton, 1996).

It is important that we work in partnership with users of services to explore and examine our possible different expectations and purposes and how we may come to a shared agreement about tasks involved and interventions required. This is not to suggest that we will always agree but we need to be clear when we are disagreeing. If there is disagreement it also needs to be clear and transparent about how we might try to reach consensus. If this is not possible we need to be clear about who has the authority to make a decision on the way forward and how the detailed implementation of this is to be negotiated and agreed in an inclusive and empowering way (Smale *et al.*, 2000).

Assessment and a contractual approach in social work

The use of a contractual approach to assessment is a potential way of addressing clashes in perspective but will not solve the problems identified earlier in the chapter unless the value base of transparency and clarity, also discussed earlier, supports it. However, considering a contractual approach may offer a discipline to social workers and social care workers which runs counter to potential hidden agendas, unchecked assumptions and unspecific or unclear communication of expectations and procedures. As Trevithick (2005) argues, '[d]rawing up contracts provides an opportunity to formalise and structure the nature of the contract between ourselves and service users in relation to the purpose of the work and the roles, responsibilities and expectations of those concerned' (p. 224). The process involved in arriving at this working agreement is as important as the task itself and acts, as Aldgate (2002) suggests, 'as a tangible manifestation of working in partnership'.

A contractual approach may also act as a check on assumptions about professional authority which do not include a commitment to openness, mutuality, reciprocity and partnership. A useful question for us always is to consider ourselves as the user of services, e.g. in relation to the law, medicine or social services, and how our views are taken into account when we are, in a subjective way, the 'expert' on our own situations.

While this book is not a text on social work methods (see Coulshed and Orme, 2006), assessment is clearly a crucial underpinning for choice of method of intervention (Coulshed and Orme, 2006; Trevithick, 2005). Historically in the literature about communication there has been limited explicit reference to assessment, even though assessment clearly underpins the concept of clear shared agreement about purpose of contact, and expected outcomes and contracts. For example Robb *et al.* (2004) do not explicitly refer to assessment or contracts and this may reflect a wider problem in writing and learning about communication skills in that they are often presented in a context of relationship building and therapeutic engagement. For social workers in roles carrying financial and legal accountability in care management, and also statutory authority in child care and criminal justice, communication skills have to be used sensitively to engage sometimes with reluctant users of services and to ensure that assessments are clear and shared (although not necessarily agreed in the case of involuntary users of services or clashes between users of services and their requirements and the availability of resources). Assessment and the concept of contracts are interlinked and should be underpinned by skilled communication.

The principles of good assessment in social work and social care are dealt with in depth by Milner and O'Byrne (1998) and Smale *et al.* (2000). Milner and O'Byrne (1998) make an analogy between assessment and sound qualitative research. The process of assessment includes 'a clear statement of intent, which also demonstrates how one can be held accountable for one's values' (p. 36). They also argue that an assessment or contract has to set out clear desired outcomes so that we can evaluate whether they have been achieved. For Smale *et al.* (2000), assessment includes the need to negotiate with a range of people about 'specific problems and their potential solutions' and 'to address both the change, care and social control tasks' (p. 132).

Smale *et al.* (2000) examine three potential assessment models: Questioning, Procedural and Exchange. The Questioning Model assumes the worker as expert, asking questions in order to assess need: it provides information about basic needs but, the authors argue, it does not promote choice and empowerment. The Procedural Model, in a sense, has the worker as a technician 'gathering information to see if the person meets certain criteria that make them eligible for services' (p. 142). The worker fills in a form, the questions of which will form an assessment of whether the applicant or service user meets the organization's criteria for resource allocation. Neither the Questioning nor the Procedural Model used rigidly will promote reciprocity between users of services and a social worker or social carer or enhance and utilize their joint skills for problem resolution. However, used sensitively and with good engagement skills, the Questioning Model is often most appropriate to achieve a full detailed assessment, for example, in criminal justice. Neither model particularly values the concept of shared agreement which underpins the use of contracts in social work and social care.

The Exchange Model is particularly relevant to community care if government policy requiring a *needs-led* and personalized rather than a *service-led* provision is actually to occur (Hunter and Ritchie, 2008). In the Exchange Model assessment is a much wider, less individualized process using expertise from all relevant people, including users of services, other professionals and volunteers. It does involve shared and active participation and agreement by all involved about the potential problems and the options for resolution or management. Smale *et al.*

(2000) address, in describing this model, the potential for a 'clash in perspective'. 'Those sending communications may be clear about what they intend to say, but they can never prejudge what the other person receives' (p. 136). The use of a contractual approach can underpin the Exchange Model of assessment because of its emphasis on negotiating agreement and open discussion and recording of agreements and disagreements.

A further issue in relation to assessment, which has become a dominant theme in social work, is the assessment of risk (Kelmshall, 2007). The emergence of the focus on risk assessment and management arises from failures such as the Caleb Ness case (O'Brien, 2003) but itself runs the risk that an emphasis on assessing dangerousness or the possibility of harm may be at the expense of positive benefits from risk. (A recent example was a resident in residential care who had to fight for his right to go to the pub one evening a week to meet his friends.) In a paper on training professionals in risk assessment and risk management, Titterton (1999) found that skills in assessing, taking and managing risk involved communication skills: 'the ability to communicate risk calculation effectively to others and provide support for risk taking partnerships' (p. 237). Whether with informal support networks or formal agencies, communication skills were necessary to share the complexities of risk assessment with users of services in a way that did not disempower them and, where appropriate, with their families and support networks. They were also necessary for wider interprofessional and interagency communication skills: 'how to convey our perception of risk to other agencies' (Titterton, 1999, p. 238).

A contractual approach

Discussion in this chapter about the concept of contracts and issues relating to their potential use must be seen in the wider context of assessment. Davies (1994) defined the use of contracts in social work as involving the worker and user of services making a specific agreement to work towards clearly specified goals. According to him a contractual approach has the following advantages:

> it encourages honesty in the working relationship; it encourages the explicit identification of some focus for action; and it encourages an element of reciprocity in the exchanges between worker and client. (p. 160)

For Davies a contractual approach is likely to avoid clashes in perspective. Before discussing a critique of the use of contracts or identifying the skills involved some examples of contracts are described.

A woman had been homeless following physical abuse from her husband and psychiatric inpatient treatment. She was offered her own council tenancy but arrived for an interview with the duty social worker in great distress saying that she was going to return to her husband because she had no material or financial resources with which to manage her new accommodation or independent life. The duty social worker clarified the problems:

- no transport to take her furniture and possessions into her new accommodation;
- no bedding;
- no response about a grant which would have provided 'comforts' for her new accommodation to ease the transition to independent living;
- anxiety about independent living.

Verbally this user of services and worker acknowledged the anxiety inherent in her becoming more independent. The worker agreed:

- to find transport to take her furniture and possessions to her new accommodation;
- to get the necessary bedding delivered from a voluntary organization;
- to ring to find out about the grant.

The worker then discovered that the user of services had not filled in the appropriate form, so:

- the service user agreed to go to the appropriate office and fill in the form;
- the worker agreed to support the application, as urgent, in a telephone call.

The worker and the user of services each successfully completed the tasks and she took possession of the accommodation.

Egan (2007) describes a different kind of contract. A woman's son had disappeared and she became depressed. 'She shunned both relatives and friends, kept herself at work and even distanced herself emotionally from her other son' (p. 273). Following confrontation from a close relative and her counsellor about her preoccupation with her own misery she engaged in a series of contracts to 'recommit herself' to her other son, herself and her life.

> For instance, she contracted to opening her life up to relatives and friends once more, to creating a much more positive atmosphere at home, to encouraging Jimmy to have his friends over and so forth. The counsellor worked with her in making the patterns of behaviour clear, detailed and realistic. (p. 274)

The use of a contractual approach: complications and reservations

The previous discussion was not intended to suggest that contracts provide a relatively straightforward and unproblematic means of discussing and resolving clashes in perspective. Inevitably further critical examination reveals the complexity of issues involved.

1. A caveat about the term 'contract' between social worker and user of services is that its use in social work is not intended as a legal contract drawn up by lawyers (Collins, 2000) but as a mutual agreement between social worker or social care worker and a user of services. This is not to say that, as a social worker or social care worker, we are not accountable for what we promise, organizationally and to the user of services. If we fail to deliver what we have promised a user of services may rightly wish to use complaints procedures which, at the highest level, involve the Public Services Ombudsman.

2. Underlying the concept of contracts lie assumptions of freedom, choice and self-determination for the user of services and the worker. In reality these are limited. For example, the worker's 'agency function in probation, child care or mental health ... requires him [sic] to use coercion, persuasion or pressure or to have recourse to legal sanctions' (Davies, 1994, p. 153).

3. Underlying the concept of contracts in social work is an assumption, conveyed in terms such as mutuality and reciprocity, of equality between the worker and the user of services. Rojek and Collins (1987) questioned this: 'Social workers have accumulated expertise, knowledge and skill through training and work experience. Most clients have not had equivalent experience and cannot draw upon similar knowledge and skills' (p. 202). In contrast Smale *et al.*'s (2000) argument that '[p]eople are, and always will be the experts on themselves, what they want and need' (p. 137) reminds us of the need in many social work encounters to engage in a mutual, reciprocal relationship where social work expertise is used in partnership with users and carers to ensure an agreed outcome.

None of these reservations should be taken as dismissive of a contractual approach: rather they spell out the contextual constraints within which contracts are negotiated. Perhaps a more useful way of understanding the use of contracts is as a shared agreement.

There are more specific issues about the use and formulation of contracts or shared agreements which include:

1. *Mutual agreement*: we have seen that disagreement between worker and user of services about goals or the means of achieving them has been associated with dissatisfaction and a poor outcome. However total agreement may be difficult, if not impossible, to achieve.

   Potential sources of disagreement are clear. Current examples are:

   - In care management, the difficulty in reconciling what a user of services, as expert in their own lives, want and need and what the social services department can provide in a constrained resource climate.
   - In criminal justice, what the legal processes require and what the user of services wishes, for example avoidance of a recommendation of a prison sentence.
   - Similarly, in child protection, a parent's wish to keep his or her child may conflict with a professional assessment that the risk for the child is too great.

2. *Explicitness*: this means being open, clear and explicit. The value of being explicit lies in the avoidance of confusion or clashes in perspective. Corden (1980) questioned whether explicitness is always necessary or desirable: 'some features of interaction between social workers and clients are capable of being acknowledged, appreciated, and understood without being described in the spoken or written word' (p. 155). For example, in working with a couple whose daughter had died, I made no formal contract beyond saying, 'I have come to see if I can be of any help' and making clear to them that grief work was necessary. I cannot imagine setting specific explicit goals and yet in each session there was a focus we all implicitly agreed on and the work of grieving took place (Lishman *et al.*, 1990).

Clearly the use of contracts or shared assessments is not a panacea for all problems in communication about purpose and outcomes which arise between social workers and users of services. However contracts and shared assessments can be a means of clarification of expectations, roles, purposes, and ways of tackling problems which may go some way to lessening the feelings of confusion, dependency and powerlessness frequently experienced by users of services. While the use of contracts is most closely associated with task-centred casework, cognitive behavioural work, family therapy and family group conferences, it is not limited to these methods of intervention. We need to use the concept of negotiating shared agreement of purpose in all our social work and social care interventions, including criminal justice in pro-social modelling (Trotter, 2007), and not assume that users of services and social services workers understand or share our models of social work intervention.

For example Beresford *et al.* (2006) found that, in palliative care, service users initially had overwhelming negative views of social work and social workers based on media accounts, direct experience and a view of social workers as professionals who removed children from parents. The actual experience of service users of social workers in palliative care was different and they valued it. The use of relationships, personal qualities of the social worker (including kindness, warmth, sensitivity, and empathy) and the importance for service users of being able to determine their own agenda, i.e. achieving a shared agreement about purpose of contact with the worker, led to high level of satisfaction about the contact and its outcomes.

Skills for using a contractual approach

What are the skills involved in the making of a contract or explicit shared agreement? Initially the worker and user of services need to discuss the reasons for professional contact, for example the problems the user of services is encountering, or the resources he or she requires access to or the legal requirements for contact. Egan (2007) calls this 'screening' and Marsh (2007) refers to it as 'an initial general scan of all the areas that may need help' (p. 159). Discussion of these problems or issues requires the social worker's use of engagement skills (see Chapter 5), listening skills (see Chapter 6) and exploration skills (see Chapter 7).

All these skills are involved in the first part of making a contract or shared agreement: what Egan (2007) calls 'helping clients tell their story'. However, the literature about views of users of services shows that, while such ventilation or unburdening might initially provide relief, if it is to be helpful and effective it had to lead to a useful outcome. Here the concept of problem identification, used in a task-centred approach (Coulshed and Orme, 2006; Marsh, 2007) is relevant. The social worker here needs the skills of summarizing, focussing and negotiation which are a necessary part of the assessment process as well as making a contract.

Problem specification

Unburdening by users of services may often appear confusing and overwhelming both to themselves and to the social care workers or social workers in terms of the range, multiplicity and apparent hopelessness of the problems involved. Payne (2005) usefully summarized steps in the process of problem specification which are relevant to the formulation of contracts. These include:

- helping people describe difficulties in their own way, and then summarizing and checking out the worker's perception of the problems;
- trying to reach agreement with users of services about what they see as the main problems;
- raising other potential problems, although accepting the definition of priorities by the user of services;
- getting details of when, where, and how the problems arise.

The key issue for the social worker, or indeed any helping professional, is to work with a user of services to focus on specific issues to be addressed and outcomes to be achieved: this problem specification also allows clear evaluation of effectiveness (Milner and O'Byrne, 1998). Marsh (2007) usefully argues that there are two major factors in prioritizing problems: the wishes of users and services and statutory requirements, e.g. about the care of children. This reminds us of the context in which contracts in social work are made: they may reflect a tension between the wishes of the users of services and statutory or social control.

In order for problem identification or clarification to occur the worker needs to probe, question, clarify and paraphrase (see Chapter 3). Written techniques (see Chapter 4) can also be useful in helping users of services to identify, clarify and prioritize their problems. The following are some of the techniques we can usefully use in problem identification and clarification.

Sentence completion

Priestley and McGuire (1983) suggested the 'simplest and most effective way' of helping a user of services to identify and clarify problems is to ask him or her to complete the following sentences:

'My biggest problem is …'
'I also have problems with …'

While this can be done verbally, it may usefully be written and provide a baseline on which agreement about assessment and possible action may be made.

Brainstorming

Brainstorming is a technique usually used in groups to generate ideas. Priestley and McGuire (1983) suggested that it is particularly useful for 'creating lists of concerns'. All ideas are written down on a blackboard or sheets of paper and the basic rules are:

- as many ideas as possible;
- any ideas, however crazy, are valuable;
- all judgement to be suspended at this stage;
- everything to be written down.

Ideas thus generated can be discussed, discarded, prioritized and acted on. The absence of judgemental attitudes may free participants to be more creative.

While this is generally used in groups it may be a means for an individual to create a list of concerns, or of solutions to problems, freed from judgemental responses normally accompanying such activity.

Checklists

Here the worker may give the user of services a checklist of problems, e.g. about family, relationships, health, work, and attempt to identify the frequency with which such problems occur, for example:

	Often	Sometimes	Never
I worry about money	✓		
I worry about my substance misuse		✓	
I worry about being overweight	✓		
I criticize my boss			✓
I shout at my children	✓		
I lose my temper	✓		

This provides a more private way than brainstorming for a user of services to review his or her concerns and again may be a basis for discussion and prioritizing with the worker.

Checklists can also be used to identify skills, e.g. for employment or in relationships, for example:

	Often	Sometimes	Never
I show warmth	✓		
I am friendly	✓		
I am assertive			✓
I am reliable		✓	
I turn up in time		✓	
I write clearly			✓
I use IT communication			✓

This is a useful starting point in helping someone to identify skills he or she would like to develop or for challenging: if a user of services fails to recognize social skills the worker has observed in her or him, this discrepancy can be pointed out as a positive challenge.

Ranking, prioritizing and goal setting

As with checklists, this set of activities can also help a user of services to identify changes he or she would like to achieve. Once a list of concerns or problems has been drawn up by a user of services the list can then be prioritized, both in order of importance and of amenability to change. Again this can be done on paper: a written record of priorities is clearer and better remembered than ideas floating around in one's head. However we should not assume that all service users are comfortable with using written communication. A written record of concerns and priorities can facilitate goal setting and making a contract and provides a useful baseline to which the worker and user of services can return in order to review progress in achieving desired and agreed outcomes, to recognize obstacles in achieving these outcomes, and if necessary amend early goal setting (Doel and Marsh, 1992; Marsh, 2007).

For example, a user of services listed her concerns as debt, being overweight, irritability with her children and poor care of her house. After discussion she was asked to rank her problems in terms of importance to her and did so as follows:

- debt
- irritability with children
- poor care of house.

When she ranked her concerns in relation to amenability to change the order was different:

- poor care of the house
- debt
- irritability with children.

The ranking processes helped her and worker to begin to negotiate a contract which included initially a home support worker working with her to improve the care of her home, and the social worker arranging and accompanying her on a visit to the local welfare rights organization for advice on rights and debt reduction strategies. Once progress had gradually been achieved in these initial problem areas, the user of services was clear that she wanted to address specific child care issues and a Sure Start worker became involved.

In order to work in partnership with the user of services to identify and prioritize their problems the social worker requires further skills: she or he will need to summarize and to focus in order to draw together the concerns of the user of services, to feed them back and to test whether their understanding continues to be shared.

Summarizing and feedback

The *Shorter Oxford English Dictionary* defines 'to summarize' as 'to sum up' or 'to state briefly or succinctly'. In summarizing (see also Chapter 3) we try to 'sum up' what the other person has been telling us or feed back 'briefly and succinctly' what we understand to be their concerns. Summarizing is rather like paraphrasing on a grander scale. It involves selecting out the most relevant and significant themes and issues and discarding the less important ones. It indicates, if properly done, that we have been listening attentively and have been understanding. Summarizing can focus what has been a rather rambling and scattered range of thoughts, concerns and feelings in order to give greater coherence and meaning to them. It can act as an overview and highlight important issues. It can facilitate the transition from exploration to shared goal setting, and it can help the discussion shift from exploration and, perhaps, ventilation to clarification and thereby a new perspective.

Because of the selection involved in summarizing it is important that the social worker checks with the user of services that the summary is accurate and ensures mutual participation in summarizing. The worker can invite the user of services to modify the summary, or in a more participative way to lead summarizing, for example in a discussion in which he or she is asked, 'What would you say are the main issues we've talked about today?'

Nelson-Jones (2005) distinguishes between two dimensions of summarizing: reflection and feedback. Reflection involves summarizing entirely, from the user of service's perspective, an empathic responding to their thoughts and feelings.

In contrast the feedback element of a summary also includes the worker's view. It is never adequate alone: it will always be in addition to reflection and engaging with and accepting the view of the user of services, but cautiously and carefully trying to extend it, otherwise we are in danger of a clash in perspective again. Here the worker adds an element of interpretation: 'You've been talking about how your family are not supportive enough: they are too interested in their own lives. Similarly your friends are not enough. Perhaps it goes back to your grief; no-one is as good as 'X' was.'

Offering feedback such as this may help the user of services, as Egan (2007) suggests, to develop a new perspective or frame of reference. It can therefore be a useful part of negotiating a shared assessment which involves the user of services in moving on from her or his current perception of the problem into alternative ways of approaching and dealing with it.

Egan (2007) suggests that summarizing can clarify the wider picture, offering a different perspective, and implicitly asking, 'What now?' or 'Where do you/we go from here?'. This question is an integral part of making a contract on shared agreement: it conveys the requirement to shift from a description of how things are now to a focus on what differences are desirable (goals) and how these changes might be achieved (techniques of intervention).

Trevithick (2005) raises interesting and related issues in relation to giving feedback. It can be used to 'check whether we are agreed about achieving shared outcomes and how we may do this.' It can also help users of services, as well as colleagues from social work and interprofessional colleagues from other agencies, to understand a little more about how they are perceived by other people. Egan (2007) distinguishes three different types of feedback:

- confirmatory, i.e. letting users of services know when they are on track;
- corrective, i.e. to help them to get back on track;
- motivating, i.e. to help them improve how they are trying to achieve desired outcomes.

We need to be sensitive in our use of feedback. Many users of services will have received negative and hurtful feedback as a regular part of their life experience. Trevithick (2005) helpfully reminds us that the balance between being honest and facilitative is difficult:

> When faced with this tension, it can help to remember that some things can be left for some time and that feedback is more likely to be taken on board if it is brief and to the point, and it focuses on behaviour as opposed to statements about the individual. (p. 170)

Focussing

Focussing involves prioritizing: users of services frequently come with multiple, complex problems and focussing is about finding criteria to decide what should be worked on first.

Egan (2007) describes a focussing technique used by Lazarus (Rogers et al., 1977). First he asked a user of services to use one word only to describe her problems, and then put the word into a simple sentence. In working with children, it is not uncommon to ask, as part of the initial assessment, for them to give three wishes. For adults an equivalent is, 'What is the main problem just now?' or, alternatively, if we focus on change, 'What aspect of your situation would you most like to change?'.

Workers and users of services can feel bombarded and overwhelmed with problems. Egan (2007) suggests some useful principles about where to start or what to focus on first which remain useful and practical:

- If there is a crisis, deal with it first: a user of services in crisis will have no spare capacity to deal with other concerns until the crisis has been resolved. For example, someone on the point of eviction will not appreciate a focus on her previous management of rent payment, although in the longer term her future ability to manage it will be crucial. This reinforces the findings from Mayer and Timms (1970) about the need for social workers to focus on immediate problems, such as finance, rather than longer-standing problems such as relationships, although family relationships may also be a contributory factor in managing financial problems.
- Focus on the issues the user of services sees as the most important. Consider here the evidence from the client-based research literature where clients had felt the workers did not understand the severity of their problems, particularly financial and material ones. Evidence from research about user views reinforce this.

- Begin with the problems that seem to be causing the most distress because the motivation of the user of services to deal with these is likely to be higher.
- Begin with a manageable sub-problem.
- Begin with a sub-problem which is likely to lead to a successful outcome since success in one area can generate success in other areas.

A manageable sub-problem is more likely to lead to a successful outcome, so the last two items are often interlinked. For example, a user of services was having problems with her three year old who was not sleeping and had frequent temper tantrums. She also felt her husband was unsupportive and that their relationship was deteriorating. The worker and she agreed to focus on the child's behavioural problems and a behavioural programme was drawn up involving 'time out' when there were temper tantrums, and no reinforcement (in the form of drinks, stories or conversation) for failure to go to sleep. The husband agreed with a focus on managing the child's behaviour and agreed to take part in the behavioural programme. The programme was successful: the child went to bed at an appropriate time and had only occasional temper tantrums. Both parents felt they had successfully cooperated in managing their child's problems and each felt their relationship had improved.

Focussing can help the user of services and worker pinpoint both major problematic areas and areas most amenable to change. However, as we saw earlier, the worker and user of services will not always necessarily agree on a focus. Here the skills of negotiating are essential.

Negotiation

The *Shorter Oxford English Dictionary* defines negotiation as 'a course or treaty with another (or others) to bring about some result' or 'the action of getting over or around some obstacle by skilful manoeuvring'.

Too often the obstacle in making a contract or shared agreement may lie in disagreement between worker and user of services (a clash in perspective) about:

- the target for change;
- the goals;
- the means of intervention.

If we take child care as an example the disagreement may be expressed as follows:

Agenda	The view of the user of services/parent	The view of the worker
Anxiety about child care and potential child protection	Anxiety about statutory power in relation to the removal of children	Anxiety about risk and child protection
Target for change	The child	The parent or family
The goals	Improvement in child's behaviour	Improvement in family relationships
The means of intervention	Punishment or increased control of the child, e.g. by removal into care	Family therapy or family group conferencing as a means of improving communication

We should note that this disagreement does not include the view of the child.

The example is taken from child care but the issues of disagreement occur equally, for example, in community care where an older person may disagree with a spouse or their children about problem definition, perhaps in relation to the need for residential care, and where the care manager has to negotiate between these very different and firmly held views.

Where the contract is voluntary, negotiation appears appropriate to try to find some common ground to provide a way out of these disagreements. Where legal requirements constrain choice, e.g. in child abuse or criminal justice, negotiation remains relevant but may not be possible.

In a voluntary context how may fundamental disagreements be dealt with? How can a contract be negotiated? First, we should remember Egan's principles of focussing: if the focus on which the contract is based does not begin with the issues the user of services sees as most important, and is most willing to work on, his or her motivation for work and change is likely to be low.

Second, we have to start with and understand the perspective of the user of services; this does not necessarily mean agreeing with it. Rather we need to explore it, accept it as far as possible, and reciprocate by sharing our own perspective and if necessary our disagreement. We must try to avoid a major issue, raised in the client-focussed research literature, of hidden agendas in which perspectives of clients and workers were not openly discussed but operated as hidden assumptions which confused and distorted communication. Obviously in a disagreement about purpose of contact and assessment, timing is important, as is the skill with which the worker may need to disagree with the user of services. If we immediately 'leap in' and 'shout down the user of service' he or she will be left feeling resentful and not understood.

Third, we need to hold onto and highlight mutual areas of agreement. In child care areas of agreement between parents and social worker are more likely to be about long-term goals. We need to hold onto the optimistic view that parents frequently want the best for their children even when they realize they are struggling to provide it, although we also need to be realistic in our assessment of whether they do or not (Aldgate, 2007; Platt, 2006). In relation to families struggling with parental substance misuse, for example, we should not assume that parents do not have their children's welfare at heart, but need to be cautious in assessing the impact of substance abuse on their child-care abilities.

Shared assessment may also be problematic in community care for older people, where their children's desire for safety in residential care may conflict with the older person's wish to remain at home and the care manager's professional accountability to provide for care in the community. However, the importance of trying to find areas of mutual agreement is crucial where achievable. We need to emphasize that all are concerned about the older person's welfare.

Negotiation involves each side being prepared to give, so that some kind of compromise is reached which is acceptable to each party but not their ideal starting point. It does involve clarity about the starting point, and about what is being compromised; it also involves each party being committed to the compromise without feeling short-changed. So, for example, in child care, the worker might initially hope to work with the whole family to improve communication and relationships; the parents, on the other hand, might focus on the need for changes in the behaviour of one child. The negotiations involved might be complex: the social worker might accept the desirability of the child's changed behaviour, the child might demand more positive reinforcement and attention from the parents and the parents might have to accept that any behavioural change on the part of the child would involve them heavily in administering the programme and giving reinforcement to improved behaviour.

Sometimes negotiation may be unsuccessful and a shared agreement may not be possible. This may be because the worker does not have the resources, e.g. financial or material help which the user of services needs and requires. Here it is important that the worker is honest and does not string the user of services along. It may also be helpful to acknowledge the validity of the request even though the worker cannot respond with the resources.

The discrepancy between the goals of the user of services and the worker may be too great. If the parents require behavioural change in a child without any willingness to be involved themselves a social worker may feel pressure to collude in a scapegoating process and, thereby, be unable to form a contract. If a family want residential care for an older parent but the older person does not agree, and is not at risk, a contract may not be possible.

The discrepancy may be about means of intervention. If a group of tenants want to deal with the issue of damp housing by exposing the landlord and protesting by demonstrations against him, and the worker would wish to begin by establishing channels of communication (i.e. to use a collaborative model rather than a conflict one), a contract between tenants and workers may not be possible. Sometimes a worker may be unable to enter into such a shared agreement because of an agency's reluctance to allow her or him to engage in any activities which might be seen as political or to jeopardize sources of funding.

Contracts can be limited or constrained by the legal framework, and mutuality, reciprocity or negotiation then play little part. For example, the social worker's use of legal authority in relation to the protection of the children will predominate. However, even in this setting the expectations of parents can be clearly and explicitly set out, and choice promoted where possible. In criminal justice, statutory legal requirements will limit the extent to which negotiation about shared purpose and a contract can fully be achieved.

Working with resistant or reluctant users of services

Not all users of services who are involved with social workers have chosen the involvement: as indicated, some encounters are constrained by statutory requirements. Reluctance or resistance to contact does not necessarily render the contract of mutual agreement or another type of contract impossible. Rather we should consider how we may attempt to work with such reluctant users of services.

Egan distinguished between *reluctant* clients – people who have been more or less forced to come, e.g. because of a supervision or probation order, or when dragged along by a spouse – and *resistant* clients who may have referred themselves or overcome initial reluctance but 'balk' at the implications of the work at some point.

Egan (2007) gives examples of reasons why people may be reluctant and/or resistant to help, including the following:

- seeing no reason for going for help in the first place;
- feeling resentful at third-party referrals, e.g. in child abuse it is common for the parents to express anger that the referral was mistaken;
- fear of the unfamiliar;
- uncertainty about expectations;
- ambivalence about change;
- seeing no advantage in change;
- once change has started, seeing more costs than benefits;
- feeling that having to come for help involves weakness, failure or inadequacy – 'losing face'.

For people who have committed offences, all these reasons for resistance may apply but the accountability of the social worker to the criminal justice system and the court is a further reason. For parents involved in child protection social work contact, their anxiety about the authority of the social worker to remove their child into care will be paramount and may make them defensive if not reluctant and resistant.

In what ways may we most usefully respond?

- It is important to acknowledge feelings of reluctance of a user of services about engagement and to explore them rather than deny them.
- It is important to discuss what is going to be involved in the contact.
- It is important to see that resistance is usual.
- It is important not to view resistance as deliberate ill will or a personal rejection. If we think, instead, in a positive way of reasons for 'defensiveness', we may more productively think of why users of services need to use it and what incentives might help them not to.
- It is equally important for us to examine our own resistance and potential for defensiveness: the more we understand our own the more we can understand and help users of services.
- It is important to examine our own behaviour: are we eliciting resistance? Sometimes someone who is hostile can elicit our defensiveness or get under our skin in such a way that we attack in return. It is important to consider our own behaviour and interactions. How do I as a white, older, middle-class woman appear to a young, black,

unemployed man? Probably as potentially patronizing, unhelpful, different and critical. However, this is an example of wider issues about how we need to be aware of the way in which structural issues, age, class, gender, ethnicity, religion, sexual orientation may become blocks to effective working with users of services.

● It is important not to attack resistance, rather we need to accept it, respect it and work round it. Egan (2007) says, 'befriend the resistance'.

● It is also important to use challenge and confrontation when our assessment indicates that we should be cautious about possible manipulation by an involuntary user of services.

In criminal justice, the empowering approach to assessment, and thereby, to contract setting envisaged by Smale *et al.* (2000) is restricted by policy agendas which emphasize the risk to society in not taking a very cautious approach to offences and how we deal with them, for example in terms of prison rather than community sentences, and how we approach decisions about parole (Beaumont, 1999). A contractual approach in criminal justice with clearly defined and linked goals should not be dismissed. For offenders entering the criminal justice system, practical goals which include getting supported accommodation, work-related and social skills training, drug or alcohol reduction programmes and employment are elements of a contractual approach to which they may readily subscribe and in the longer term may empower them to manage their lives more successfully.

Overall the use of a contractual approach, while realistically not a success with every user of services, may, by its emphasis on openness, shared decisions and participation, help resistant users of services to feel more engaged and more in control of the process.

Verbal or written contractual approaches

One question is whether contracts in assessment should be written or verbal. The value of a written contract is that it is explicit, open equally to worker and user of services and neither can deny it at a later stage. Writing down the problems renders them concrete and may be the first stage for a user of services in confronting and taking responsibility for them.

When a contract is more appropriately viewed as a verbal shared agreement between user of services and social worker it is nevertheless important to keep a written record. Verbal agreements may not always reflect shared perceptions.

Sometimes, however, the problems and issues to be worked on may be less specific, e.g. ventilation of mixed feelings. Here a written contract may be too concrete and simplistic, running the risk of devaluing the significance of what is being shared. For example, a key worker and a twelve-year-old boy in residential care drew up a written contract:

1. defining desirable and unacceptable behaviours;
2. setting out realistic goals for the reduction of unacceptable behaviours;
3. defining the consequences (withdrawal of particular privileges) if the goals in (2) were not achieved;
4. defining rewards for performance of desirable behaviours.

The definitions, goals and consequences were mutually agreed.

Simultaneously, the key worker and the boy had an informal, verbal agreement that he had access to the worker whenever she was on duty for half an hour before his bedtime. He regularly availed himself of this time and used it to talk about home, in particular his distress after his mother's death, and his anger that his father did not seem to care for him. In this second assessment scenario the contract was implicit but mutually agreed: a written contract or even a more formal explicit verbal contract seemed almost too crude to address the delicacy, depth and sensitivity of this child's agenda.

Such a contractual approach, both formal and informal, can often help to prevent the clashes in perspective outlined at the beginning of this chapter, and, while they are not always relevant to every social work and social care encounter, the awareness and conscious use of a contractual approach is a useful discipline for the worker in ensuring that she or he clarifies, checks out and negotiates with users of services about the purpose of contact. In any assessment we need to pay attention to these principles (Coulshed and Orme, 2006; Milner and O'Byrne, 1998; Smale *et al.*, 2000).

Conclusion

This chapter has examined critically the continuing relevance of a contractual approach in facilitating greater clarity between the worker and user of services about expectations, goals, means of intervention and outcomes and, thereby, reducing the risk of a clash in perspective. It can be a means of enhancing partnership working between social workers and users of services (Smale *et al.*, 2000).

However it is not a panacea for all communication and assessment problems between workers and users of services. Differentials in power between workers and users of services can mean the relationship is unequal and reduce the opportunity for mutuality and reciprocity.

The tensions between the social control and social care purposes of social work and social care need to be recognized. In the authority role for social work, power is clearly unequal. In the social care role, the emphasis is on partnership and empowerment – a more equal sharing of power.

A contractual approach is not a unitary phenomenon: the context and purposes of social work vary enormously and influence the potential for contracts. However, in all of these contexts and purposes we need to try to apply the concept and principle of contracts or mutual agreement about purpose to improve the possibility of shared agreement, mutuality of purpose and clarity of expectations for all users of services.

In the early client-based research some people were highly motivated to seek help, knew what they required and saw that as legitimate, and themselves as partners in the helping process (Rees and Wallace, 1982). For them, contracts were a natural means of negotiating mutually agreed roles and tasks. More recently, users of services who are 'experts by experience' would continue to take this approach (Beresford et al., 2005; Reid and Reynolds, 1996). Other people were more reluctant, and felt stigmatized and powerless at having to seek help. For them mutuality in contract making was more difficult, but the clarification of expectations, of goals and the ways these might be achieved, via a contract, was a means of increasing their commitment to the process and increasing their sense of power and choice. Some users of services had no choice about their contact with social work. They were legally required to do so: the contract was not a mutual one but specified legally what they were required to do. As we have seen, this tension between empowering users of services and statutory authority in social work and social care remains, and influences how we use a contractual approach and how much we may achieve shared agreement about purposes of contract and assessment (Coulshed and Orme, 2006; Trevithick, 2005).

Contracts or mutual agreements may perhaps be most clearly seen as useful in crisis, task-centred or behavioural work. Here the problems to be addressed are clearly defined, the goals clear and specific, and the tasks discrete, specific and incremental. The task-centred model involves a commitment to partnership in the sense of a respect for the views of users' of services: a great deal of effort is put into good communication, a preference for joint actions on problems, and a focus on the abilities and strengths of the users of services (Marsh, 2007).

However a contractual approach is not limited to these models. It is also appropriate in care management, in counselling, and in working with families and groups (Coulshed and Orme, 2006). It is also important in cognitive, behavioural work with people who have offended. Its value lies in the discipline it requires of workers in terms of clear communication, of clarification of expectations, of negotiation of mutually agreed goals and therefore a mutual commitment to the work, and of discussion and negotiation about how the worker and user of services may best achieve the goals. It carries the implication of time limits but this does not necessarily limit the work to short-term goals and approaches: the use of a contract, short-term work, periodic review and evaluation and a further contract can be useful in longer-term work in reducing aimlessness in purposeful contact between worker and users of services. However, as already suggested, an explicit contractual approach may not be helpful in certain social work contexts, e.g. working with the dying or bereaved or in admission to residential care for an old person. However, the principles of a contractual approach can still usefully underlie assessment practice in social work and social care, e.g. in clarifying expectations, discussing the purpose of contact, or considering 'where do we go from here?'

We also need to think about the underlying principles and techniques in relation to agreeing, focussing and prioritizing our work with colleagues from other disciplines. How do we ensure that we do not have a 'clash in perspective' in our dealings with colleagues from other professions? How may the technical suggestions in this chapter about developing shared purpose help us to work better interprofessionally, and work to ensuring successful outcomes for users of services?

---

putting it into practice

Have you ever been a resistant or reluctant user of services? If so, think about why?

Think about a recent contact you have with a GP. Did you feel you had a shared purpose and agreement?

In working with a user of services who has substance abuse problems, in particular in relation to alcohol, and is concerned about her three children who are under the age of seven, how would you engage with her in a shared assessment, about her substance abuse, risk to her children and overall child care? What kind of a contract might you make with her and how might you jointly prioritize the children's needs, food, school and nursery and a reliable lifestyle and her need to deal with her alcohol abuse problem? What other agencies might you and she agree to involve?

Recommended reading

Smale, G., Tuson, G. and Stratham, D. (2000) *Social Work and Social Problems*, Basingstoke, Macmillan – now Palgrave Macmillan. Help in examining the empowering elements of assessment.

Coulshed, V. and Orme, J. (2006) *Social Work Practice*, 4th edn, Basingstoke, Palgrave Macmillan. A critical analysis of relevant issues in assessment which underpin appropriate use of intervention.

Milner, J. and Byrne, P. (1998) *Assessment in Social Work*, Basingstoke, Macmillan – now Palgrave Macmillan. A comprehensive review of approaches to assessment linked to specific methods of intervention.

Lishman, J. (2007) *Handbook for Practice Learning in Social Work and Social Care*, London, Jessica Kingsley. See Section 2 on Assessment with chapters on Models of Assessment, Assessment and Children, Assessment and Reflexivity, and Assessment in Criminal Justice.

9 | Intervention: non-verbal and verbal techniques for enhancing behavioural and attitudinal change

Historically, client-based research (Maluccio, 1979) and social work theory (Fischer, 1978) has been critical of the undue emphasis in social work on the relationship or process at the expense of effectiveness or outcomes. This tension between process and outcome continues to be problematic in social work and the provision of social services. A social worker still, unfortunately, can remain relationship- and process-orientated at the expense of thinking about the outcomes of what we engage in. Outcomes for users of services must be a focus: however, relationships and processes are a means to achieving this, and users of services testify to this (SCIE, 2004c). For the worker to be optimally effective she or he must:

● establish trust and a caring relationship

before it is possible to:

● employ techniques of change.

These lessons from early research have not changed (see Macdonald, 2007; Trotter, 2007) but need to be reviewed in the current contexts of social work and social care practice.

Relationships, process and outcomes

Chapter 2 showed how users of services value and anticipate that they will experience sensitive user-friendly relationships and processes, and also that they expect effective outcomes.

Currently the requirement for evidence-based practice and evaluation of the outcomes of any intervention we do attempt is an essential component of our practice (Macdonald and Sheldon, 1998; Sackett *et al.*, 1996). In criminal justice a clear and precise measure of success of intervention is a reduction in an individual's offending behaviour (McGuire, 1995).

In child protection a crucial measure of success of an intervention is the prevention of child abuse. However, this apparently simple outcome measure is, in practice, complex. To argue, as a senior civil servant did (personal communication), that successful performance management in child protection requires that no child is abused while living at home and that no child is taken into care unnecessarily, reveals an impossible juxtaposition of criteria for judging a successful outcome and ignores the complexity of risk assessment (Kelmshall, 2007). For example, a community-based project which provides a creative range of support for children and families where parents had drug misuse problems, had an outcome measure of reducing the number of children on the child protection register by improving safe parenting. However the project became increasingly concerned about the safety of one child and had to ensure that social services engaged in child protection measures which led to the removal of the child from her family. The project saw this outcome as the best possible in terms of the safety of the child, but this was not a part of the outcome measures against which they were being judged. In community care, successful outcomes may also be difficult to define and may more usefully be evaluated by how a user or carer views the service they have received: did they feel empowered as part of a partnership which fully used and enhanced their problem solving skills? (SCIE, 2005; Smale et al., 2000).

Historically social workers and social care workers did not pay sufficient attention to the purpose and outcomes of their work. At the beginning of the 21st century we must do so and therefore incorporate evaluation into our practice. Why is this a priority? We need to demonstrate professional accountability, accountability to the organizations we work in (public, voluntary or private), responsibility and accountability to users of services. We also need to show that we are meeting government imperatives and to demonstrate that we do make a difference to the lives of people who require the services we provide (see, for example, *Changing Lives*, 2006; Shaw and Lishman, 1999).

Realistic approaches to social work: structural or personal intervention

We need to consider whether personal change (of attitudes or behaviour) is a realistic and valid goal of social work, given the importance of structural influences in/on the lives of service users (see also the Preface). Practical changes for individuals, for example in relation to better housing or personal care, are an important part of the social work task and previous chapters on attending and listening, sharing information and shared purpose and assessment focus on skills which can help and empower users of services to access better services. This chapter, while relevant to those skills, focusses on how intervention may help individuals in their personal and psychological functioning. It would seem a loss of an important element of social work skills if this function of social work is seen as more appropriately undertaken by counselling. Previous chapters have shown how users of social work services, for example in community care, want not just a practical approach to service provision but also an understanding of issues of loss, bereavement and attachment.

In relation to intervention aimed at changing interpersonal and psychological functioning the following questions are relevant:

● Is change of any kind (personal, social or political) a valid aim of social work?
● Is personal change a valid aim given the significance of structural factors, e.g. of poverty and discrimination, in the problems users of services bring to us?
● More specifically, how much are changes in attitudes or behaviour relevant to users of services?

Davies (1994) remained critical of the emphasis in social work literature on change, personal or political. He argued that a more realistic goal was maintenance: 'maintaining a stable, though not a static, society, and maintaining the rights or providing opportunities for those who in an unplanned uncontrolled community would go to the wall'. In contrast, radical social workers promoted the concept of change in social work, but the change involved was of the system and not the individuals. Radical social work challenged social work's preoccupation with individualistic explanations of social problems and focussed instead on social, economic and political solutions and collective action (Langan, 2002; Trevithick, 2005). From such a perspective, attempting to help an individual to make personal changes ignores the powerful structural influences defining her or his situation and problems and runs the risk of 'blaming the victim'.

Both the radical social work perspective and the maintenance perspective remain relevant to the context of any discussion of skills involved in bringing about change for individuals. Many changes which social workers and users of services would wish to bring about are not within their individual control: for example, relief of poverty, reversal of unemployment, provision of adequate housing and removal of discrimination on the basis of race, gender or disability. It is important to be clear in our assessments about what problems are structural in origin and within our combined abilities to change. It is also important that we make clear to users of services (whether in children and families, adult or criminal justice services) when these problems are within their personal control and responsibility: being poor may not be the fault of an individual as a 'poor' person or because of 'poor' management but instead reflect a social and economic structure in which unemployed people or people in low-income jobs are inadequately resourced to live their lives (Becker and MacPherson, 1988).

To assume that we can help users of services to change or solve these problems is unrealistic or even arrogant: the solution is political. However, as social workers and social care workers we cannot ignore the impact of poverty and discrimination on people's lives. How may we address this? Langan and Lee (1989) stressed that we need to work in a more structural and adversarial way. We need to acknowledge with users of services the social, political, economic and structural pressures which disadvantage them (see Preface). When faced with structural problems for users of services, we need to work in ways which are empowering and do not individualize structural problems.

Payne (2002) expands and develops the debate I have described between Davies' maintenance view of social work and Langan and Lee's radical social work perspective. He suggests that:

> Practice Theories are about *effective* behaviour with clients, just as values are about *ethical* behaviour with clients. A theory cannot tell us how to be effective unless we can say what our aim is and therefore what direction we want to be effective 'in'. (p. 128)

He proposes three potential purposes for social work and social care, also considered by Shaw and Lishman (1999) in their critique of evaluation and social work practice.

Payne's first perspective of the purpose of social work is emancipatory or socialist–collectivist: 'rather than helping people to adjust to society to deal with their problems, we should change fundamental structures in society, which are the origins of most people's problems' (Payne, 2002, p. 130). Structural differences, including ethnicity, gender, age and disability, create oppressions and problems which cannot be dealt with on an individual basis.

His second perspective is an individualist–reformist approach which sees 'social work as providing services effectively to help individuals' personal problems and adjust well to the society around them' (Payne, 2002, p. 129). Care management is a good example of this approach, where a managed package of services coordinated by a care manager who may be social work or occupational therapy trained enables a vulnerable older person, or an adult with learning disabilities or mental health problems to maintain and sustain an independent life in her or his own community.

His third perspective is a reflective–therapeutic approach which sees social work and social care 'as helping individuals (and perhaps groups and communities) to achieve personal growth, self actualisation and personal power over their environment' (Payne, 2002, p. 129).

Smale *et al.*'s (2000) model of 'change agent activity' provides a useful integration of individual and structural change perspectives. It stresses that in social work and social care participants (voluntary or involuntary users of services or providers of services) will have different perceptions of the processes involved, assessment, interventions or evaluation (as the 1970s client studies revealed). Smale *et al.* (2000) argue that problem formulation, assessment and intervention need to be 'a joint enterprise between people involved and the social workers' (p. 107). In order to achieve change we need to reframe problems, relocate resources, and facilitate and empower behavioural change. The issue of resources is critical if users' and carers' perspectives are really to influence social policy, social work and social services.

Effective intervention skills

In this chapter I draw on the individualist–reformist or reflective–therapeutic perspectives to examine intervention skills which may increase our effectiveness in helping users of services to problem solve or make changes in their attitudes or behaviour. I do so because many people still bring to social work and social services, including criminal justice, problems which they would like personally to solve or to manage better, for example child care or offending behaviour. For them, simply acknowledging their structurally disadvantaged position or promoting collective action to address it may not meet their current individual needs. Negotiation about goals within their personal control may enable them to manage current problems more effectively. Changes in behaviour and attitudes, in this context, are ways of problem solving within the reality of a disadvantaging and discriminatory social structure. Following Smale *et al.* (2000), however, we can also extend this rather individual, therapeutic approach to intervention to consider what techniques may also be relevant in a more collective and emancipatory approach and in working with other professionals in interdisciplinary teams.

If we subscribe to a view that promoting and enabling change is a part of social work and social care we still need to ensure that when we make any intervention, in group care, community care, child care or criminal justice (McIvor and Raynor, 2007), we employ, as an integral part of assessment and intervention, reflective practice and ongoing evaluation.

A useful set of questions which address Schon's (1983) distinction between reflection (and evaluation) *on* action and *in* action are:

- How am I doing what I am doing?
- Why am I doing what I am doing?
- How could I be more effective?

Reflective practice is an essential component of effective practice and communication (Fook, 2007). Evidence-based practice includes reflective practice but also the need for evaluation and research-mindedness in practice (Lishman, 2007). What does the research literature tell us about relevant, effective intervention skills?

Some of the answers to effective intervention lie outside the control of the individual practitioner or user of services: they lie in questions and answers about service delivery from a particular organization or from interprofessional service delivery. However, users of services have clear views about what they find relevant and effective intervention skills in social work (Chapter 2).

We have already seen that social workers and social care workers in all settings need to build relationships with users of services and to enable them to tell their stories. Sometimes the combination of empathy, active listening, probing and clarification may be enough to help a user of services to gain a new perspective on his or her problems and to engage, without further intervention, on problem solving. More frequently, offering users of services a supportive relationship and the opportunity to unburden is not enough (Maluccio, 1979) and intervention skills aimed at problem solving and changing attitudes and behaviour are essential.

What skills and techniques have been found to be effective in promoting such change? Reid and Hanrahan (1981) found the following factors to lead to greater effectiveness:

- the use of focussed intervention methods;
- the adaptation of behavioural approaches;
- contract-based programmes;
- careful matching of target problem and users of services with a particular style of intervention.

This chapter and the following one examine non-verbal, verbal and written communication skills and techniques which may be useful in work with users of services around change and problem solving. They are not concerned with particular models of social work practice: the skills involved are relevant to a range of intervention models (Coulshed and Orme, 2006; Trevithick, 2005). Both chapters refer back to skills introduced in Chapters 3 and 4 but develop and apply them. Underlying this chapter is the assumption that a social worker is a source of influence and persuasion for users of services and colleagues and that, where the social work task involves helping people to change, the process must involve the social worker's use of influence to promote that attitudinal or behavioural change, whether with colleagues or users of services.

What is important about influencing is to know when we are doing it (see Chapter 3). We need to be aware of when we reinforce other people's behaviour, when we slip into giving opinions, when we may be trying to control people. If we are aware of how and when we are influencing we can use this more responsibly and more openly to achieve goals agreed with users of services.

Non-verbal influence

Chapter 3 examined non-verbal behaviours and explored the impact of social workers' non-verbal behaviour on users of services. It was suggested that non-verbal communication is extremely influential: where there is conflict between verbal and non-verbal messages it is the non-verbal ones which predominate. It was also suggested that there are problems in interpreting or decoding non-verbal behaviour: one behaviour can convey more than one emotion, clusters of behaviour can convey a different meaning from the meaning of each individual behaviour, and the meaning of non-verbal behaviour may vary according to culture and to context. We also saw that interpreting or decoding non-verbal behaviour was strongly influenced by our culture, ethnicity and gender and that we need to be cautious about interpretations that may have been based on research which reflected primarily a male, white, middle-class world.

Are there non-verbal behaviours which may be influential in terms of the focus of this chapter – changing attitudes and behaviour? Status and power, responsiveness, persuasiveness and reinforcement may all be conveyed non-verbally and are relevant to exercising influence.

In Chapter 3 we saw that people of higher status tended to adopt a more relaxed posture, conveying our assumptions of status and power. Sitting behind a desk or in a higher chair also signifies higher status or greater power; sitting in the lower seat can feel quite disempowering and disabling. Power or status can be conveyed by an 'expanded' bodily posture with an expanded chest, erect head and body and raised shoulders, and low power by a bowed head, dropping shoulders and a sunken chest.

We need to consider how much power we do wish to convey non-verbally. If we are engaging in a partnership with the users of services where we wish to emphasize mutuality, reciprocity and empowerment, any assumption of unequal power will be perceived as inappropriate, counterproductive and ineffective, and a complementary posture and seating arrangement (similar height chairs arranged at right angles) should be chosen. Sometimes, however, it may be relevant to convey power non-verbally. It can reinforce the use of firmness and authority and enhance direct guidance and influence which is sometimes required and appreciated by users of services: 'They've got to be strong. They should be able to take control of the situation' (Sainsbury, 1975). When we are giving advice or guidance (see Chapter 6), for example about child management, the assumption of power may non-verbally serve to strengthen and emphasize our verbal message, thereby increasing its influence.

More generally, in statutory work, whether in child protection, criminal justice (McIvor and Raynor, 2007) or mental health, we may need to convey power non-verbally, and thereby our authority. In dealing with colleagues from other disciplines, e.g. the police, law and health, we need non-verbally to convey confidence and authority in order to ensure social, structural and individual factors are taken into account in interdisciplinary assessment and intervention. Interdisciplinary work is an area where social workers have been perceived as not able to use authoritative and confident communication skills (*Changing Lives*, 2006).

Responsiveness is an ingredient of the non-verbal behaviours found to be involved in persuasiveness and influencing people. In Chapter 3 we saw that responsiveness is conveyed by activity which includes: bodily movement, facial expression and quality of verbalization, including longer communications, unhalting quality and faster speech rate. Immediacy is another element of persuasiveness, involving shorter distances between people, more eye contact, moderately relaxed posture and frequent head nodding.

A final non-verbal means of influence is reinforcement. As we saw in Chapter 3, smiling, nodding one's head, leaning forward and brief verbal recognitions (e.g. mm ... mmm) act as reinforcers of opinions or attitudes. Argyle (2007) argued that:

> operant conditioning of verbal behaviour, and probably of other behaviour too, is an important process of influence in dyadic encounters. The effect is rapid and can occur without the awareness of the person influenced. It may also occur without the knowledge of the influencer... (p. 179)

We need to retain awareness of these elements of our non-verbal behaviour in our interactions with both fellow professionals and users of services.

It is important that we are aware of when we are using *reinforcing* non-verbal behaviour and that we do not use it indiscriminately or to reinforce undesirable behaviour. More positively we can consciously use such reinforcers to encourage attitude or behaviour change. In working with a user of services with very low self-esteem I consciously reinforced non-verbally any statement in which she expressed a positive attitude to herself, and nodded approvingly when she told of an instance where she had been able to assert herself at work. Such non-verbal reinforcements need to be used, for example where someone is successfully beginning to combat an alcohol or drug abuse problem, reduce offending or improve their child care. With interprofessional colleagues we need to think carefully about our non-verbal behaviour. How can we convey non-verbally our own professional confidence and competence, and also recognition of other interdisciplinary colleagues' confidence and competence and thereby influence colleagues from other professions? (*Changing Lives*, 2006).

Verbal techniques

Some of the techniques discussed in earlier chapters on relationship building, sharing information and making a contract are also means of intervention to promote change, for example empathy, reflection, clarification, questioning and probing, giving advice, summarizing and focussing. In this chapter they are re-examined as potential ways of helping people change and problem solve. We also look at challenging, which specifically addresses the task of helping people change their attitudes or behaviour and may usefully be employed with interprofessional colleagues.

Empathy

Empathy was defined and its use explored in Chapter 5. How can its use help people solve problems or make changes? In criminal justice, research on pro-social modelling approaches has found that these were most effective when workers displayed high levels of empathy, but were also more pro-social in terms of positive reinforcement (Trotter, 2007).

Empathic responses can help someone who feels stuck to move forward. Feeling understood and having problematic feelings and experiences accepted can help people to leave them behind. A frail, vulnerable older woman cherished her rather fragile independence but recognized the need for a community care alarm. Confronted with a single, shared assessment form she felt overwhelmed by its level of detail for services she did not see as relevant. The care manager recognized her concerns and ambivalence about seeking help and with empathy enabled her to make the application.

A frail elderly man had several times begun the process of applying for residential care and then withdrawing. He again approached the local social work department. The worker explored his current situation and then commented that it sounded as if he had very mixed feelings about such a move. She was able to convey to him her understanding of his current need to be cared for, but also his apprehension about dependence and his feelings of loss, of his independence, his home and, in a way, his past. Taking time to explore and acknowledge these feelings, and the empathic responses with which they were met, enabled him to move on to a positive decision about his need for greater security and care – a decision he did not subsequently regret.

Empathic responses can help validate and confirm a person's perceptions which they experience as previously having been ignored, disqualified or disconfirmed. While this cannot 'heal' or solve the past hurt it may reduce its power in the present by helping the person to recognize the hurt and live with it, perhaps even to 'lay it to rest' and move on. A young woman had been self-mutilating. Her self-esteem was low and she had had a series of relationships which had always ended in rejection. She talked about her mother whom she had found powerful and controlling but who had also helped her practically and financially. She mentioned that as a child, whenever she had tried to touch or embrace her mother, she had been pushed away. The worker said how hurtful and rejecting this must have felt: the woman looked surprised and then relieved and agreed. The worker's empathic confirmation of the rejection she had felt (but which had always been denied by her mother) began a process whereby she acknowledged that her mother had been rejecting but that this was not her (the child's) fault. The worker's empathy and confirmation of the young woman's perceptions helped her self-esteem to rise a little and she began to see connections with her current difficulties.

In residential or group care empathic responses can be an important means of intervention. Here workers have to be able to respond to critical incidents or significant statements by residents as they arise without preparation (Keenan, 2007). If we can convey empathic understanding of what the resident is trying to communicate this may be therapeutic, whereas simply to respond to the overt behaviour or words may leave the resident feeling that he or she has not been understood and that real communication is not possible.

An elderly resident in a home for older people, who was seen as bitter and disagreeable, was complaining to a worker about the food and the other residents. The worker neither ignored her nor rebuffed her but acknowledged how difficult she seemed to be finding life in the home. The older woman began to talk about how difficult her life had always been, particularly as a child when she felt her parents had preferred her younger sister. The worker commented on how upset and angry she seemed to be feeling and how hard it must have been as a child to feel less loved. The older woman spoke with great distress about how she had felt that no-one understood what she had gone through. Over time she talked more with the worker about her past life and, while she was still perceived as a rather difficult person, some of her bitterness seemed to be alleviated.

Reflection and clarification

Reflection and clarification are not only a means whereby we check out, convey or increase our understanding of the problems of user of services. They are also a means of helping people to develop new perspectives about their situation or of reframing a problem (Smale *et al.*, 2000), an essential component of problem solving and change.

A woman arrived at an intake team in considerable agitation. She poured out an almost incoherent jumble of problems and the social worker felt quite overwhelmed. She reflected this feeling back to the woman and wondered if she felt like this too. The social worker then began a process of trying to clarify the major problems or concerns. Gradually the woman became less distressed and began to identify three problems which concerned her most: debt, her partner's drinking and her children being out of control. The worker used further clarification to establish concretely and specifically:

- what debts were owed;
- when the husband drank;
- how the children behaved.

What emerged for the user was that the debts were the main problem: whenever a demand for payment or a bill came in she felt overwhelmed and depressed, her partner went for a drink, and the children's behaviour deteriorated. She, therefore, decided that the problem she wished to address with her partner was the debt management. The worker agreed to a limited contact with this focus, to negotiate on the couple's behalf manageable repayment schedules, and to explore the possibility of charitable help.

A young man on a criminal justice supervision order left his work because he felt he was being picked on by his foreman. The social worker clarified exactly what the foreman had done and said, and the young man began to realize how touchy he had been about any feedback even if it was constructive criticism.

Questioning and probing

Like clarification and reflection, questioning and probing may enable a user of services to gain a new perspective about a problem. Skilful questioning and probing can involve them in examining their attitudes, values, perceptions, and assumptions and, in a sense, defending them or revising them.

An enraged father appeared before the duty social worker asking for his teenage daughter to be taken into care. His only concern was that she was involved in a relationship with a young Chinese boy at the same school. The worker used probing techniques to examine what this concern was about, and the following picture emerged. The father had no worries that a sexual relationship was involved. The boy's family was prosperous and united, integrated within a predominantly white neighbourhood, although prominent members of the Chinese community. As the father responded to the worker's probes, his anger and anxiety appeared increasingly unrealistic and prejudiced and he left, more accepting of his daughter's choice and aware of his own stereotypes, although with continuing anxiety about the development of the relationship.

Probing for what is missing as someone tells a story is important as a means of intervention. A resident in a centre for people with physical disabilities was describing, with amusement, being asked to leave a pub. The worker probed about the reasons: the resident had been told that because she was in a wheelchair she was a fire risk. The worker probed further about whether the resident thought that was true or the real reason, and the resident identified prejudice and discrimination as the probable reasons for exclusion. The worker probed further: what had the resident felt? The resident said she was used to it, but on further probing said it was hurtful and made her angry. The worker and she then looked at whether she could use these feelings to try to challenge the situation, given that disability discrimination is illegal. They agreed to go back to the pub together and jointly try to educate the publican and challenge his prejudice.

Giving information and advice

Sometimes a user of services may not be able to deal with a problem because of lack of relevant information or misinformation. New information can lead to a new perspective, i.e. reframing a problem (Smale *et al.*, 2000).

In working with people who have experienced loss or bereavement I have found that giving information about normal reactions, e.g. anxieties about going mad or 'seeing' the lost person, has helped people to accept that this is what has to be undergone, and reassured them that they are not crazy. While this does not relieve the pain it frees the bereaved person to tolerate the processes of grief without additional anxieties, and to be more prepared to face the pain rather than try to avoid it.

Similarly, for carers dealing with people with dementia, clear information about how dementia may develop, progress or be contained and what services are available can provide both a useful realization of what the range of 'normal' reactions are and more importantly what services might be available (Hunter, 1997; Killick and Allan, 2002). For carers who are supporting people with mental health problems, similar advice about their origin, medication and prognosis and about services available is essential.

Where parents bring problems in dealing with their children's behaviour, giving them information about normal child development and behaviour at different stages can be helpful, in a preventative way, by providing them with a new perspective (Aldgate and Simmonds, 1988). Temper tantrums, bed wetting or difficulties in getting to sleep are examples of behaviour which parents often see as problematic and deviant, and try to punish or eradicate. Information about the normality of such behaviour at certain ages can relieve parental anxiety that the child is disturbed or the parents have gone wrong. They are then more open to considering alternative ways of responding to normal, if irritating, behaviour. Practical information can help parents to problem solve. Information about the use and availability of a bell and buzzer can help a child and parents to deal constructively and effectively with a bed-wetting problem. Information about respite care and sitter services can help the parents of a child or adult with severe learning difficulties in making decisions about ongoing care. A parent who feels desperate and overburdened by the demands of basic care for an adolescent with learning disabilities may reluctantly contemplate long-term residential care. The provision of information about alternatives may lead to more effective decision making and problem solving where the parent gets some respite from the demands of care without the necessity of what would have felt like rejection, and the young person makes the journey to adulthood via, for example, supported but independent accommodation.

Giving advice is an explicit social influence technique and an intervention which can contribute to problem solving. In Chapter 3 we looked at considerations involved in deciding whether it was appropriate to give advice. In particular we have to be careful that the advice is not simply a reflection of our own need to feel useful or of our values, but does respond to the need for a user of services for some structure and direction.

Giving advice effectively can only be done when we have established an influence base and when users of services expect and are receptive to it (Kadushin and Kadushin, 1997; Maluccio, 1979; Mayer and Timms, 1970; Trevithick, 2005). As Kadushin and Kadushin (1997) argue:

We are expected to have some knowledge, some expertise, about social problems and the variety of alternatives to their amelioration. We are supposed to have had some repetitive experience with the probable consequences of the various solutions available. All this gives the social worker the legitimate grounds for offering advice. (p. 11)

However our advice must come from knowledge, expertise and experience. Users of services have also expressed their wish for and appreciation of advice and guidance (Mayer and Timms, 1970; SCIE, 2004a and c).

There are different degrees of directiveness and explicitness in giving advice. 'I think you should do X' is more directive than 'Have you thought of doing X?' but each can be relevant and useful. If I am working with someone who appears to be depressed and not eating or sleeping I will say, 'I think you should go to your GP' and I will follow that up by trying to ensure that the advice is taken. If someone is having problems with benefits I will say, 'I think you should go to the Welfare Rights office' and I would, with permission, ring to try to arrange an appointment. Explicit, directive advice can be empowering for a user of services. If someone was being sexually harassed at work I would say that I think she ought to contact her trade union and consider formal complaint procedures. I would advise someone equally firmly if they were experiencing racial discrimination.

In other circumstances I would use a more tentative form of advice. For example, if a carer is becoming increasingly worn down by looking after an elderly frail parent, I would say, 'Given how frail your mother is, have you thought about a care package?' If a parent is complaining about a toddler's temper tantrum I might ask, 'Have you ever thought of ignoring it?' or 'Have you ever thought …?' and describe the use of time out.

Summarizing and focussing

Summarizing and focussing are intervention skills as well as ingredients of making a contract (see Chapter 8). They also give a user of services a new perspective on his or her situation, reframing the problem (Smale *et al.*, 2000) and providing 'leverage' on problem identification and solving (Egan, 2007) by helping someone identify and prioritize major areas for change. When we summarize effectively, we feed back to a user of services their story, but in a selective way, highlighting what we see as major issues. This selection is a form of influence. So, for example, a parent has multiple concerns about her four-year-old son's behaviour. The worker selects and summarizes:

'So you are worried about lots of aspects of Jack's behaviour but it seems to me your main concerns are:
- first, he nips the baby
- second, he won't go to sleep at night and comes into your bed
- third, he has temper tantrums when he doesn't get his own way.'

Here the worker selects from an overwhelming catalogue of complaints what she perceives as the major concerns and in doing so renders the problems more discrete, specific, identifiable and thereby manageable. The mother begins to sense that the problems are not completely uncontrollable and selects the failure to go to sleep as the most immediate one to address. The change is her feeling that the problems are not insoluble but that she and the worker can jointly begin to identify ways in which she can manage them.

Focussing, similarly, can reframe complex and overwhelming problem situations by identifying and selecting the major concerns. Focussing can also identify themes, e.g. rejection, loss, discrimination, abuse or dependency, which may underly a myriad of apparently unconnected presenting problems. For a user of services to realize that a theme is persistent and recurrent may offer a different perspective on current problems, which begin to make sense in the light of past experience. Equally importantly, with that understanding, they may also put aside the 'emotional baggage' of the past and be freer to deal more competently with here-and-now problems. A woman was extremely self-critical and lacking in trust in herself and others. Over time she brought numerous problem situations where her negativity sabotaged her own actions and abilities and her relationships. The worker focussed on the theme of her harsh self-criticism and excessive demands of herself and others. This focus brought home to her the pattern of her behaviour and she began to explore what had led to it. Gradually she became able to stop herself being so self-critical on significant occasions and was more able to live with herself and manage what she had previously experienced as insurmountable problems.

Interpretation

Interpretation involves more than reflection or clarification: using these techniques we stay within the frame of reference of the user of services.

When we interpret, however, we extend or challenge that frame of reference by using alternative ones to suggest explanations of behaviour or attitudes. Kadushin and Kadushin (1997) suggest:

> A clarification, paraphrase or reflection stays close to the message presented by the client. Interpretation takes off from the message and includes an inference derived from it, one added by the interviewer. It is what the interviewer heard plus what the interview inferred. (p. 175)

Interpretations do involve inference; they will vary according to theoretical orientation (Payne, 2002). A structural orientation would emphasize structural influences such as poverty, gender or ethnicity or disability. A psychodynamic orientation would stress the unconscious influence of the past on present attitudes and behaviour. A cognitive orientation would emphasize the influence of faulty cognitive processes on behaviour. These orientations are not incompatible: both outer structural influences and inner emotional and cognitive influences affect our behaviour.

An interpretation from a different perspective can challenge someone's current perspective, attitudes or behaviour. For example, a colleague working in an intake team with users of services who predominantly are poor interprets their current difficulties as structural: this challenges their conviction that poverty is their personal responsibility and due to mismanagement. This structural perspective frees both worker and service users to be more realistic about financial management, in particular about prioritizing. It does not solve the problem of poverty but it challenges their feelings of personal responsibility and guilt.

Interpretation involves making connections for people between apparently random current behaviours, between thoughts, feelings, attitudes and behaviours which have not previously been seen as connected or between past influences and present attitudes and behaviour.

Our ability in social work and social care to integrate very different perspectives (structural, social and individual) about origins of problems for users of services gives us a potential considerable influence in interdisciplinary assessment and intervention. We need to use this interpretation to articulate, verbally, the different possible factors leading to the current problematic situation and the implications for partnership working between users of services, ourselves and interdisciplinary colleagues.

Interpretations are conjectures or hypotheses but we have to be careful to make them on the basis of sufficient information. Otherwise they are simply random guesses. They have to be made tentatively, since they reflect our perceptions which may not tally with the other person's view of the situation, what is wrong or needs to be changed. In my own research which involved directly observing social workers' behaviour (1985), I found that they varied enormously in the way they offered interpretation. Some appeared arrogant: failing to check that they were understanding correctly or putting comments in such a way as to override the client and leave no room for disagreement. Others checked out that they were understanding or put an interpretation more hesitantly or as a question.

Interpretations which are pure guesses or leave no room for disagreement are likely to lead to clashes in perspective, whereas tentativeness and checking out reduce the risk of this. This applies to verbal communication with users of services but also our colleagues, where a tentative 'Is this what you are thinking?' is much more enabling than 'I gather (assume) this is what you are thinking'.

To be effective in problem solving, an interpretation has to be seen as valid by the other person. Kadushin and Kadushin (1997) suggest it is more likely to be effective if it introduces only a slight discrepancy from the other person's view of the situation.

Winnicott (1971) conveyed clearly the importance of a person's perception of how valid an interpretation is: 'An interpretation that does not work always means that I have made the interpretation at the wrong moment or in the wrong way and I withdraw it unconditionally' (p. 9). Users of services can disconfirm workers' interpretations either by disagreeing or more commonly ignoring them. Often if an interpretation is ignored the worker unhelpfully assumes that it is accepted without checking.

A successful interpretation occurred when a worker made a verbal link between a mother's current anxieties about her eight-year-old son's behaviour, including soiling and stealing, and her residual feelings about her brother who had the same name as her son and had been a bad lot and ended up in prison. The mother began to see that her anxieties about her son did not belong to him and were more about the past. She also saw that she might be engaged in a self-fulfilling prophecy: the more anxious she was about her son's behaviour the more he behaved in ways which justified her anxiety. As she began to see her son more realistically his behaviour improved.

In summary, Kadushin and Kadushin (1997) highlight useful overall guidelines for offering effective interpretations:

- We need to have established a positive working relationship.
- We need to view and present the interpretation as a hypothesis which may not be accepted.
- We need to be sensitive to concerns about it and accept rejection.

Challenging or confrontation

Challenging and confrontation were defined in Chapter 3 as ways of feeding back discrepancies to users of services about their behaviour, thinking or feelings, to be used sensitively and cautiously and not in ways which might escalate a clash in perspective or stand-off.

Kadushin and Kadushin (1997) aid our understanding about using confrontation as an effective intervention: in particular, 'confrontation deals with incongruities' and 'stimulates self examination'. While it does not directly lead to changes in behaviour it confronts users of services with inconsistencies and distortion in their self-perceptions and behaviours, and can be a way of questioning problematic behaviours, for example in terms of substance abuse, offending or child care.

In an analysis of social workers' behaviour (Lishman, 1985) I defined confrontation as 'statements which face the client either with behaviour of which he/she is not aware, or which he/she wishes to avoid looking at, or with some discrepancy in his or her behaviour between words and deeds, attitudes and behaviour'.

For example, a social worker confronted one offender in the criminal justice system – a probationer who had been on a stealing 'binge' and then given himself up to the police – as follows: 'What if I say to you that behaving as you did almost sounds to me as if you were asking to be taken back inside?'. Confrontation may also be necessary in working with parents whose substance abuse is impacting negatively on the care of their children although parent and child attachments and concern remain strong.

Smale *et al.* (2000) propose that 'challenging refers … [to] the ability of staff to confront people effectively with their responsibilities, their problem perpetuating or creating behaviours and their conflicting interests' (p. 226).

Egan (2007) stresses the importance of challenging in helping people change and problem solve. He suggests it can involve the following:

- stimulating awareness of relevant experiences, attitudes or behaviour;
- feeding back people's incomplete interpretation of experiences, behaviours or attitudes;
- feeding back to them their lack of understanding of the consequences of their behaviour;
- feeding back discrepancies in their lives, e.g. between attitudes and behaviour;
- challenging them when they hesitate to act on their new understanding.

In these different ways of confronting or challenging we are facing users of services with contradictions, distortions, inconsistencies or discrepancies and inviting or stimulating them to reconsider and resolve the contradictions. While such a reconsideration does not in itself change behaviour, the readjustment of interpretations and attitudes involved can lead to behavioural change. The ultimate goal of challenging, however, is problem reformulation, action and change. We also need to remember that we may find it helpful to use these skills with our colleagues as well as users of services. If a medical colleague, engaged with a family where substance abuse is damaging child care, is using an entirely medical model, how may I use challenging, as problem reformulation, to include in the assessment structural and social issues which need also to be addressed for change to occur?

Confronting or challenging needs to be sensitively and carefully done. As Trevithick (2005) argues, 'people who have experienced too many "put downs" or too much humiliation in their lives can be extremely sensitive to challenges of any kind' (p. 238). Trotter (2007), in relation to child protection, points out that confrontation was most effectively used if it focussed on positive rather than negative reinforcement. We should not assume that this applies only to users of services, but remember our colleagues may also have difficulty in dealing with confrontation.

We now examine some different components of challenging: stimulating awareness, exploring and outlining consequences of behaviour, challenging discrepancies, distortions, self-defeating thoughts and omissions and challenging people about hesitancy to act.

Stimulating awareness

We are all sometimes unaware of our behaviour and its impact, and also our thought processes and our feelings and these blocks may be a major contribution to our problems. If shyness is presented as aloof or arrogant behaviour it may be difficult to make relationships. If we think (faultily) that whatever we do is doomed to failure we may never start anything. If we feel unlovable or lacking in self-esteem we may withdraw from relationships, or fail to pick up any positive messages from other people. Stimulating awareness may be about behaviour, thoughts or feelings.

1. *Behaviour*: if a user of services trusts the worker and values her or his opinions, the worker's feedback about how they behave or present may be a useful challenge. I worked with a young woman who had very low self-esteem and very little trust in other people for good reason. (She had had very unreliable parenting but her strength had been that she was academically very able and

successful.) Over time she began to trust me and gradually I was able to feed back to her how suspicious and hostile she had initially appeared to me. She was able to see that she did behave like this with people who were new to her and that it was threatening and offputting to them. This awareness helped her to change her behaviour: quite consciously she practised and began to give more positive verbal and non-verbal messages, even to new acquaintances, and she found them reciprocated.

DVDs and audiotapes can also feed back to users of services about their presentation and behaviour. However, care has to be exercised: to use a DVD to feed back to a depressed person their negative presentation is likely to further reinforce the depression. In contrast, to show a rather abrasive person the impact of their presentation may help her or him decide to modify it.

2. *Thoughts or cognitions*: faulty or irrational beliefs or cognitive states can lead to problems of anxiety, depression, negative self-esteem, and general inability to problem solve. Ellis (1962) suggested that often people have ways of thinking which keep them locked into their problems: we can call these self-limiting or self-defeating thoughts. Dryden and Scott (1991) usefully summarize these self-defeating thoughts as follows:

- 'I must do well or very well!
- I must be approved or accepted by people I find important
- I am a bad person if I get rejected
- People must treat me fairly and give me what I need
- People must live up to my expectations
- My life must have few major hassles or troubles
- I cannot stand very difficult people or issues'

As workers in social care or social work we may want to reflect on whether we ever apply these self-limiting thoughts to our own situation. When we pick up evidence of these ways of thinking in ourselves or users of services we can question them or challenge them by providing an alternative more rational belief. Essentially life is not always fair and people may at times let us down but that does not mean we are bad or unworthy, i.e. that we deserved what has happened.

3. *Feelings*: people who use our services bring to us horrendous stories of loss, deprivation or abuse. Quite often they present appalling histories with little affect. They have learned that certain feelings such as anger or sadness are unacceptable to their families and must never be expressed, or that they are so vulnerable that expression would have little point. However hidden or 'repressed' anger

at persistent abuse or deprivation is likely to affect current functioning: it may lead to depression, low self-esteem, or inability to sustain relationships and a general unease with the emotional or relationship aspects of life. It may also lead to repeating the pattern of rejection and abuse in relation to their own children. I have found it useful to feed back an emotional response, 'Listening to your story makes me feel extremely angry' or 'extremely sad' and I always mean it. Often the users of services look quite shocked, but my response stimulates them to think back to how they might have felt: it gives permission to experience feelings they have repressed. Similarly it can be useful to say, 'Often, in your circumstances, people feel X'. Again this introduces the possibility of hidden or forbidden feelings and the normality of experiencing them.

Finally it can sometimes be useful to say, 'You have told me about your childhood but it is almost as if you have no emotion. If your daughter (aged 8) told you she was being treated in this way what would you feel?' Putting the user of services into a more distanced position of a child other than themselves may help them to experience feelings on behalf of a vulnerable other which really belong to their own childhood.

4. *Missing thoughts or feelings*: here we draw attention to what is important but avoided or left unsaid. For example if a single parent is referred to us because of concerns about her or his child care, and then he or she focusses on the difficulty of getting the local authority to deal with juvenile delinquency on the housing estate we need to be able to challenge and refocus on the concerns about parent's child care.

5. *Incomplete perceptions or interpretation*: here we sense that the user of services is seeing things in a very limited or incomplete way. For example an adolescent girl had run away from home and complained of her mother's nagging and very restrictive rules. The social worker examined the mother's expectations in more detail: gradually the girl began to acknowledge that the restrictions arose from the concern about her safety and were not punitive in intent.

Helping people to explore consequences of behaviour or actions

Here we invite users of services to explore or confront themselves with the potential consequences of what they choose to do. Exploring the likely consequences of a range of decisions is a means of making decisions based on predicted outcomes. A woman who was pregnant was discussing the option of termination, adoption or keeping the baby. Although she was in a long-term relationship with a partner she made no mention of him. The worker questioned this and invited her to think of the consequences of a decision made without consulting the baby's father, her partner.

Exploring consequences may be very important in work where we carry statutory authority. People who offend and who do not turn up for supervision need to be confronted with the consequences of their action: potentially recall, a court hearing and possible imprisonment. Similarly, where we have concerns about child care we will have to confront parents with any failure to meet conditions of supervision and its consequences. For example, failure to be available weekly for a home visit with the social worker where the child is present or failure to have the children at nursery on a regular basis will result in an early review at a child protection conference and may lead to the possibility of the children being taken into care.

Challenging discrepancies, distortion, self-defeating beliefs, games and excuses

We need to challenge a range of attitudes and behaviours including the following:

1. *Discrepancies*: discrepancies occur between verbal and non-verbal behaviour, between what we think or say and what we do, between our own views of ourselves and others' views.

   Often we are not aware of discrepancies and here challenges may provide useful feedback and the opportunity of reviewing our behaviour and choosing to alter it. The worker may comment on discrepancies between verbal and non-verbal behaviour. A man maintained that he did not see the value or purpose of becoming angry: he always maintained calm. As he spoke he looked and sounded more and more angry and became quite flushed: the worker pointed out the discrepancy between what he said and how he looked. The comment led him to think about why he found it so important not to be angry and the impact on his family (with whom he was having difficulty) of these rather mixed messages.

   We may challenge statements which do not seem consistent with normal behaviour. For example, a woman said consistently that she never felt angry with her children. The worker challenged this by expressing surprise: never to feel angry seemed unusual for parents! Again this led to exploration around anger, and the woman gradually became more able to express appropriate anger to her children and set appropriate boundaries. In response, gradually their behaviour became more manageable.

We may challenge someone's perception of self: 'You see yourself as funny: other people have been saying you are sarcastic'. We may challenge when a user of services says one thing and appears to do very differently: a man protested how much he cared for his wife and children but the worker challenged how little time he seemed to spend with them.

Finally we may challenge discrepancies in a very positive way. A user of services may present a catalogue of failures and disasters. In contrast the worker is aware of considerable strength and achievements and feeds these back: 'You say you've achieved nothing. Over the last six weeks you've told me about your pay rise at work, your daughter getting an apprenticeship and you and your partner having a night out for the first time in ten years and enjoying it. Is that nothing?'.

We also need, in a commitment to reflection and evaluation (Fook, 2007; Lishman, 2007; Schon, 1983; Shaw and Lishman, 1999), to ensure that we check and challenge our own behaviour. For example, can we be entirely confident that our non-verbal behaviour corresponds with our verbal communication or that we have not allowed our own experiences, for example of poverty, discrimination, parental negativity or loss, to skew our interpretations of what users of services say in what might be a distorting way?

2. *Distortions*: here users of services may find it difficult to see other people in realistic ways. A young man had been brought up by a powerful domineering grandmother. In relationships with women he always experienced them as overpowering and critical. The (female) social worker observed this pattern and fed back to him how he always interpreted her remarks as critical. This made her feel quite helpless and powerless. Her perception was a direct challenge to his distortion of her. He was taken aback and then began to examine when and how he interpreted her comments and distorted them. This began a process whereby he more often perceived women more realistically. Someone may have a distorted view of how their behaviour is perceived and received and might need to be challenged about how other people experience it, for example as abruptness, aggressiveness or potentially threatening.

3. *Self-defeating beliefs*: we examined these earlier in terms of raising awareness of when people were engaging in self-defeating beliefs. It is also important for the worker to challenge a user of services whenever he or she slips back into self-defeating beliefs, even after

having become aware of them. For example, a mother felt responsible for everything in her family and that she had to do everything and do it right. Not surprisingly, she felt exhausted and depressed. She was aware of her self-defeating beliefs but still got caught up in them. The worker challenged, 'There you go again, expecting 100% of yourself and punishing yourself when you don't quite make it. What about the 99% done well?'.

The more we pick up on and challenge self-defeating beliefs, the more likely users of services are to be aware of when they are beginning a self-defeating sequence and to challenge themselves out of it. People can use thought stopping (simply refusing to think about the particular negative set of thoughts) or self-talk (talking oneself out of them) as a means of self-challenge (Egan, 2007). In working with a user of services with a very self-destructive history I always picked up on statements about his badness, worthlessness and unloveableness, fed them back to him and challenged their accuracy in the light of his current behaviour and performance. Gradually he took this on board for himself: when he started to think such self-defeating thoughts he would question or challenge them or practise thought stopping until his current pessimistic mood had passed.

4. *Games*: Berne (1968) identified 'games people play' in relationships and interactions: the games have a manipulative element and the danger is of getting hooked into the game, and thus being restricted in one's ability to help. One game is the 'Yes, but' game where a user of services presents as helpless and desperately needing the worker's help, advice and guidance, but then deskills the worker by conveying that whatever she or he offers is ineffective: there is always a 'but'!

Initially we have to set up a climate which discourages all of us from playing games. For example, in the 'Yes, but' game we are more vulnerable if we present as the expert, whose wisdom is then never quite right. In contrast, if we are clear where responsibility for the problems and their solutions lies, the 'yes but' game is less effective.

Sometimes, however, a user of services will persist in attempting games even if the atmosphere is not encouraging, and we have to challenge the games playing. A very passive young man would present his difficulties and problems, look helplessly at me and then sit and wait. If there was a silence he would look helpless and wait for me to fill it, which initially I did. I began to feel I was doing all the work and I challenged him with the game I felt he was attempting to hook me into of 'Rescue me'. I saw this as a game he played in other aspects of life, taking little responsibility but then feeling resentful at other people taking over. Within sessions I refused to 'rescue': we sat out some long silences and he began to be more active in considering his difficulties and potential ways of managing them. In interprofessional communication we also need to be aware of potential unconscious games being enacted, including who enacts the role of the expert and who is the 'yes but'. Another interprofessional game is 'not my responsibility' or 'passing the buck'.

5. *Excuses*: we all make excuses for ourselves at times, but excuse making can be problematic if it leads to avoidance of problems or disowning of responsibility. Excuses leading to avoidance include complacency ('It won't happen to me') and procrastination ('It doesn't need to be dealt with now') (Egan, 2007). Both need to be challenged as ways of avoiding problems or problem solving. They are no basis for work or changing attitudes or behaviour or problem solving.

Disowning responsibility is expressed by 'I'm not the person responsible' (Egan, 2007). This is often expressed when there are problems in relationships, for example between parents and children, in partnerships, or in intergenerational conflicts, and has to be challenged if there is to be work to improve the relationships. One colleague, when faced with a parent or partner who said, 'It's not me …, it's her/him', would say 'It takes two to tango' and then go on to set out the way he worked: that a breakdown in a relationship was the responsibility of each person involved. The task now was to work on ways where each person could contribute to improving it. Family group conferencing similarly uses the solution-focussed approach (Lupton, 1998). Similarly, interprofessional colleagues can all work in organizational and funding silos: bed blocking is an example of the wish to transfer financial responsibility from one budget (health) to another (social care) where the interests of both service user and carer get lost.

Recognizing the use of discrepancies, distortion, games and excuses is an important element of statutory work in criminal justice and child care.

Challenging can be an effective way of helping people to reconsider attitudes and behaviours and to change them. However it always needs to be done with care.

Challenging can only take place on the basis of a good relationship. The user of services has to trust the worker and to feel properly understood otherwise a challenge may be heard as a criticism. Challenges are better delivered tentatively like interpretations; they are then more likely to be seen as a basis for discussion rather than a criticism. We must combine challenges with understanding and empathy. The other person needs to feel that the worker is 'with' him or her and that the challenge is based on positive regard and a realistic appreciation of the client's difficulties and potential for change.

Challenging strengths rather than weaknesses is more effective (Egan, 2007; Trotter, 2007). This means challenging people with their assets or resources, which they may not recognize. Challenging or confrontation is not the same as criticism, putting people down or *making* them face things: these activities are unethical and will arouse anxiety, hostility and defensiveness.

Good challenging or confrontation arises out of our concern and respect for other people, our understanding of their predicament and our desire to help them to deal more effectively with their problems. Kadushin and Kadushin (1997) suggest that '[t]he best confrontation mirrors the Bible's admonition to "speak the truth in love"' (p. 166).

We really need to be better in applying this admonition in working with our colleagues, whether in social work, social care or other disciplines. We also need to use challenging in relation to ourselves and our attitudes. Such challenging or confrontation may become the basis of agreed and shared longer-term intervention with users of services whether in counselling, advocacy, task-centred or behavioural work (Coulshed and Orme, 2006). In the literature on interdisciplinary work (Barrett *et al.*, 2005, Quinney, 2006), challenging does not appear as a major feature in communication between colleagues from different disciplines – but it is. How do I as a social worker or social care worker promote and support an assessment of a user of services which is holistic, including their impairment or disability *and* their social circumstances, and involves, at least, housing, income and family and other support, if the dominant assessment is medical. I, as a social worker or social care worker, need to challenge this medical model (Oliver, 1996) and use the skills identified in this chapter to do so.

Conclusion

In conclusion we need to reflect on how we use these skills in terms of power and authority. Generally users of services have little power and authority in their relationship with us as service providers. On the other hand, medical consultants do. We need to take care that in our use of challenging and confrontation we do not use these skills differentially in terms of relative power and authority.

putting it into practice

Once more, think about a recent encounter with a 'helping professional' for example GP or lawyer. Reflect back on whether they used any of the intervention techniques identified in this chapter, for example clarification or challenging, and, if so, how effective these were in helping you to think, problem solve and behave differently.

You might want to think about this in relation to friends who in general support our long-held modes of dealing with life and family. Currently I am dealing with family health and relationship problems. Friends are incredibly supportive but would I be better helped by a more challenging approach?

Now think of yourself as the professional social worker or social care worker. Which of Payne's (2002) models of intervention is your main starting point? In which social work or social care area do you work – child care, criminal justice or community care? What are the specific applications to your field?

In terms of non-verbal influence use video feedback to observe how you behave, for example in terms of empathy, responsiveness, power and authority.

In terms of verbal influence and intervention consider how you convey empathy and how you challenge. I find being empathic much easier than challenging but know that challenging needs to be done. List recent examples of when you have challenged someone, when and why it worked or did not.

Recommended reading

Kadushin, A. and Kadushin, G. (1997) *The Social Work Interview*, 4th edn, New York, Columbia University Press. While examining social work interviewing in an American psychotherapeutic context, this book continues to have huge relevance in how we may use communication to contribute to effective outcomes for users of services.

Trevithick, P. (2005) *Social Work Skills: A Practice Handbook*, Maidenhead, Open University Press. An essential textbook on the social work skills required for understanding, assessment and effective intervention.

Barrett, G., Sellman, D. and Thomas, J. (2005) *Interprofessional Working in Health and Social Care: Professional Perspectives*, Basingstoke, Palgrave Macmillan. This book about interprofessional work helps us to understand where each of the professions comes from in terms of values, professional culture, knowledge and research. To understand and appreciate these differences can help us to engage in better interprofessional communication including the use of response, empathy and challenging.

Lishman, J. (2007) *Handbook for Practice Learning in Social Work and Social Care*, London, Jessica Kingsley. Section 3 examines models of intervention in detail, including cognitive behavioural, task centre, crisis intervention, family therapy and group care.

10 Intervention: written techniques for changing attitudes and behaviours

This chapter draws on the literature review in Chapter 4 but applies it more specifically to effective social work intervention. How can we use written techniques in helping users of services to problem solve or change attitudes or behaviour? As we discussed previously, putting things in writing makes them concrete. Words spoken can disappear: we forget or lose what seemed important in a previous interview. Writing things down can be a way of holding onto difficult or complex attitudes or feelings while they are being worked on and can make it difficult to avoid them. If we write down problematic, promised actions, the paper represents a commitment (although we can of course tear it up!). It also is a means of review. If we write down strong or forbidden feelings we are more likely to acknowledge them and face them: in talking they can drift away. Sometimes a user of services may write a letter to a worker in order to share difficult feelings or experiences, for example about abuse or sexuality, which he or she would find too threatening to begin to explore face to face. Similarly communicating in writing using a website, we have seen, can offer anonymity and confidentiality to a user of service who feels harmed, abused or ashamed, for example, about mental health problems, child abuse or sexual abuse. As we saw in Chapter 4, we also need to be aware of the longevity and legal status of written communication whether paper-, email- or web-based. It is rightfully a record which may be used to hold us accountable.

Written techniques can help in the following areas: decision taking, changing attitudes, monitoring and changing behaviours and dealing more effectively with feelings, or with the past.

Decision taking

Users of services and colleagues can be encouraged to use brainstorming (see Chapter 8) to generate ideas about action to bring about change or problem solving. Brainstorming is a creative activity in which all ideas, however crazy, are written down and judgement is suspended. It helps free people from the tramlines of conventional thinking which probably have been limited in addressing the needs or solving the problems which I, as a user of services or a colleague, am experiencing.

It can generate a feeling of enthusiasm or hope. A woman was moving out of psychiatric care into an unfurnished flat. She had very few possessions and very little money. She brainstormed possible ways of getting furnishings and appliances. Her list included the following:

- take out a loan;
- rob a bank;
- ask friends for the contents of their attics;
- apply to social services;
- go to the minister;
- ask her sister to lend her some money.

While we don't judge ideas when they are being brainstormed because this inhibits creativity, once the written list is complete we can begin to evaluate the ideas. Some will be discarded as wild or impractical, but from the reduced list we can begin to weigh up pros and cons of each action in order to decide the most feasible and potentially effective. Here we can evaluate the potential actions in terms of priorities and goals, and if a decision is reached it will be owned by all and not imposed.

A useful way of evaluating potential actions is to draw up a list of costs and benefits for each. A service user was offered a job several hundred miles away and was confused and ambivalent about whether to take it or stay where he was. The worker encouraged him to draw up a list of costs and benefits for each alternative action. His list included the following:

Option	Costs	Benefits
Moving to take the job	Distance from family Homelessness? Housing Unsure Whether I can do it	More money Challenge Opportunity to make friends
Staying in current job	Boring Lower pay Loneliness	Security Near family Know what I'm doing

How we weigh up such a list of costs and benefits will depend partly on temperament and personality. If we value change and excitement they are likely to outweigh a number of costs: similarly the importance of security may outweigh other costs. Reality about the likelihood of costs and benefits also needs to inform decisions.

Finally in deciding on actions it can be useful to write down a timescale for achieving them. This has to be realistic but writing down when we will do things acts as a pressure to do them: 'I will go to the Job Centre on Tuesday' holds more commitment than 'I will go to the Job Centre.'

Brainstorming is also a very useful technique for team working whether in social work, social care or interprofessional settings. It enables us to consider a range of perspectives, for example about assessment and intervention or resource allocation, and to challenge and evaluate them and thereby potentially agree shared action. Written agreement about timescales and individual responsibilities is also essential for effective team and interdisciplinary action and intervention. A written record (paper or email) holds us to our professional accountability to undertake this action by a specific deadline.

Changing attitudes

In the previous chapter we discussed self-defeating beliefs. Writing is a very useful way of challenging them. For example, I have often asked users of services to write down a list of the good things about themselves. Sometimes I would give this as homework and ask them to bring it back to the next session. Sometimes I would ask them to do it with me in the interview. Frequently they would say how much easier it was to write down the negatives. Many of them had to do this before they could start on the positives. The written list of the negatives could then be used to examine their perception in more detail and challenge them. Some users of services really struggled to find positive things about themselves or if they did disqualified them:

'Well, I work hard but it makes me irritable.'
'I am a good housekeeper but I shout too much at the children.'

While many users of services do not suffer from low self-esteem or a negative self-image but simply require a service which social work and social care may (or may not) be able to provide, other users of services do battle with a negative self-image. Working with them to challenge this and identify their strengths is an important skill in social work which draws on working with their resilience and social work values of the worth and uniqueness of every person (Clark, 2000).

Questioning and prompting are useful skills in reminding a user of services of what we have perceived as his or her strengths. When I have used these techniques and successfully persuaded users of services to complete an analysis of their strengths and weaknesses but highlight their strengths they express a sense of achievement: somehow forcing them to think of their *positives* had helped them to own them and believe in them.

It is important to acknowledge how difficult users of services find the task of changing self-image. A negative self-image may represent a major contribution to the problems many users of services bring to social work and social care. We need to remain aware of this and challenge them about how they need to recognize positive attitudes and behaviours. For example, young people, who are homeless and may be using illegal drugs, may have experienced a lifetime of parental abuse and rejection, changes in care plans and little or no educational stability and achievement, and may be more likely to commit crime. Project workers, for example in voluntary organizations' projects, can effectively help these young people to change by agreeing a contract and change programme and providing support in housing, employment, social skills and substance misuse programmes. Putting this in writing reinforces the reciprocal requirements on the service user and the project.

Monitoring and changing behaviour

This book is not about detailed techniques of behavioural and cognitive behavioural intervention. Such an analysis is dealt with in the work of, for example, Sheldon (1995), Hudson and Sheldon (2000) and Macdonald (2007) and is particularly relevant in terms of criminal justice (McIvor, 2007; McIvor and Raynor, 2007). However, the principles involved in behavioural and cognitive behavioural work may usefully be used as a written tool for communication and intervention, in particular when the worker and user of services are clear about which behaviours are problematic and distressing, but also recognize which are potentially amenable to change. If we agree about this (and Chapter 8 on assessment and contract setting stresses how crucial this agreement about purpose and desired outcome is), we also need a baseline as to when and how often undesirable behaviours occur. Such a baseline may be recorded by using a graph or, as Sheldon (1995) suggests, by diaries kept by users of services in which they can record 'both occurrences and reflections'. Sometimes the act of recording baselines can in itself be helpful. To discover that a problematic behaviour, e.g. an adolescent shouting at a parent (which has come to assume major proportions for the parent) in reality occurs only once in two days, may enable the parent to see the behaviour as less overwhelming in the context of the rest of the time (the majority) spent in more positive interaction.

Even where such recording of the baseline is not in itself therapeutic, it is necessary in order to identify whether over time the problematic behaviour improves. If it does, the recording of the improvement may itself be therapeutic and reinforce positive change. For example, star charts for children operate on the principle that an observed and recorded decline in problematic behaviour, accompanied by parental praise, will reinforce continued more acceptable behaviour.

A second aspect of baseline diary keeping is for the user of services to record what precedes the problematic behaviour and what follows it. In behavioural terms, what is the stimulus to which particular behaviour is a response and what reinforces the behaviour. For example, such a diary might show that a child's temper tantrums were generally preceded by his baby sibling waking up, or it might show that they were reinforced by being given a sweet, by parental attention, or by being allowed to stay up later. This sequence is known as the ABC of a behavioural approach (Coulshed and Orme, 2006): A is the antecedent, B the behaviour and C the consequence. When they are recorded in detail we may jointly with the users of services begin to identify the components most amenable to change, e.g. not rewarding problematic behaviour by sweets or attention.

In cognitive behavioural intervention not only is behaviour and its antecedents and consequences recorded but also feelings and interpretations of users of services. According to Dryden and Scott (1991) the cognitive model suggests that 'people are less disturbed by events in themselves and more by the way they view events' (p. 177). In the cognitive behavioural approach, A is the antecedent or stimulus, B the interpretation or evaluation of the event and C the emotional response. A user of services will, therefore, be asked to record not only behaviours but 'events between sessions they experience as upsetting. These may be external events (or interpretation of events) such as being criticised by a spouse (or partner), or internal events' (Scott and Dryden, 1991, p. 178) (see also Trevithick, 2005; Coulshed and Orme, 2006). The recording in itself may be therapeutic. Users of services are also asked to identify and record what they might have said to themselves to get so upset, i.e. to find the B of the ABC model. They are thus helped to begin to recognize any pattern of interpretation which is self-destructive and the worker may be able, from the recording, to identify and challenge such a pattern.

We can also use written techniques to identify alternative responses and behaviours. Hall and Lloyd (1989) suggested an exercise to help women who have been abused to become more assertive but which could be adapted for other desired behavioural change. They propose the following areas as being useful to put down in writing in relation to a situation which the user of services does not handle assertively but would like to change:

- situation/action/words of other person;
- my response;
- my feelings;
- what I wanted to say;
- how I would have chosen to handle the situation assertively.

Dealing with the past

It must be clear that in writing this book I take for granted that communication skills are essential whatever the context of social work and social care, and we need continually to work to improve our skills in using them. Some of effective communication in social work and care draws on behavioural and cognitive theory about current behaviours and attributes, but effective communication also involves a recognition and understanding of how the past influences us.

Written exercises can be more helpful in dealing with the past than face-to-face communication. Written exercises can also be thrown away when the insight they provide is integrated and they are no longer useful.

Some pencil-and-paper tasks may be useful, not just in assessment, but in helping a user of services understand the relevance of the past and perhaps lay some ghosts.

Life snakes or lifelines

This is a line drawn on paper to represent someone's life or part of life.

Priestley and McGuire (1983) suggest that the 'snake' represents our life. So, starting from our childhood, we need to think of events, people or places that were turning points for us and mark these on the snake. We need to mark in things that were important to us at different times and consider how these led to where we are currently. So my snake might begin as shown in Figure 10.1.

For an adult, drawing out a life history in such a way may show more clearly than verbal discussion the impact of past events or 'patterns' of events or behaviour previously unrecognized. For example, the pattern of illness in my male relatives in my childhood emerged clearly.

For children, snakes may be a means by which worker and child try to find out and make sense of the child's history and to acknowledge breaks and discontinuities in care and relationships. They can provide a simple, pictorial alternative to the use of life-story books (see below) (Fahlberg, 1994) although, for children in care with complex histories, a life-story book may be a means of doing greater justice to the child's past and may be necessary in order for the child to have the kind of tangible history (photos, mementos, memories) usually held by parents.

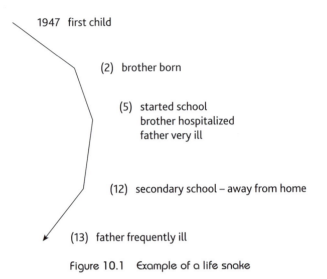

1947 first child

(2) brother born

(5) started school
brother hospitalized
father very ill

(12) secondary school – away from home

(13) father frequently ill

Figure 10.1   Example of a life snake

Genograms

Genograms are like family trees and can fulfil a similar function to life snakes in helping family members to understand past events in their history and to see 'patterns' of events or behaviour previously unrecognized. They can be done by children and may help them to communicate with their parents about aspects of family relationships they have not known or were confused about. Genograms usually start with children of the current family, working from the bottom of the page up. Family members are invited to discuss and write salient issues as they arise in drawing the genogram.

Family trees or genograms become quite complicated. The finished product is not an end in itself but may help a family to communicate better about the past and understand its significance. For example, in my children's genogram, the premature death of their paternal grandfather, whom they never met, had a profound influence on my son who was anxious that the same might happen to his father, particularly after a huge offshore accident in which the father of his friend died. Genograms, by putting complex family history in writing in diagrammatic form in one place, can help families make connections and understand the significance of patterns of behaviour which continue to influence them, e.g. absent men, dominant women, even where all the individual bits were known and remembered by individual family members. Recording by genograms of family separations and reconstituted families also can play

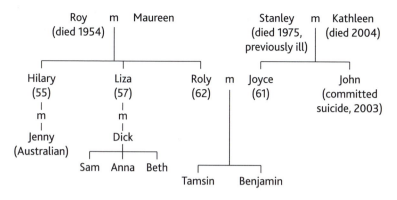

Figure 10.2 Example of a genogram

a major part in helping children and their carers and professionals to understand how the past may have contributed to the present.

Genograms change over an individual's or family's life cycle but understanding our own family history, including its emotional component, is necessary both for social work and care workers so that we can understand other families we work with, without generalizing from our own (Coulshed and Orme, 2006). My own genogram, presented rather starkly and factually in Figure 10.2, may not seem illuminating.

However, used as a written technique to explore the impact of family history on my personal and professional life, it suggests both themes and paradoxes, for example men may historically be vulnerable by death or illness and more recently, separation, divorce or suicide. How may these personal experiences affect how I deal professionally with male and female users of services. In my genogram men may also be strong and robust in long-term marriages with able, successful women.

Throughout this exploration themes of resilience and depression compete. As professionals we need to be aware of how our personal history may influence our professional response (Lishman, 2002). For users of services, family trees or genograms may also provide themes, positive and negative attachments, bonds and potential problems. Coulshed and Orme (2006) refer to the work of Hill (2002) on using networking in social work: 'it is these networks of relatives, friends and neighbours to whom people with problems often turn' (p. 201).

Hill (2002, p. 244) extends the concept of the family tree or geneogram to other diagrams, for example, the ecomap or star diagram where we put the key person in the centre and show how others are connected, and then by concentric circles show how family members view distance and closeness in relation to a key person. (In written communication this is somewhat similar to the non-verbal technique of family sculpting.) Coulshed and Orme (2006) stress the importance in working with families, of recognizing diversity in terms, for example, of class, ethnicity, religion, age or gender but also of recognizing the importance of life cycles, family patterns and networks (genograms are one way of exploring the importance and impact of these on current behaviours and problems brought to social work and social care, and not therefore, unconsciously repeating unhelpful patterns from the past). Another important way of exploring in written communication is the use of Life Story Books.

Life story books

Fahlberg (1994) saw the life story book as 'an opportunity to identify strong feelings about past events, to resolve issues, to correct misperceptions'. This seems to me a useful definition of purpose for each of the written techniques identified in this chapter as ways of exploring and understanding people's personal, family, social and structural histories.

Fahlberg (1994) specified further the purposes of the life story book. It can help a child:

- to organize past events in the chronological schema;
- to aid ego development;
- to increase self-esteem;
- to re-read at her or his own pace;
- to share in an orderly fashion her or his past with selected others;
- to build a sense of trust in the worker who aids in compiling the book;
- to gain acceptance of all facets of her or his life and help the child to accept his or her own past;
- to facilitate bonding (see Aldgate, 2007).

Again these purposes seem equally applicable to other written forms of exploring the past. Writing down a history makes it more tangible and identifies themes. Common themes which emerge for people – children and adults – are of discrimination, rejection, deprivation, loss, stigma and abuse. Listening to and recording such histories can be painful in the extreme and the worker has to be trustworthy, sensitive and empathic. She or he must understand how her or his own personal history might influence her or his interpretation of accounts of users of services and take time to explore with the person the thoughts and feelings which arise for them. A major issue for some users of services is what to do with these feelings from the past: if an abusing father is dead he cannot be challenged and he cannot accept responsibility. For some people identifying the feelings, verbalizing them, understanding where they come from and having them accepted by a trusted worker may be enough. Writing them down (see the next section on dealing with feelings) may be useful. Writing down a history identifies gaps more clearly than oral accounts where some bits get lost in the telling anyway. It may be possible to find the information from other family members or it may be lost: such a loss of history almost has to be grieved for before it can be accepted. Writing down a history identifies distortions and misperceptions, e.g. a child may have thought he was unwanted. The history reveals that his mother was ill and had to go into hospital so he was put into foster care. While the child/adult may question why no other family member was able to take him, and why this was never explained, his mother's concern to have him adequately cared for was not rejection and this misperception can usefully be clarified. The 'child' may now be an eighty-five-year-old man or woman, where the resonances of early rejection make adult choices about future care difficult.

So, finally, for an adult to construct his or her own written history enables her or him to experience some of the feelings which accompanied the original events and heightens the person's awareness of childhood feelings. My experience is that often adults need to grieve over painful childhood experiences, e.g. of inadequate parenting or rejection and the losses involved. Written histories can be a means to begin this process: experiencing the anger and sadness of their losses and the way they were (mis)treated can help adults to resolve some of their childhood pain, to accept some of their past and to be freer of the burden of this pain in adult life.

Dealing with feelings

Lists, diaries and letters are written techniques which aid therapeutic exploration and expression of feelings.

Lists

While checklists have already been discussed, here we discuss how a user of services may be asked to generate his/her own list as a therapeutic intervention. For example, Hall and Lloyd (1989, p 228) suggested it can be helpful to ask a woman who has suffered abuse:

- to write down a list of all the ways in which she is still affected by the abuse;
- to write down the ways she coped with the abuse as a child;
- to write down how she feels she has come to terms with the abuse since coming for help. The list should include her achievements and successes as well as any difficulties;
- to make a list of all the things she did right today;
- to write down what she has done to make herself feel better.

Generally, writing lists remains relevant to users of services (including victims of abuse). Hall and Lloyd (1989) however, remind us of a more generic difficulty: women who have been abused (or have low self-esteem for other reasons) find it difficult to appreciate and acknowledge their strengths. As we have already seen, this is also true for wider groups of users of services, many of whom may find writing a list of problems or weaknesses much easier than a list of strengths. For them, to insist on a list of strengths or achievements may be the beginning of challenging their negative self-image.

For users of services who have difficulty in acknowledging their anger, I have also found that writing a list of 'things that make me angry' can help them to feel safer in expressing such anger than they would do in verbalizing it. This can be helpful in working with carers where admitting to feeling angry may be seen as taboo. Similarly for more anxious or depressed users of services, a list of 'things that make me sad' or 'anxious' may be the beginning of identifying and managing such painful feelings.

Diaries

Diaries and logs have already been considered in relation to providing baselines of problematic behaviour and monitoring cognitive and behavioural changes. Hall and Lloyd (1989) saw other functions of diaries: enhancing self-expression and empowerment, acknowledging change and development, and identifying issues which have been dealt with and those which still recur.

Thus diaries can provide a useful record of the helping process in general including (Hall and Lloyd, 1989):

- expectations of a session or meeting;
- good or bad experiences during sessions;
- new memories;
- connections with the past made during sessions;
- reflections on relationships past and present. (p. 231)

Such a record of thoughts and feelings, like life snakes and genograms, acknowledges and makes concrete and real issues from the past or from current therapeutic work, whereas thoughts come and go and can be forgotten. Diaries can be a valuable means of self-expression in a much wider range of social work settings. For example, an offender in a criminal justice setting may be required to keep a diary of activities and potential anti-social wishes and thoughts. A carer may use a diary to record problematic issues in relation to the care services a user of services is, or is not, receiving.

Letters

Letters also allow the expression of difficult feelings. Hall and Lloyd (1989) suggested:

> Incest survivors can find it very helpful to write letters to significant people from their childhood. It allows them to express feelings which they might never have the courage to express verbally. (p. 229)

It also allows them to express feelings to someone who is dead or to someone they feel will be unable to respond. Again Hall and Lloyd are referring specifically to women who have been abused, but writing a letter can be cathartic and therapeutic for someone who:

● experienced their parenting as unloving, unresponsive, or unreliable;
● has difficulty in confronting or expressing anger verbally;
● finds it difficult to communicate verbally about feeling, with a parent, child or partner;
● has unresolved feelings about someone who is dead;
● is currently more generally dealing with issues in current life which arise from these including ageing parents and adolescent children.

I sometimes ask 'What would you like to say to X?' (parent or partner or child, dead or alive), 'Write it down in a letter'. It may also be useful as a child or parent to do this. For children writing such a letter can be a useful catharsis.

However, if we choose to use email, we need to be cautious: once we press 'send' our angry message goes to the recipient. A letter does not have to be sent. Often the process of putting angry or painful feelings out on paper is enough and the letter is then consigned to the bin. If written to a dead parent, it may be thrown on the grave. Sometimes it may actually be given to the parent or partner and, in conflict, a letter (rather than an email) may have value. It can be read slowly, with time to try to understand the underlying message, rather than responded to immediately or defensively in the heat of an angry confrontation. Even where a letter is not understood, it may help the writer to come to terms with the lack of understanding and to move on to accept that the desired responses will never come but should not govern the rest of the writer's life and relationships.

Drawing

For children drawing may be a way of expressing and trying to deal with complex and difficult feelings. A child whose parents were emotionally estranged drew a picture of each on the edge of a cliff, distant from each other but holding out a hand towards the other. A child whose sister had died drew a picture of a car crash and an ambulance. He talked about the picture, about going to hospital and about dying (as his sister had done). The worker commented that that sounded like his sister and that it seemed very frightening. The boy looked relieved, nodded and stopped drawing. Enough had been said for the time being.

As workers we can use particular techniques to explore and discuss feelings and relationships with children. We can draw faces and for each family member ask the child whether it should be a happy or a sad face. We can then explore why in the child's view each person is happy or sad. What would make a sad person happy? We can use sad and happy faces for a child in different care situations. Where was he or she happy/where sad? We can ask a child to draw his or her house and who lives there. This can be a way of exploring family relationships and problems from the child's point of view. Who is close to who, who fights with who? Are mother, father or partners there? Are other members of the extended family included? It can also be a useful means of exploring the child's world when abuse is suspected. We can ask what happens in each room: how easy and open is the child in doing this task? Is there any room which seems to cause anxiety, tension, apprehension or out of character refusal to speak? Here we may probe a little more specifically: who is usually in this room? Is it the child? Is it scary? Without being inquisitional, the use of drawing may help a child to express forbidden or frightening anxieties, feelings or experiences, although again the adult with whom this is done has to be perceived as trustworthy.

We can also play squiggles with a child or adolescent (Winnicott, 1971). The game is played by two people, the 'helping' adult and the child. One participant draws a random squiggle which the other person must turn into a picture, then the players swap roles. The child quickly becomes interested in the game and relaxes. He or she may then start to draw pictures without needing a squiggle as a starting point, and will probably do so more freely than if he or she had been asked by a relative stranger to 'draw whatever you like'. Perhaps the most important feature of the game is that it is shared. Squiggles can be just a game, but it can also be a means for a child to draw and communicate themes and issues which are important for them.

This chapter has perhaps appeared to focus on the needs of vulnerable users of services, adults and children. However the techniques described can also have an important place in effective intervention with involuntary users of services. Life snakes and genograms, for example, may be used to help people who have committed serious offences to understand how their past experiences may have influenced their current attitudes and behaviour and to encourage a recognition of the need to change. Letter writing has been found to be a means of increasing empathy among sexual offenders for their victims: 'Offenders write hypothetical letters both from the victims to themselves and in the form of a reply from the offender to the victim' (Fernandez and Serran, 2002). 'These letters are meant to express the victim's distress and the offender's acceptance of this and his responsibility for the offence' (Marshall *et al.*, 2004, p. 120).

Conclusion

Chapters 9 and 10 have examined non-verbal, verbal and written communication skills and techniques which may be used to help people who require our services to problem solve and change attitudes or behaviour. They have emphasized that to do this the worker is engaged in influencing, and they have focussed on specific skills and techniques rather than broader models of intervention (Coulshed and Orme, 2006). However, we should also be aware that one of the ways we may implicitly influence users of service is by modelling. Fischer (1978) says, 'Modelling refers simply to a change in behaviour as a result of the observation of another's behaviour, i.e. learning by vicarious experience or imitation' (p. 169). Modelling is used consciously as one technique in behaviour modification by which a worker 'repeatedly demonstrates desired responses, instructs the client to reproduce them, prompts the behaviour when it fails to occur and administers potent reinforcers to the client' (Fischer, 1978, p. 169).

We have noted that users of service themselves appreciate workers having 'some standing' (relationship skills, authority or expertise) and some areas of commonality.

If these conditions are met and we can establish both a relationship base and an influence base it is at least possible that some of our communication and behaviour acts as a model for users of service even if we do not consciously seek this. The use of communication skills examined in this book may therefore fulfil two functions for users of services (voluntary or involuntary) to facilitate them in dealing more effectively with their problems and to model behaviours and communication skills which in themselves may increase problem solving abilities.

putting it into practice

Do you as student or social worker keep a reflective diary? If not, how do you envisage meeting regulatory body requirements about your continuing professional development?

Have you used any of the written techniques outlined in this chapter with a user of service? If you have, how useful did you find it and, more importantly, how useful did the user of services?

How do you think some of these techniques might be applied to practice in child protection and criminal justice?

In general do you think that written techniques identified in this chapter can help change behaviour or attitudes and, if so, how?

Recommended reading

Coulshed, V. and Orme, J. (2006) *Social Work Practice*, 4th edn, Basingstoke, Palgrave Macmillan. Detailed and practical application of how in social work and social care we may best use communication skills in social work.

Trevithick, P. (2005) *Social Work Skills: A Practice Handbook*, 2nd edn, Maidenhead, Open University Press. Again, a general, important textbook about social work skills, which locates written communication in the necessary repertoire of intervention skills.

11 | Conclusion

In this edition of *Communication in Social Work* I have reflected on change and continuity in communication in social work and social care. The context continually changes but some essentials of communication do not (although the tools do, for example email, internet and text messaging). While in the middle of drafting this I prepared a Christmas cake using a recipe which is at least twenty years old. Why have I continued to use the recipe? The simple answer is that it works; occasionally I have tried other recipes and the result was less good. So in this book, I have drawn on what worked from the past but also tried to recognize that contexts change and new knowledge needs to be incorporated into our repertoire of skills. We need to embrace change critically but not abandon what has been tried and tested.

I hope this book introduces the reader to a range of communication skills which underlie effective social work practice and social care in child care, criminal justice, community care and in mental health social work whether practised in the statutory, voluntary or private sector. It can only be an introduction. Skills have to be practised, applied and developed on the basis of feedback from users of services, voluntary or involuntary, carers and colleagues, or, in training, from peers, tutors and video. I hope, however, that this book challenges readers to reflect on, examine and apply to their own practice, and therefore raise an increased understanding and awareness of their skills and weaknesses in communication, and encourage them to apply this awareness to ensure that they practise, improve, extend and develop their communication skills.

The skills involved in attending and listening, engaging and relating, giving and getting information, negotiating agreements or contracts and helping people to make changes in their attitudes, beliefs or behaviour continue to be relevant to social work and social care in all contexts. Each context will influence the way in which communication occurs, both enhancing and encouraging the use of some skills and constraining or limiting the use of others.

In group or residential care the skills of attending and listening, of sharing information, of agreeing shared goals and targets for change, and of clarification, interpretation and challenging are employed in the context of daily living rather than in a formal time-limited interview. The concept of the life space is relevant, defined by Keenan (2007) as a 'therapeutic and institutional environment wherein residents or attenders enact both existential and historical aspects of their lives in the context of relations with each other, professional and other staff, their systems and subsystems' (p. 220). Within the life space the daily patterns of residential or group care – washing up, meals, bed time – offer the opportunity at times for purposeful and meaningful communication.

Much of the communication in residential or group care is the everyday stuff of normal living, but sometimes the communication has a significance for the resident or user which the worker has to pick up and respond to. This requires the worker to understand the meaning underlying the interaction and to communicate that understanding. An adolescent boy was particularly abusive to a young Scots male care worker. It emerged, coincidently, that his mother was just about to marry a much younger man, a Scot. The residential worker took time to explore the boy's feelings and to reflect back the link between his aggressive behaviour in care and his anger about his new stepfather. The capacity to respond appropriately depends not just on the worker's communication skills, but also on the constraints of the setting, including difficulties about privacy and the needs and demands of other residents or users.

The context also constrains communication in social work and social care in interdisciplinary settings, for example in health. If an interview has to be conducted at the bedside of someone in a public ward, privacy is impossible and the person may well feel inhibited from sharing real concerns or feelings, e.g. of anxiety, distress or anger, because of the public nature of the setting. Interruptions are also frequent and can inhibit real communication. I became particularly aware of the impact of interruptions when I was sitting in a cubicle with a terminally ill child and his parents. He was asleep and they were preparing for his death, partly by talking about the practical arrangements for his funeral, partly by sitting silently and partly by grieving openly. They needed peace and privacy but ward routines continued and there were frequent interruptions to check the child's condition.

Referrals to social work in interdisciplinary work are often made by someone from another discipline, e.g. a nurse, doctor, teacher or headmaster, and can be made without the knowledge of the person referred. It is, therefore, essential for the social worker to clarify whether the potential user of services knows about the referral or wishes for social work contact. The skills of engagement, clarification of purpose, giving information about the role and resources of social work, and negotiation of a mutually agreed contract are essential for a social worker practising in an interdisciplinary or multidisciplinary setting.

The very nature of an interdisciplinary setting may constrain effective social work communication because the primary purpose of the organization may not be the practice of social work. The priorities, values, professional beliefs and ideologies of the different disciplines involved will vary, for example, between education and health. Because of its lack of relative status and power, social work and social care may sometimes not be in a position to assert and achieve the primacy of its beliefs and values, although individual social workers may achieve personal influence within their multidisciplinary teams (*Changing Lives*, 2006). Given the policy requirements for integrated services (*Changing Lives*, 2006), we need in social work to use communication skills to articulate clearly and authoritatively our ability to take a view which incorporates a structural, social and individual perspective and takes on board the perspectives of users of services.

This conflict in professional beliefs can constrain both the social work role and social care and communication between worker and users of services. For example, social workers in psychiatric hospitals may be viewed by nursing and medical colleagues only in terms of their mental health officer role, or of their welfare rights expertise. Nursing and medical staff may still show disapproval of the social worker for 'upsetting' the patient if the social worker's appropriate use of listening, probing, empathy and reflection results in a patient sharing distress.

Social work fieldwork settings provide their own constraints, some of which have already been discussed; the power and authority of the social worker or whether the user of services is seen on a voluntary or statutory basis is crucial, although the issue of power is highlighted when the basis of the contract is a legal requirement. In child care, it has been argued that social workers operate within the constraint of the fear of the user of services about the power of social work to remove children into care.

The physical setting of fieldwork may interfere with effective communication. An office is not a natural setting, but rather an alien and artificial one. It is the social worker's territory, not that of users of services and therefore the social worker retains control. It conveys professional power, authority and distance reminiscent of other offices and interviews, with GPs, lawyers or DHSS officials. We also, therefore, need to remember the importance of visits to people's homes, in child protection and community care but also in criminal justice: in child protection and criminal justice, which frequently involve work with involuntary clients, we need to make a careful and cautious risk assessment of the potential value and risk of a home visit.

Perhaps the main constraint on communication in fieldwork is the time limit. In contrast to residential or group care, a fieldwork interview is a brief episode in the life of the user of services; used for assessment it is inevitably limited, a snapshot of what a user of service is prepared to reveal. Even a more regular contact, for example on a weekly basis, has to be seen in the context of the other relationships, commitments and networks. Inevitably there are severe limitations on the influence of a social worker's hour a week contact with a user of services, set in the context of the complexity of the rest of his or her life, including immediate family, social networks and, most influential of all, structural position in society. In particular, as acknowledged in the introduction, an individual social worker's communication skills can do little to address the structural problems of poverty, class, gender and race which face many of social work's clients.

In concluding any book, the author has to examine and review critically its content and omissions. I am particularly aware of three major problems in this volume. First, as I indicated in the introduction, writing about communication cannot do it justice. Communication is an activity that has to be practised, reviewed and thereby improved in order to do it effectively. This book can only be a tool and an impetus, and not, in itself, a means to effective communication. Second, it is difficult to do justice to the diversity of social work and social care, its settings, its different user and carer groups, its purposes and aims, and its individual users of service in relation to their class, gender, ethnicity, age and personality. In particular, the analysis of communication and culture in relation to ethnicity, social class, age and gender may appear limited. I have only been able to highlight key issues; dealing with them in depth would require a separate volume. Third, the main focus of this book has been about communicating with users of services, in a range of settings which include the local authority, voluntary and private sectors in social work and social care. However, the skills involved are just as relevant and necessary to effective communication with colleagues both from social work and from other professions, disciplines and occupations.

Within these limitations, what are the requirements of effective communication in social work and social care?

First, it requires the development and use of a range of skills and techniques examined in this book, with users of services and interprofessional colleagues:

- engaging and establishing rapport;
- attentive listening to the meaning of people's communication;
- exploration, questioning and probing;
- summarizing and focussing;
- establishing a shared purpose, mutually agreed between a user of service and the worker, or interprofessionally;

- giving information or advice;
- reflection and clarification;
- challenging and confrontation.

These are the technical components of effective communication. Without the knowledge or ability to practise this repertoire of skills, the social worker is unlikely to use encounters with users of services or colleagues for purposeful communication.

Such technical expertise is necessary for effective communication in social work and social care, but it is not enough. Social work involves entering into the lives of people who are in distress, conflict or trouble. To do this requires not only technical competence, but also qualities of integrity, genuineness and self-awareness.

Both social workers and workers in social care have to begin from a value base which entails basic respect for all human beings. While I recognize that individual users of services may sometimes be dishonest, destructive or dangerous, social work and social care in child care, working with adults and criminal justice has to start from humanistic principles or values about the worth and dignity of each individual. Social workers and social care workers also need to possess the Rogerian qualities of warmth, genuineness and authenticity. If we are not honest and authentic and real in our practice, the skills outlined in this volume become hollow and mechanistic. Skills have to be based on integrity. In part this is a moral consideration: it represents my belief that the potential vulnerability of users of services requires a personal response and commitment from me as a person, as well as my professional technical competence. It is also an empirical issue: research has highlighted genuineness or authenticity as a necessary, but not sufficient, condition of effective helping. Our value base also needs to underpin our communication with all our colleagues.

The other major requirement for effective communication is the worker's self-awareness. Communication, verbal, non-verbal or symbolic, is about our use of self. In order to communicate effectively we have to be aware of what we are doing, why we are doing it, how we are presenting ourselves to users of services and interprofessional colleagues, and, on the basis of this self-knowledge or awareness, what changes in our communication are needed if we are to be more effective.

Skilled and effective communication is not a static state. It will always involve change and development and consolidation, learning from our past behaviour and from our mistakes. I hope this book stimulates and challenges its readers to do just that: to learn, to develop and to consolidate their communication skills in a reflective and evidenced-based way.

References

Aiello, J. and Jones, S. (1971) 'Field Study of the Proxemic Behaviour of Young School Children in Three Sub-Cultural Groups', *Journal of Personality and Social Psychology*, 119: 351–6.

Aldgate, J. (2002) 'Family Breakdown', in M. Davies (ed.) *The Blackwell Companion to Social Work,* 2nd edn. Oxford, Blackwell.

Aldgate, J. (2007) 'The Place of Attachment Theory in Social Work with Children and Families', in J. Lishman (ed.) *Handbook for Practice Learning in Social Work and Social Care*, London, Jessica Kingsley.

Aldgate, J. and Simmonds, J. (eds) (1988) *Direct Work with Children: A Guide for Social Work Practitioners.* London: Batsford/BAAF.

Alexander, C., Edwards, R., Temple, B. *et al.* (2004) *Access to Services with Interpreters: Users' Views.* York, Joseph Rowntree Foundation.

Argyle, M. (1975) 'Non-verbal Communication', in M. Brown and R. Stevens (eds) *Social Behaviour and Experience: Multiple Perspectives.* London, Open University Press.

Argyle, M. (2007) *Social Interaction.* London, Aldine Transaction.

Argyle, M. and Dean, J. (1965) 'Eye Contact, Distance and Affiliation', *Sociometry*, 28: 289–304.

Ashdown, M.T. and Clement Brown, S. (1953) *Social Service and Mental Health: An Essay on Psychiatric Social Workers.* London, Routledge.

Baldock, J. and Prior, D. (1981) 'Social Workers Talking to Clients: A Study of Verbal Behaviour', *British Journal of Social Work*, 11(1).

Balloch, S. McLean, J. and Fisher, M. (1999) *Social Services: Working Under Pressure.* Bristol, Policy Press.

Barnes, D., Carpenter, J. and Bailey, D. (2000) 'Partnerships with Service Users in Interprofessional Education for Community Mental Health: A Case Study', *Journal of Interprofessional Care*, 14(2): 189–200.

Barrett, G. and Keeping, C. (2005) 'The Processes Required for Effective Interprofessional Working', in G. Barrett, D. Sellman and J. Thomas (eds) *Interprofessional Working in Health and Social Care: Professional Perspective.* Basingstoke, Palgrave Macmillan.

Barrett, G., Sellman, D. and Thomas, J. (eds) (2005) *Interprofessional Working in Health and Social Care: Professional Perspective.* Basingstoke, Palgrave Macmillan

Beaumont, B. (1999) 'Assessing Risk in Work with Offenders', in P. Parsloe (ed.) *Risk Assessment in Social Care and Social Work*, London, Jessica Kingsley.

Becker, S. and MacPherson, S. (1988) *Public Issues and Private Pain: Poverty, Social Work and Social Policy*. London, Social Service Insight Books.

Beresford, P., Adshead, L. and Croft, S. (2006) *Service Users' Views of Specialist Palliative Care Social Work*. York, Joseph Rowntree Foundation.

Beresford, P. with Page, L. and Stevens, A. (1994) *Changing the Culture: Involving Service Users in Social Work Education*. CCETSW Paper 32.2, London, Central Council for Education and Training in Social Work.

Beresford, P., Shamash, M., Forrest, V. and Turner, M. (2005) *Developing Social Care: Service Users' Vision for Adult Support*. Bristol, Policy Press/SCIE.

Berne, E. (1968) *Games People Play*. Harmondsworth, Penguin.

Bichard, Sir M. (2003) *The Bichard Inquiry Report* (www.bichardinquiry.org. uk). London, Home Office.

Biestek, F.P. (1965) *The Casework Relationship*. London, Unwin University Books.

Blaxter, M. (1976) *The Meaning of Disability*. London, Heinemann.

Blom-Cooper, L. (1985) *A Child in Trust: The Report of the Panel of Enquiry into the Circumstances Surrounding the Death of Jasmine Beckford*. London, London Borough of Brent.

Bowlby, J. (1984) *The Making and Breaking of Affectional Bonds*. London, Tavistock, Social Sciences Paperbacks.

Breakwell, G.M. and Rowett, C. (1982) *Social Work: The Social Psychological Approach*. Wokingham, Van Nostrand Reinhold.

Buckley, R. (2007) 'Social Work with Children and Families: A Case Study of the Integration of Law, Social Policy and Research in the Development of Assessment and Intervention with Children and Families', in J. Lishman (ed.) *Handbook for Practice Learning in Social Work and Social Care*, London, Jessica Kingsley.

Butler, I. and Drakeford, M. (2001) 'Which Blair Project? Communitarianism, Social Authoritarianism and Social Work', *Journal of Social Work*, 1(1), April.

Butler, N. (1977) 'Uncovering a Gap in the Service', *Community Care*, 3, Aug 14–16.

Byrne, P.S. and Long, B.E.L. (1976) *Doctors Talking to Patients: A Study of Verbal Behaviour of General Practitioners Consulting in Their Surgeries*. London, HMSO.

Carkhuff, R.R. (1969) *Helping and Human Relations*. New York, Holt.

Changing Lives: the 21st Century Review of Social Work in Scotland (2006).

Clark, C. (2000) 'Values in Social Work', in M. Davies (ed.) *The Blackwell Encyclopaedia of Social Work*. Oxford, Blackwell.

Clough, R. (2000) *The Practice of Residential Work*. Basingstoke, Macmillan.

Clyde, J.J. (1992) *Report of the Inquiry into the Removal of Children from Orkney in February 1991*. London, HMSO.

Cohen, A. (1971) 'Consumer View: Retarded Mothers and the Social Services', *Social Work Today*, 1(12): 35–43.

Collins, S. (2000) 'Contracts between Social Workers and Service Users', in M. Davies (ed.) *The Blackwell Encyclopaedia of Social Work*. Oxford, Blackwell.

Cook, M. (1968) *Studies of Orientation and Proximity*. Oxford Institute of Experimental Psychology.

Corden, J. (1980) 'Contracts in Social Work Practice', *British Journal of Social Work*, 10: 143–61.

Coulshed, V. and Orme, J. (2006) *Social Work Practice: An Introduction*, 2nd edn. Basingstoke, Palgrave Macmillan.

Cox, J. (2008) 'Family Group Conferencing and "Partnership"', in S. Hunter and P. Ritchie, *Co-Production and Personalisation in Social Care: Changing Relationships in the Provision of Social Care, Research Highlights, 49*. London, Jessica Kingsley.

Cree, V. and Davis, A. (2006) *Social Work: Voices from the Inside*. London, Routledge.

Croft, S. and Beresford, P. (2000) 'Empowerment', in M. Davies (ed.) *The Blackwell Encyclopaedia of Social Work*. Oxford, Blackwell.

D'Ardenne, P. and Mahtani, A. (1989) *Transcultural Counselling in Action*. London, Sage.

Dale, P. (2004) 'Parents' Perceptions of Child Protection Services', *Child Abuse Review*, 13(2): 137–57.

Davies, M. (1994) *The Essential Social Worker: A Guide to Positive Practice*. Aldershot: Wildwood House.

Davies, M. (ed.) (2000) *The Blackwell Encyclopaedia of Social Work*. Oxford, Blackwell.

De Lange, J. (1995) 'Gender and Communication in Social Work Education: A Cross-cultural Perspective', *Journal of Social Work Education*, 31(1): 75–81.

DfES (Department for Education and Skills) (2001) *Special Educational Needs, Code of Practice*, London, HMSO.

DHSS (Department of Health and Social Security) (1974) *Report of the Inquiry into the Care and Supervision provided in relation to Maria Colwell*. London, HMSO.

Dickson, D., Hargie, O. and Morrow, N. (2003) *Communication Skills Training for Health Professionals*, 2nd edn. Cheltenham, Nelson Thornes.

Diggins, M. (2004) *Teaching and Learning Communication Skills in Social Work Education*. London, SCIE.

Dillon, J. (1997) 'Questioning', in O.W.D. Hargie (ed.) *The Handbook of Communication Skills*. London, Routledge.

Doel, M. and Lawson, B. (1986) 'Open Records: The Client's Right to Partnership', *British Journal of Social Work*, 16: 407–30.

Doel, M. and Lawson, B. (1989) 'A Paper Dialogue', *Community Care*, 8 May: 26–7.

Doel, M. and Marsh, P. (1992) *Task Centred Social Work*. Aldeshot, Ashgate.

Drakeford, M. (2000) *Privatisation and Social Policy*. London, Longman.

Drakeford, M. (2002) 'Social Work and Politics', in M. Davies, *The Blackwell Companion to Social Work*. Oxford, Blackwell.

Dryden, W. and Scott, M. (1991) 'A Brief, Highly Structured and Effective Approach to Social Work Practice: A Cognitive Behavioural Perspective', in J. Lishman (ed.) *Handbook of Theory for Practice Teachers in Social Work.* London, Jessica Kingsley.

Egan, G. (2002) *The Skilled Helper.* Pacific Grove, CA, Thomson/Brooks-Cole.

Egan, G. (2007) *The Skilled Helper: A Systematic Approach to Effective Helping.* Pacific Grove, CA, Brooks-Cole.

Ekman, P. and Friesen, W. V. (1968) 'Non-verbal Behaviour in Psychotherapy Research', in J.M. Schlien (ed.) *Research in Psychotherapy Vol 3.* Washington, DC, American Psychological Association.

Ellis, A. (1962) *Reason and Emotion in Psychotherapy.* New York, Lyle Stuart.

Evans, C. and Fisher, M. (1999) 'Collaborative Evaluation with Service Users: Moving Towards User-Controlled Research', in I. Shaw and J. Lishman (eds) *Evaluation and Social Work Practice.* London, Sage.

Exline, R.V. (1963) 'Explorations in the Process of Person Perception: Visual Interaction in Relation to Competition, Sex and the Need for "Affiliation"', *Journal of Personality*, 31: 1–20.

Fahlberg, V. (1994) *A Child's Journey Through Placement.* London, BAAF.

Fakhoury, W.K.H and Wright, D. (2004) 'A National Survey of Approved Social Workers in the UK: Information, Communication and Training Needs', *British Journal of Social Work*, 34: 663–75.

Fernandez, Y.M. and Serran, G. (2002) 'Empathy Training for Therapists and Clients', in Y.M. Fernandez (ed.) *In their Shoes: Examining the Issue of Empathy and its Place in the Treatment of Offenders.* Oklahoma City, Wood 'n' Barnes Publishing.

Fischer, J. (1978) *Effective Casework Practice: An Eclectic Approach.* New York, McGraw-Hill.

Fisher, M., Marsh, P. and Philip, D. with Sainsbury, E. (1986) *In and Out of Care.* London, Batsford.

Fook, J. (2007) 'Reflective Practice and Critical Reflection', in J. Lishman, *Handbook for Practice Learning in Social Work and Social Care: Knowledge and Theory.* London, Jessica Kingsley.

Foote, C. and Stanners, C. (2002) *Integrating Care for Older People: New Care for Old – A Systems Approach.* London, Jessica Kingsley.

Freeth, D. (2001) 'Sustaining Interprofessional Collaboration', *Journal of Interprofessional Care*, 15: 37–46.

Furnham, A. and Bochner, S. (1986) *Culture Shock: Psychological Reaction to Unfamiliar Environments.* London, Taylor & Francis.

Gandy, J.M., Pitman, R., Stretcher, M. and Yip, C. (1975) 'Parents' Perception of the Effect of Volunteer Probation Officers in Juvenile Offenders', *Canadian Journal of Criminology and Corrections*, 17(1): 5–19.

GSCC (General Social Care Council) (2002) *Codes of Practice for Social Care Workers and Employers.* London, GSCC.

Grampian Regional Council: Grampian Health Board (1991) *Draft Joint Community Care Plan.*

Greenspoon, J. (1955) 'The Reinforcing Effect of Two Spoken Sounds on the Frequency of Two Responses', *American Journal of Psychology*, 68.

Gurin, G., Keroft, J. and Feld, S. (1960) *Americans View their Mental Health*. New York, Basic Books.

Gurney, M. (1990) 'Anxiety Overload', *Community Care*, 15 November.

Halberstadt, A.G. (1985) 'Race, Socioeconomic Status, and Non-verbal Behavior', in A.W. Siegman, and S. Feldstein (eds) *Multi Channel Integration of Non-verbal Behavior*. Hillsdale, NJ, Lawrence Erlbaum.

Hall, A.S. (1974) *The Point of Entry*. London, Allen & Unwin.

Hall, E.T. (1966) *The Hidden Dimension*. New York, Doubleday.

Hall, E.T. (1974) *Handbook for Proxemic Research*. Washington DC: Society for the Anthropology of Visual Communication.

Hall, E.T. (1976) *Beyond Culture*. New York, Anchor Press/Doubleday.

Hall, L. and Lloyd, S. (1989) *Surviving Child Abuse: A Handbook for Helping Women Challenge their Past*. London, Falmer.

Harper, R.G., Wiems, A.N. and Matarazzo, J.D. (1978) *Non-verbal Communication*. New York, Wiley.

Henley, A. (1979) *Asian Parents in Hospital and at Home*. London, King Edward's Hospital Fund.

Hill, M. (2002) 'Network Assessments and Diagrams: A Flexible Friend in Social Work and Education', *Journal of Social Work*, 2(2): 233–54.

HMSO (1984, 1988) *The Data Protection Act*. London, HMSO.

HMSO (1987) *Access to Personal Files Act*. London, HMSO.

HMSO (1989) *Children Act*. London, HMSO.

HMSO (1990) *National Health and Community Care Act*. London, HMSO.

HMSO (1991) *Criminal Justice Act*. London, HMSO.

Hoffman, W.P.F. (1975) 'Expectations of Mental Health Centre Clients Related to Problem Reductions and Satisfaction with Services', University of Pennsylvania DSW. Summary from *Abstracts for Social Workers*, 11(3) No. 700.

Horobin, G. and Montgomery, S. (1986) *New Information Technology in Management and Practice: Research Highlights in Social Work*. London, Jessica Kingsley.

Hudson, B. and Sheldon, B, (2000) 'The Cognitive Behavioural Approach', in M. Davies (ed.) *The Blackwell Encyclopaedia of Social Work*. Oxford, Blackwell.

Hunter, S. (1997) 'Dementia: Challenges and New Directions', *Research Highlights in Social Work, 37*, London, Jessica Kingsley.

Hunter, S. and Ritchie, P. (2008) 'Co-production and Personalisation in Social Care. Changing Relationships in the Provision of Social Care', *Research Highlights in Social Work, 49*. London, Jessica Kingsley.

Joinson, A.N. (2003) *Understanding the Psychology of Internet Behaviour: Virtual Worlds, Real Lives*. Basingstoke, Palgrave Macmillan.

Kadushin, A. and Kadushin, G. (1997) *The Social Work Interview*, 4th edn. New York, Columbia University Press.

Keenan, C. (2007) 'Group Care', in J. Lishman (ed.) *Handbook for Practice Learning in Social Work and Social Care: Knowledge and Theory*. London, Jessica Kingsley.

Kelmshall, H. (2007) 'Risk Assessment and Management: An Overview', in J. Lishman (ed.) *Handbook for Practice Learning in Social Work and Social Care: Knowledge and Theory*. London, Jessica Kingsley.

Kendon, A. (1973) 'Some Functions of Gaze – Direction in Social Interaction', in M. Argyle, *Social Encounters: Readings in Social Interaction*. Harmondsworth, Penguin.

Killick, J. and Allan, K. (2002) *Communication and the Care of People with Dementia*. Buckingham, Open University Press.

Koprowska, J. (2006) *Communication and Interpersonal Skills in Social Work*. Exeter, Learning Matters/Macmillan.

Koprowska, J. (2007) 'Communication Skills in Social Work', in M. Lymberry and K. Postle (eds) *Social Work: A Companion to Learning*. London, Sage.

Lago, C. and Thompson, J. (1996) *Race, Culture and Counselling*. Buckingham, Open University Press.

Laming, W. (2003) *The Victoria Climbié Inquiry: Report of an Inquiry*. London, HMSO.

Langan, M. (2002) 'The Legacy of Radical Social Work', in R. Adams, L. Dominelli and M. Payne (eds) *Social Work: Themes, Issues and Critical Debates*, 2nd edn. Basingstoke, Palgrave.

Langan, M. and Lee, P. (1989) *Radical Social Work Today*. London, Unwin Hyman.

Leadbetter, C. (2004) *Personalisation through Participation*. London, Demos.

Ley, P. (1977) 'Communicating with the Patient', in J.C. Coleman (ed.) *Introductory Psychology*. London, Routledge & Kegan Paul.

Lindow, V. (2000) 'User Perspectives on Social Work ', in M. Davies (ed.) *The Blackwell Encyclopaedia of Social Work*. Oxford, Blackwell.

Lishman, J. (1978) 'A Clash in Perspective', *British Journal of Social Work*, Autumn: 301–11.

Lishman, J. (1985) *An Analysis of Social Work Interviews Using Videotape: Behaviour, Effectiveness and Self-fulfilling Prophecies*. PhD Thesis, University of Aberdeen.

Lishman, J. (1988) 'Social Work Interviews: How Effective Are They?', *Research, Policy and Practice*, 5: 1–5.

Lishman, J., Macintosh, L. and Macintosh, B. (1990) 'A Child Dies', *Practice*, 3(3–4): 271–84.

Lishman, J. (2000) *Evidence for Practice: The Contribution of Competing Research Methodologies* , in the ESRC-funded seminar series *What Works as Evidence for Practice? The Methodologies Repertoire in an Applied Discipline*. Cardiff, Seminar 4, 27 April.

Lishman, J. (2002) 'Personal and Professional Development', in R. Adams, L. Dominelli and M. Payne (eds) *Social Work: Themes, Issues and Critical Debates*, 2nd edn. Basingstoke, Palgrave.

Lishman, J. (2007) 'Research, Evaluation and Evidence Based Practice', in J. Lishman (ed.) *Handbook for Practice Learning in Social Work and Social Care*, London, Jessica Kingsley.

Lott, R.E., Clark, W. and Altman, I. (1969) *A Propositional Inventory of Research on Interpersonal Space*. Washington Naval Medical Research Institute.

Lupton, C. (1998) 'User Empowerment or Family Self-reliance? The Family Group Conference Model', *British Journal of Social Work*, 28(1): 107–28.

Macdonald, G. (2000) 'The Evidence Based Perspective', in M. Davies (ed.) *The Blackwell Companion to Social Work*, 2nd edn. Oxford, Blackwell.

Macdonald, G. (2007) 'Cognitive Behavioural Social Work', in J. Lishman (ed.) *Handbook for Practice Learning in Social Work and Social Care*, London, Jessica Kingsley.

Macdonald, G. and Sheldon, B. (1998) 'Changing One's Mind: The Final Frontier', *Issues in Social Work Education*, 18(1): 3–25.

Maluccio, A.N. (1979) *Learning from Clients: Interpersonal Helping Viewed by Clients and Social Workers*. New York, Free Press.

Marris, P. (1974) *Loss and Change*. London, Routledge & Kegan Paul.

Marsh, P. (2007) 'Task-Centred Practice', in J. Lishman (ed.) *Handbook for Practice Learning in Social Work and Social Care*. London, Jessica Kingsley.

Marsh, P. and Fisher, M. (1992) *Good Intentions: Partnership in Social Services*. York, Joseph Rowntree Foundation.

Marshall, B., Serran, G. and Moulden, H. (2004) 'Effective Intervention with Sexual Offenders', in H. Kemshall and G. McIvor (eds) *Managing Sex Offender Risk*. London, Jessica Kingsley.

Mayer, J.E. and Timms, N. (1970) *The Client Speaks*. London, Routledge & Kegan Paul.

Mayo, C. and Henley, N. (1981) (eds) *Gender and Nonverbal Behavior*. New York, Springer Verlag.

McGuire, J. (1995) (ed.) *What Works: Reducing Reoffending. Guidelines from Research and Practice*. Wiley, Chichester.

McIvor, G. (2007) 'Assessment in Criminal Justice', in J. Lishman (ed.) *Handbook for Practice Learning in Social Work and Social Care*, London, Jessica Kingsley.

McIvor, G. and Raynor, P. (eds) (2007) *Developments in Social Work with Offenders*. London, Jessica Kingsley.

McLean, T. (2007) 'Interdisciplinary Practice', in J. Lishman (ed.) *Handbook for Practice Learning in Social Work and Social Care*. London, Jessica Kingsley.

Mehrabian, A. (1971) *Silent Messages*. Belmont, CA: Loadsworth.

Mehrabian, A. (1972) *Non-verbal Communication*. Alberta, Aldine.

Mehrabian, A. and Williams, H. (1969) 'Non-verbal Concomitants of Perceived and Extended Persuasiveness', *Journal of Personality and Social Psychology*, 13.

Millar, M. and Corby, B. (2006) 'The Framework for the Assessment of Children in Need and their Families – A Basis for a Therapeutic Encounter', *British Journal of Social Work*, 887–9.

Miller, R.L., Brickman, P. and Boch, D. (1975) 'Attribution versus Persuasion as a Means of Modifying Behaviour', *Journal of Personality and Social Psychology*, 31.

Milner, J. and O'Byrne, P. (1998) *Assessment in Social Work*. Basingstoke, Macmillan.

Morago, P. (2006) 'Evidence Based Practice: From Medicine to Social Work', *European Journal of Social Work*, 9(4): 461–77.

Morgan, G. (1986) 'Welfare Benefits Computing', in G. Horobin and S. Montgomery, *Research Highlights in Social Work 13*. London, Jessica Kingsley.

Mullen, E. (1968) 'Casework Communication', *Social Casework*, 49.

Munro, E. (1998) 'Improving Social Workers' Knowledge Base in Child Protection Work', *British Journal of Social Work*, 28: 89–105.

Nelson-Jones, R. (2005) *An Introduction to Counselling Skills*. London, Sage.

Neville, D. and Beak, D. (1990) 'Solving the Case History Mystery', *Social Work Today*, 28 June.

Nicolson, P., Bayne, R. and Owen, J. (2006) *Applied Psychology for Social Workers*, 3rd edn. Basingstoke, Palgrave Macmillan.

O'Brien, S. (2003) *Report of the Caleb Ness Enquiry*. Edinburgh, Edinburgh and the Lothians Child Protection Committee.

O'Hagan, K. (1986) *Crisis Intervention in Social Services*, London, Macmillan – now Basingstoke, Palgrave Macmillan.

Oliver, J. (1990) 'The Customers' Perspective Campaign: Reception Areas', *Social Work Today*, 5 April.

Oliver, M. (1996) *Understanding Disability: From Theory to Practice*. Basingstoke, Macmillan – now Palgrave Macmillan.

Oliver, M. (1998) 'Social Work: Disabled People and Disabling Environments', *Research Highlights in Social Work, 21*, London, Jessica Kingsley.

Parkes, C.M. (1975) *Bereavement Studies of Grief in Adult Life*. Harmondsworth, Penguin.

Payne, M. (1978) 'Users of Social Work Records', *Social Work Today*, 9(33): 254–78.

Payne, M. (2002) 'Social Work Theories and Reflective Practice', in R. Adams, L. Dominelli and M. Payne (eds) *Social Work: Themes, Issues and Critical Debates*. Basingstoke, Palgrave Macmillan.

Payne, M. (2005) *Modern Social Work Theory*, 3rd edn. Basingstoke, Palgrave Macmillan.

Petch, A. (2000) 'Work with Adult Service Users', in M. Davies (ed.) *The Blackwell Encyclopaedia of Social Work*, 2nd edn. Oxford, Blackwell.

Pithouse, A. (1987) *Social Work: The Organization of an Invisible Trade*. London, Gower.

Platt, D. (2006) 'Investigation or Initial Assessment of Child Concerns', *British Journal of Social Work*, 36(2).

Porporino, F. and Fabiano, E. (2007) 'Case Managing Offenders within a Motivational Framework', in G. McIvor and P. Raynor (eds) *Developments in Social Work with Offenders*. London, Jessica Kingsley.

Preece, J. (1999) 'Empathic Communities: Balancing Emotional and Factual Communication', *Interaction with Computers*, 12: 63–77.

Priestley, P. and McGuire, J. (1983) *Learning to Help: Basic Skills Exercises*. London, Tavistock.

Prince, K. (1996) *Boring Records: Communication Speech and Writing in Social Work*. London, Jessica Kingsley.

Rafferty, J. (2000) 'Information and Communication Technologies (ICT)', in M. Davies (ed.) *The Blackwell Encyclopaedia of Social Work*. Oxford, Blackwell.

Randall, P. and Parker, J. (2000) 'Labelling Theory and Role Theory ', in M. Davies (ed.) *The Blackwell Encyclopaedia of Social Work*. Oxford, Blackwell.

Reece, M.M. and Whitman, R.N. (1962) 'Expressive Movements, Warmth and Verbal Reinforcements', *Journal of Abnormal and Social Psychology*, 64.

Rees, S.J. (1974) 'No More Than Contact in Outcome of Social Work', *British Journal of Social Work*, 4(3): 255–79.

Rees, S.J. (1978) *Social Work Face to Face*. London, Edward Arnold.

Rees, S. and Wallace, A. (1982) *Verdicts on Social Work*. London, Edward Arnold.

Reid, J. and Reynolds, J. (1996) *Speaking our Minds: An Authority of Personal Experiences of Mental Distress and its Consequences*. Basingstoke, Macmillan – now Palgrave Macmillan.

Reid, W.J. (1967) 'Characteristics of Client Intervention', *Welfare in Review*, 5.

Reid, W.J. and Hanrahan, P. (1981) 'The Effectiveness of Social Work: Recent Evidence', in E.M. Goldberg and A. Connelly (eds) *Evaluative Research in Social Care*. London: Heinemann.

Reimers, S. and Treacher, A. (1995) *Introducing User Friendly Family Therapy*. London, Routledge.

Reith, D. (1975) 'I Wonder if You Can Help Me?', *Social Work Today*, 6(3): 66–9.

Reith, D. (1984) 'Evaluation of Practice', in J. Lishman, *Evaluation; Research Highlights in Social Work Practice 8*. London, Jessica Kingsley.

Robb, M., Barrett, S., Komaromy, C. and Rogers, A. (2004) *Communication, Relationships and Care: A Reader*. London, Routledge.

Robinson, L. (1998) *Race, Communication and the Caring Professions*. Buckingham, Open University Press.

Robinson, T. (1978) *In Worlds Apart*. London, Bedford Square Press.

Rochford, G. (2007) 'Theories, Concepts, Feelings and Practice: The Contemplation of Bereavement within a Social Work Course', in J. Lishman (ed.) *Handbook of Practice Learning in Social Work and Social Care*. London, Jessica Kingsley.

Rogers, C.R. (1957) 'The Necessary and Sufficient Conditions of Therapeutic Personality Change', *Journal of Consulting Psychology*, 21.

Rogers, C.R. (1980) *A Way of Being*. Boston, MA, Houghton Mifflin.

Rogers, C. (2004) 'The Necessary and Sufficient Conditions of Therapeutic Personality Change', in M. Robb, S. Barrett, C. Komaromy and A. Rogers (eds) *Communication, Relationships and Care*. London, Routledge.

Rogers, C.R. and Truax, C.B. (1967) 'The Therapeutic Conditions Antecedent to Change: A Theoretical View', in C.R. Rogers (ed.) *The Therapeutic Relationship and its Impact*. Madison, WI, University of Wisconsin Press.

Rogers, C.R., Shostroun, E. and Lazarus, A. (1977) *Three Approaches to Psychotherapy II*. Orange, CA, Psychological Films.

Rojek, C. and Collins, S.A. (1987) 'Contract or Con Trick?', *British Journal of Social Work*, 17: 199–211.

Rozelle, R.M., Druckman, D. and Baxter, J.C. (1997) 'Nonverbal Behaviour as Communication', in O.D.W. Hargie (ed.) *Handbook of Communication Skills*. London, Routledge.

Russell, K.M. and Hymans, D. (1999) 'Interprofessional Education for Undergraduate Students', *Public Health Nursing*, 16(4).

Sackett, D.L., Rosenberth, W.M., Gray, J.A.M., Haynas, R.B. and Richardson, W.S. (1996) 'Evidence Based Practice: What Is and What Isn't', *British Medical Journal*, 312(7023): 71–2.

Sainsbury, E. (1975) *Social Work with Families*. London, Routledge & Kegan Paul.

Sainsbury, E. and Nixon, S. (1979) *Organisational Influences on the Ways in which Social Work Practice is Perceived by Social Workers and Clients*. Unpublished first draft. University of Sheffield.

Sainsbury, E., Nixon, S. and Phillips, D. (1982) *Social Work in Focus*. London, Routledge & Kegan Paul.

Schon, D.A. (1983) *The Reflective Practitioner: How Professionals Think in Action*. New York, Basic Books.

Schon, D.A. (1987) *Educating the Reflective Practitioner*. San Francisco, Jossey-Bass.

SCIE (Social Care Institute for Excellence) (2000) *Resource Guide 3: Teaching and Learning Communication Skills*. London, SCIE.

SCIE (2003) *Types of Quality of Knowledge in Social Care*. London, SCIE.

SCIE (2004a) *Has Service User Participation Made a Difference to Social Care Services?* London, SCIE.

SCIE (2004b) *Improving the Use of Research Social Care Practice*. London, SCIE.

SCIE (2004c) *Involving Service Users and Carers in Social Work Education: Knowledge Review 2*. London, Policy Press.

SCIE (2005) *Developing Social Care: The Past, the Present and the Future*. London, SCIE.

SCIE (2006) *Teaching, Learning and Assessing Communication Skills with Children and Young People in Social Work Education*. London, SCIE.

Scott, A. (1994) *Gender Segregation and Social Change*. Oxford, Oxford University Press.

Scottish Executive (1999) *Criminal Justice (Scotland) Act*. Edinburgh, Scottish Executive.

Scottish Executive (2001) *Changing for the Future Social Work Services for the 21st Century*. Edinburgh, Scottish Executive.

Scottish Executive (2003) *National Objective for Social Work Services in the Criminal Justice System: Standards, Social Enquiry Reports and Associated Services*. Edinburgh, Scottish Executive.

Scottish Executive (2004) *Single Shared Assessment – Indicator of Relative Need Operational Guidance Users' Handbook*. Edinburgh, Scottish Executive (http://www.scotland.gov.uk/Publications/2004/08/19652/40280).

Shackman, J. (1985) *A Handbook on Working with, Employing and Training Interpreters*, Cambridge, National Extension College.

Shakespeare, T. (2006) *Disability Rights and Wrongs*. London, Routledge.

Shaping our Lives National User Network (2003) *Guidelines for Making Events Accessible*. London, Shaping our Lives National User Network.

Shaw, I. (1996) *Evaluating in Practice*. Aldershot, Ashgate.

Shaw, I. and Lishman, J. (eds) (1999) *Evaluation and Social Work Practice*. London, Sage.

Sheldon, B. (1995) *Cognitive Behavioural Therapy: Research, Practice and Philosophy*. London and New York, Routledge.

SiSWE (Standards in Social Work Education) (2003) *The Framework for Social Work Education in Scotland*. Edinburgh, Scottish Executive.

Smale, G., Tuson, G. and Statham, D. (2000) *Social Work and Social Problems*. Basingstoke , Macmillan – now Palgrave Macmillan.

Smith, D. (2004) *Social Work and Evidence Based Practice, Research Highlights in Social Work*. London, Jessica Kingsley.

Social Work in Wales: A Profession to Value (2005) www.allwales.gov.uk.

Sommer, R. (1965) 'Further Studies of Small Group Ecology', *Sociometry*, 28: 337–48.

Stanbridge, R.I., Burbach, F.R., Lucas, A.S., and Carter, K. (2003) 'A Study of Families' Satisfaction with a Family Interventions in a Psychosis Service in Somerset', *Journal of Family Therapy*, 25(2).

State of Social Care in England, The (2004–5) www.csci.gov.uk/publications.

Sudberry, J. (2002) 'Key Feature of Therapeutic Social Work: The Use of Relationship', *Journal of Social Work Practice*, 16(2).

Suler, J. (2004) 'The Psychology of Text Relationships', in R. Kraus, J. Zack, J. and G. Stricker (eds) *Online Counseling: A Manual for Mental Health Professionals*. London, Elsevier Academic Press.

Sutton, C. (1994) *Social Work, Community Work and Psychology*. Leicester, BPS Books.

SWIA (Social Work Inspection Agency) (2006) *Performance Inspection: West Lothian Council*, Scottish Executive, Social Work Inspection Agency.

Tarr, J. (2005) 'Education', in G. Barrett, D. Sellman and J. Thomas (eds) *Interprofessional Working in Health and Social Care*. Basingstoke, Palgrave Macmillan.

Thompson, N. (2003) *Communication and Language: A Handbook of Theory and Practice*. Basingstoke, Palgrave Macmillan.

Thompson, P. and Foulger, D.A. (1996) 'Effects of Pictographs and Quoting on Flaming in Electronic Mail', *Computers in Human Behaviour*, 12: 225–43.

Thurlow, C., Lengel, L. and Tonic, A. (2004) *Computer Mediated Communication: Social Interaction and the Internet*. London, Sage.

Titterton, M. (1999) 'Training Professionals in Risk Assessment and Risk Management. What Does the Research Tell Us?', in P. Parsloe (ed.) *Risk Assessment in Social Care and Social Work. Research Highlights, 36*, London, Jessica Kingsley.

Trevithick, P. (2003) 'Effective Relationship-based Practice: A Theoretical Exploration', *Journal of Social Work Practice*, 2, November.

Trevithick, P. (2005) *Social Work Skills: A Practice Handbook*. Maidenhead, Open University Press.

Trevithick, P., Richards, S., Ruch, G. and Moss, B. (2004) *Teaching and Learning Communication Skills in Social Work Education*. London, SCIE with SWAP/ ITSN, Policy Press.

Trinder, L. and Reynolds, S. (1998) *Evidence-Based Practice: A Critical Appraisal*. Maidenhead, Open University Press.

Trotter, C. (2007) 'Pro-Social Modelling', in G. McIvor and P. Raynor (eds) *Developments in Social Work with Offenders*. London, Jessica Kingsley.

Truax, C.B. and Carkhuff, R.R. (1957) 'Towards Effective Counselling and Psychotherapy', *Journal of Abnormal Social Psychology*, 71.

Tunnard, J. and Atherton, K. (1996) *Family Group Conference*. London, National Children's Bureau.

Ward, H. (2001) 'The Developmental Needs of Children: Implications for Assessment?', in J. Howarth (ed.) *The Child's World: Assessing Children in Need*. London, Jessica Kingsley.

Winnicott, D.W. (1971) *Therapeutic Consultations in Child Psychiatry*. London, Hogarth Press.

Winzelberg, A. (1997) 'The Analysis of an Electronic Support Group for Individuals with Eating Disorders', *Computers in Human Behaviours*, 13: 393–407.

YIPPEE (Young Independent People Presenting Educational Entertainment) and CATS (Citizens and Trainers) (2002) *How to Consult with People who Use Services (or Anyone Else for that Matter)*. University of Salford: YIPPEE and CATS.

Index